CULTURISM

A WORD, A VALUE, OUR FUTURE

BY

JOHN KENNETH PRESS

Social Books
646-660-4684
www.culturism.us
socialbooks@gmail.com

Printed in the United States of America

ISBN: 0978577701

Library of Congress Control Number: 2007904760

Cover Image: 1585 – 6 watercolor of the Pomeiooc Indian Village by John White. A black and white image five years later shows the walls made of thicker sharpened poles. The walls here are apparently drawn to make enclosed scene visible. There while the lost colony of Roanoke existed, neither community survived their culturist challenges.

To
Joseph Eugene Press, my grandfather,
for service during World War II
and to Lillian Press, his wife,
for maintaining the home front.

TABLE OF CONTENTS

CHAPTER ONE

CULTURISM INTRODUCED

Culturism (cŭl-chər-ĭź-əm) *n.* **1.** The philosophy, art and science that values, manages and protects majority cultures. **2.** A philosophy which holds that majority cultures have a right to define, protect and promote themselves. **3.** The study of culturism

Culturist (cŭl-chər-ĭst) *n.* **1.** An advocate of culturism. **2.** One who engages in the art or science of managing and protecting majority cultures. **3.** Of or pertaining to culturism, culturists or culturist policy. - *adj.*

Culturism generally

America should re-deploy the word "culturism." The word "culturist" appeared in a Random House dictionary during the 1820s and in Webster's dictionary in 1913.[1] In 1879 the Oxford English Dictionary defined culturism as, a "systematic devotion to culture."[2] Northern women who traveled south to help newly freed Southern slaves after the American Civil War were described as "culturalists" for consciously trying to improve the culture.[3] An Internet search reveals that a smattering have recently used the word. Culturism has been around a long time and still remains in the air. Everyday news stories on topics as divergent as the arrests of Mormon polygamist to immigration can be better understood by adopting a culturist perspective. Culturism -

the word and perspective - should be re-announced and consciously
employed to advance our civilization.

America has a long culturist history to draw upon. The American
Civil War itself was an example of a culturist event. Abolitionists,
the people who started the movement to abolish slavery, sought to
purge sin from our culture. The 1918 Constitutional Amendment that
outlawed the manufacture, sale or transportation of alcohol, known
as Prohibition, resulted from a popular social reform movement that
predated the Civil War. Our cultural forefathers, the Puritans, came
here to be able to control their culture. Our political founding fathers
used culturist principles to design the democratic form of government
so central to America's identity and culture. These and other historic
events can serve as culturist inspirations.

Culturism takes diversity seriously. Culturists recognize that some
people would rather do drugs at home than go to school sober. This
preference can have ramifications for our economy. It has often been
noted that a strong middle class helps stabilize democracies. This
means that if we do not maintain a strong economy, our democracy
itself could be endangered. We must maintain our culture to maintain
our nation. Islam, for example, does not celebrate free speech,
feminism or the separation of church and state. Domestic hostility
to such values undermines them. Multiculturalism's refusal to judge
diversity can corrode our solvency and culture. Yet culturism does not
judge cultures internationally. Theocracy in other countries should
not concern us. Asian nations have a right to define themselves
racially. The more we realize how divergent cultures are the more we
appreciate that the West also has a particular culture to protect.

Culturism does not mistake the Western love of democracy and
rights for universally agreed upon truths. Other forms of social
organization and even chaos exist. Mistaking our values for universal
truths causes us to take them for granted. We think that they are so
natural that they will exist whether or not we assert them. We are led
to believe that our government can be indifferent and impartial in
regards to our cultural health and we will survive. Our mistaken belief
that our values are the universal default also results in our trying to
export them to the rest of the world. We fail to realize that others
have different visions for their societies and that democracies rest

upon specific cultural attitudes. Recognizing that our culture is just one among many will help us avoid apathy and arrogance.

We must protect our culture. Ours is an optimistic culture. It rests on a faith in the few Western societies' ability to govern themselves without heavy-handed cultural controls. Others have been following our lead. Yet, no supernatural or metaphysical guarantees of our sustainability exist. Just as debtors and alcoholics have their freedoms undermined by their inability to control themselves, our excesses can undermine our collective freedoms. Without our example worldwide diversity would increase for the worse. In our country, legal rights are used to protect anti-social behavior and the doctrine of individualism tells us no one can judge them. Multiculturalism undermines the belief that we even have a specific culture; the threat of being called racist bullies those who would discuss it. The word culturism needs to be adopted to foster badly needed values, policies, and discussions.

Definition by analogy

Using schools as an analogy for society will help make the benefits of and need for culturism clearer. If students are told that the reason they are doing homework has only to do with themselves as individuals, not doing it becomes a purely personal decision. When using individualism as the measure of all behavior, taking drugs, profanity, and scholastic failure can only be judged by the effects on the individual. If the individual wants to mess up his or her life it is no one else's business. Individualism can only provide us with a weak basis for teaching morals. Multiculturalism's celebration of diversity provides no particular values. Culturism provides coherent yet flexible values and a reason to lead a positive life. That reason being the maintenance of individualism, rights, democracy, and the culture we hold dear.

Excessive individualism can impair our personal and social mental health. Young people naturally want to join groups.[4] Being a part of a team inspires joy and great effort. Being told that you and your work have no connection to the fate of others is not ennobling or inspiring. Isolation is depressing. If we do not give young people a sense of connection, they often find it in the form of gangs and other anti-social cliques. Culturism gives you a team to root for.

Culturism provides a sense of motivation and belonging so that anti-social groups do not have to do it for us. Culturism provides collective mental health and a sense of community with those around you. As sure as loneliness hurts, culturism is more conducive to mental health than individualism.

A hypothetical culturist policy could require students who refuse to do homework being made to pay for classes they ignored if they wish to re-enroll. Unfortunately, student's rights often incapacitate efforts to protect, promote, and even sustain schools as institution. Schools where students' rights protect them from having to learn often cease to be schools in all but name. The same goes for societies in which citizens do not have to consider the public ramification of their actions. A nation of anti-social hooligan citizens cannot sustain its freedom. Our schools being zones of belligerence and ignorance threatens our economic leadership and solvency. Culturist considerations need to counterbalance rights if we are to effectively guide ourselves.

Such scenarios are not only hypothetical. Those with disabilities have rights to sue schools for not providing adequate educations if their individual needs are not met. More and more differences are being classified as disabilities and spawning lawsuits. Yet, schools may not be able to financially or physically meet every child's individual needs. In such a situation the individual has been given all the rights and the school has none. The school loses the ability to choose which programs it wants to emphasize and could conceivably be bankrupted by such lawsuits. Culturism recognizes that all Americans have rights, but social and cultural contexts must be considered legitimate concerns in policy decisions.

Though not as easy to measure as lawsuits, we must recognize the importance of cultural dynamics. Individual's actions are, in fact, never entirely divorced from the cultural milieu in which they are performed. If only one teacher battles pervasive graffiti in a school, his remarks on the subject may be seen as the obsession of an individual crank. If a school has managed to create a culture in which vandalism does not occur, the individual who vandalizes the school will seem to be the bizarre one. Individual actions are nearly always evaluated against the background of cultural norms. Culturism recognizes that individual morals cannot be divorced from the cultural setting in which they are enacted. If morals are important, the cultural setting in which we act must be considered important.

This book will remind us of many common sense culturist dynamics we know about but have been ignoring. For example, the very existence of public schools is predicated on the culturist truth that we share a common destiny. Reviewing U.S. history from Puritans to Prohibition will remind us that we have a long history of culturist practices to learn from. Studies of nature and psychology will show us that that the cliques built on exclusion and status we experienced in high school were not abnormal. Anthropology lessons will show us how these cliques manifest in the world generally. Philosophy studies will teach us to choose which cultural attributes we should push and how. Ignorance of culturist dynamics does not make the school a healthier place. This book will serve as the culturist textbook we never had.

Culturism is meant to be a corrective against excessive individualism and rights. It is, however, not opposed to individual liberty and rights. A lack of collective sentiment has been shown to undermine our willingness to fully fund public schools.[5] This lack of collective sentiment thus undermines our ability to fulfill our individual potentials. Contrary to what individualists tell you, thriving economies are the result of collective community efforts.[6] If the overall economy declines individuals have fewer opportunities and talk of rights and individualism will start to ring hallow. Reminding people of the collective nature of our success reinforces both our individual and collective potentials. A sense of collective responsibility and destiny does not interfere with personal achievement; it bolsters it. Great schools foster successful students.

Parameters of Western culturism

Western culturism is more complicated than other types of culturism. Gambling, gang membership, white collar crime, pollution, children being raised in poverty due to bad parenting decisions, profanity, drugs, and prostitution negatively affect our culture. Other cultures can outlaw and violently punish all antisocial behavior without violating their basic tenets. Western culturism must be much

more nuanced. We cannot throw out our tradition of liberty and
rights to protect our tradition of liberty and rights. Sustaining liberty
and rights in Western nations requires a nuanced understanding of
our history, culture, and traditions.

Because Western civilization is progressive, Western culturism
should seek to help America evolve and advance. It should not be
confused with the "Culture War" Pat Buchanan spoke of at the 1984
Republican convention. The Culture War is widely understood to
be an anti-homosexual, anti-abortion platform. Neither the Greeks
nor the Romans having been anti-homosexual or anti-abortion,
the culturism advocated herein is not necessarily either. Culturism
would be shallow and unstable if it were only based on recent trends
in America. That said, a thread of morality unites our secular and
Judeo-Christian traditions. Since Plato our cultural leaders have
held attributes of the mind in higher esteem than those of the body.
This tradition will, of course, be explored in greater detail later. For
now, suffice it to say that our cultural traditions provide a basis of
morality that may be able to help heal the cultural divisions implicit
in the Culture War concept. We can have morality and still embrace
progressive and evolving traditions.

Yet ultimately, every value system holds that some behaviors
are preferable to others. This cannot be avoided. Advocating
peace implies a disdain for war. Saying that people should be thin
necessarily implies that they should not be fat. Like all value systems,
culturism disparages that which is disrespectful of our traditions
and that which undermines our ability to perpetuate them. Western
culturists need not concern themselves with the morality of female
genital mutilation in other countries. Recognizing and appreciating
diversity means accepting that people in other parts of the world are
entitled to promote and enjoy their own cultural value systems. But
Western culturism must strongly and clearly denounce female genital
mutilation and other values foreign to our traditions in Western lands.
Culturism cannot help but define some practices as being outside the
scope of our traditional values.

Since a broad range of cultures exists, there are a variety of
culturisms and types of culturist practices. Our mode of culturism
will, naturally, be based on our culture's history and shared values.

Asian culturists value and seek to perpetuate Asian cultures. Muslim culturists should value and seek to perpetuate Islamic culture. While it would be inappropriate for us to force a dress code on our populace, it is not hypocritical for Muslim societies to do so. Each type of culturism uses techniques appropriate to the value system it represents. Korean culturists might be concerned with reminding people about the inventor of their alphabet, King Sejong. Mexico might instead promote folklorico. As a Westerner has written this book, it will focus on Western culturism. "Culturism," when not otherwise specified, will be used throughout this book to refer to Western culturism. This will always be done with the awareness that it is only one form of culturism.

People might reasonably raise the question of whether or not cultures can be discussed as entities. After all, cultures are multifaceted and not everyone in a culture adopts all of the values. First of all, in some heavy-handed cultures, the populations are much more culturally monolithic than in others. Secondly, as with criminals, just because a culture has nice elements does not mean we cannot discuss the elements that need change. Lastly, all policy decisions refer to groups. Advertising welfare – to – work programs makes more sense in some neighborhoods than others. Saying that it does not apply to everyone in the neighborhood is true. As our traditions would demand, we should try to think of individuals as individuals. However, such nuances cannot stop us from making generalizations; cultures are real.

The Germans' actions in World War II have made Western countries skittish about national pride. Nationalism is not a well-grounded philosophy and we should be leery of it. Western culturism's parameters are set by traditional values which are older than our nation. Western culture has been against tyranny since the ancient Greeks first defeated the Persians. It has traditionally respected the advice of individuals in governance. Our sensitivity to the prerogatives of the individual is a longstanding and justifiable source of pride. No objective criteria exist by which to say that Western culture is any better or worse than any other culture. All people get formed by their cultures. As such, we Westerners cannot help but cherish self-governance, individualism, and democracy. Nationalism's worship of the nation because it is the nation can be dangerous. Western culturism's grounding in history and traditional values protects us from the sorts of illiberal tyrannies that Western nations fear collective pride can lead to.

People who love their cultures have reasons to be happy and proud. This is a very natural and healthy state of mind. Of course, excessive self-regard can be pathological; it can make a culture overly complacent. Our ability to endlessly repeat "We are number one" as we sink in educational attainment shows that self-regard must be grounded in reality to not be delusional. Equally dangerous is the fact that overly inflated self-esteem can led you to denigrate other cultures and ignore their sovereignty. Culturism advocates respecting all cultures within their own spheres of influence. As such it has a bias towards isolationism. Our culture is special because it is not the common default of societies. Excessive self-love can undermine your ability to be realistic; it can lead to complacency and arrogance.

While excessive self-love can be destructive, not having any self-regard is both sad and pathological. We have tremendous accomplishments to proud of that should serve as the inspiration for our protection of the Western cultural heritage. Western culturism does not mean that you do not critically evaluate your society; success requires doing so. Culturism should create self-critical dialogue in our society, not stop it. However, our self-scrutiny must be done with the goal of perpetuating, not denigrating, our culture. Cultures cannot be sustained by chauvinism or self-loathing. Western culturism must be based on a realistic understanding of our history, traditions, weaknesses, and strengths.

Definition by contrasts

Currently, in English, valuing and prioritizing one's culture is associated with the words "xenophobia," "ethnocentrism," "jingoism," "patriotism," "nationalism," and "nativism." Each of these words is problematic for reasons that will be explored below. None of them can be used as the basis of a practical and grounded value system with which to guide society. Overall, the problem with these terms is that they actually stop us from having the rational discourse concerning vital social issues we must have.

Xenophobia (zĕn´ə-fo′b-ēə) *n.* An undue fear or contemptuousness of that which is foreign, esp. of strangers or foreign peoples.[7]

Xenophobia's being "undue" makes it irrational. Culturism is a rational value system. In seeking rational discourse, then, culturism will be a better fount of dialogue than xenophobia. "Phobia" is word used in psychology to denote irrational fear. One cannot base positive policy considerations on irrational phobias. While culturism also worries about the influence of foreign cultures on our country, it celebrates foreign successes in foreign lands. Culturism also creates a positive value system which the mere fear of others does not provide. Xenophobia cannot be the basis of rational policy analysis.

The real difference between culturism and xenophobia, however, are not in their dictionary definitions. The main difference between the two terms lies in their connotations. Xenophobia is a slur. In common parlance saying that someone is xenophobic is tantamount to calling them a racist or small-minded. If they do not immediately deny that they are xenophobic, nothing they say will be considered worth listening to. The same racist and irrational connotations resonate from the concepts of ethnocentrism, jingoism, and nativism. These terms cannot instigate rational conversations. Whereas they are, at best, obstacles to discussion, the word culturism can provide a basis for useful cultural guidelines, values, and discussions.

Eth·no·cen·trism (ĕth′nō-sen′trĭz′əm) *n.* **1.** Belief in the superiority of one's own ethnic group. **2.** Overriding concern with race.[8]

The problem with the term ethnocentrism comes from the fact that it not only connotes racism, it denotes it. The root, "ethno," is very closely linked to ethnicity, and ethnicity is very often linked to race. Culturism cannot amount to anything if it gets confounded with the false, dangerous, and unfruitful concept of racism. Culturists must always be careful to explain their sincere disgust with racism. That being the case, an entire section of this introduction will be dedicated to denouncing racism. Ethnocentrism is a slur that shuts down conversation and undermines positive values and rational policy formulation. This word necessitates an alternate term such as culturism.

Jin·go·ism (jĭng′o-ĭz′əm) *n.* Extreme nationalism characterized especially by a belligerent foreign policy; chauvinistic patriotism.[9]

Here again we have a word loaded with negative connotations. "Extreme" and "chauvinist" are not attributes of a reasonable ideology. And while culturism does advocate protecting one's own culture, it does not entail belligerence towards others. Chinese culturism dictates that the Chinese take pride in their culture. Iranian culturism advocates that Iranian culture be a source of joy for the Iranians. Culturism does not imply that you seek to destroy or dominate other cultures. Quite the opposite: culturism is appreciative of the Western allowance for both domestic and international diversity. Being appreciative of international diversity, culturism is compatible with isolationism in a way that the chauvinistic concept of jingoism is not.

Patriotism (pā′trē-ə-tĭz′-əm) *n.* Love of and devotion to one's country.[10]

Patriotism is an empty word because it does not convey why you value the country you value. It includes no more content than saying you are for your country just because it is yours. It is love of country regardless of that country's merits. Claiming patriotism in an argument is often a trick used to claim the upper ground and slander all those who would argue with you. Like racism, it gets invoked to protect oneself from substantive discussion. That is why patriotism has rightfully been called the last refuge of scoundrels. Patriotism is, in fact, a fine sentiment, but it cannot foster policy as affectively as culturism.

Culturism implies historical continuity. Western history provides a traditional context within which actions can be judged as worthy or unworthy. Historical and cultural precedent means that McCarthyite tactics cannot be justified in the name of culturism in the way that they can under the banner of patriotism. In fact, McCarthy was denounced for violating our cultural tradition of free speech, not for a lack of patriotism. He was denounced on culturist grounds, not patriotic grounds.

Nationalism (năsh'ə-nə-lĭz'əm) *n.* Devotion to the interests or culture of one's nation. **2.** The belief that nations will benefit from acting independently rather than collectively, emphasizing national rather than international goals.[11]

The concept of nationalism has the same problems as patriotism; it suffers from a lack of content. Though the dictionary definition refers to culture, nationalism is normally thought of as just being in favor of one's nation. Thus in common usage it is akin to "geography-ism." Being for your nation because it is your nation is not a very deep philosophy. Nationalism provides no philosophical guidance.

More importantly, the boundaries of the concept are too small. Culture transcends nations. Western civilization is larger than any one Western nation. Thus culturism gives the Western world an equivalent to the Muslim concept of "ummah" (meaning the greater transnational Muslim community). Nationalism, as the word itself indicates, sees each nation as an isolated player. In fact nations often have shared affinities and histories. Culturism can address geo-political concerns and realities in ways that nationalism cannot.

Nativism (nā'tĭ-vĭz'əm) *n.* **1.** A sociopolitical policy, esp. in the United States in the 19th century, favoring the interests of native inhabitants over those of immigrants. . . . **3.** The re-establishment or perpetuation of native cultural traits, esp. in opposition to acculturation.[12]

Nativism refers to a 19th century political movement that hated foreigners. Adopting this term for purposes of discussion would require taking on inapplicable historical baggage. More fundamentally, those who would compare culturism to Nativism completely misunderstand the term culturism. Nativism sought to separate the long standing Americans from the new arrivals. It was based on the simplistic and false evaluation of the local as good and the immigrant as evil, with no room for nuance or reconciliation. In a diverse society like ours such demonizing can only lead to disaster. Culturism's goal is unity. Certainly culturism recognizes Western civilization as the basis for our society. But Western culturist values are relatively inclusive and provide standards to which we can *all* aspire and by which we can *all* be judged.

Racism defined

Race (rās) *n*. **1.** A local geographic or global human population distinguished as a more or less distinct group by genetically transmitted physical characteristics.[13]

Racism (rā'sĭz˝ĭm) *n*. **1.** The belief that race accounts for differences in human character or ability and that a particular race is superior to others. **2.** Discrimination or prejudice based on racism.[14]

Denunciation of racism

Culturism's potential to be confounded with racism in some contexts necessitates a strong disclaimer. Culturists must do all they can to denounce racists and racism. Race is a biologically insignificant and dangerous invented category. Individuals' attainment in life has virtually nothing to do with their race. Racism can hinder people. But ultimately, peoples' beliefs and the actions that do or do not result from those beliefs determine who they are and what they will become. Cultural differences are meaningful. Race is an invalid and inconsequential factor that does not deserve the honor of having attention brought to it. Culturism gives us a means of overtly making it known that when talking about culture, we are not talking about race.

Of course, it is obvious that significant overlap between culture and race sometimes exists. It is equally obvious that culture is not the result of race.[15] Culture and race are only correlated with each other incidentally. People of Japanese descent who are raised in America speak English and have American values. The few people of non-Japanese extraction raised in Japan speak Japanese and live according to Japanese codes. To say that people are who they are because of their race is racist. Racism is wrong, constitutes definitive proof of ignorance, and a reasonable basis for disqualifying anyone from policy discussions. Race does not create or constitute culture.

Race is not even a real biological category. Biologically speaking, humans are categorized as a species. A species is commonly defined as a population that can interbreed within itself, but not with other populations. All humans are therefore of the same species. One does not ask about the race of a baboon; a baboon is a baboon. Similarly, a human is a human. Just as no two members of any species are identical, humans have superficial distinctions. It is biologically meaningless to say that cows that look different from each other are members of different races. Similarly differing environments have caused some differentiating of physical characteristics in humans. But these are not meaningful in a biological sense.

Racist books such as *The Bell Curve* are deplorable. This book purports to provide evidence that race and I.Q. are correlated. There is no reliable evidence that there are any mental differences between groups of humans.[16] Even if there were some truth to such claims (which there is not), perpetuating such ideas can only lead to horrible results. Culture and behavior are malleable; this provides a worthy justification for discussing cultural differences. But racial characteristics are not profitable basis of analysis. World War II proved that horrible results can come from talking about the concept of race. Books such as *The Bell Curve* cannot result in good and can result in a lot of horror. Racism and racists should be denounced at every opportunity.

Unlike the concept of race, meaningful conceptual distinctions can be drawn between cultures. Group values have material effects on the world those groups inhabit. Some cultures cut off the hands of thieves while others temporarily lock them in large concrete buildings. Skin color neither chops off hands nor build prisons. Race determining culture is as silly an idea as culture determining your race! Considering the dangers of racism, culturists must be very clear that cultures are *not* racially determined. Laws concerning behavior are necessary, but laws concerning race are reprehensible. Being able to safely discuss the importance of cultural differences requires clarity on the distinction between race and culture.

Western culture strives to oppose racism. Other cultures have a declared racial basis. Only those who are racially Japanese or are married to Japanese can be Japanese citizens. American culture does not have a racial basis. America was wise to cut away from its racial moorings. Western culture was almost destroyed by Hitler's racism in World War II. Neither Jesus nor Plato would sanction racism. In a multi-ethnic country like America, making racial distinctions could be destabilizing and even destroy our country. The viability of Western nations is threatened by considering racial distinctions. We cannot afford to be divided by race again. If you value the survival of the West you should fight racism in Western lands. Racists would divide us, culturists seek to unite us. Western culturists must denounce all racists, racist sentiments, racist organizations, and racial discrimination in the strongest possible terms.

Separating culture and race

The West's ability to meaningfully discuss its cultural virtues and vices has been greatly hindered by our inability to distinguish culture and race. We, rightfully, want to avoid discrimination based on race. Yet fear of being accused of racism has compromised our ability to discuss values in general. We need to be able to advocate some behaviors and disparage others. Culturism is a rational basis for discrimination.[17] Racism is not. Conversations based on cultural precepts can be very healthy. Conversations based on race are counterproductive and dangerous. We need to clearly distinguish between racism and culturism to have rational discussions concerning culture.

Racism is discrimination based on race. Hitler's policies were exemplars of racist policy and ideology. He hated non-Aryans for many historical reasons. But he ultimately thought of the historical and ideological sources of his antagonism as reflecting a genetic basis. Non-Aryans were ultimately considered evil because they were not Aryans. He hated them regardless of their achievements. Whether you were a doctor or a criminal, an artist or a beggar was not important. Racism, again, means discrimination based on racial characteristics. Closer to home, we discriminated against people who were thought to have "one drop" of "African blood." The only criterion necessary to judge people under such policies was their race. Racist policies are not only ludicrous and stupid, they are dangerous.

Education constitutes one of the many policy areas where much harm has been wrought by our not having a way to discuss cultural differences in a rational way. In a virtuous effort to avoid racism, we now emphasize race as a factor in education policy to the exclusion of other possibilities. School systems have been sued because they are said to be racist.[18] Institutional and individual racism could conceivably be reasons that higher percentages of some cultural groups go to college than others. However, there are other possible explanations that merit consideration.[19]

Culturism takes diversity seriously and thus affirms that differences in educational achievement could be the result of cultural diversity. Without being able to consider culture as significant, modern policymakers are thrown back to addressing what are termed "achievement gaps" in terms of race.[20] They correctly acknowledge that there are no differences in the innate capacities of different races.[21] Having eliminated both race and culture as significant factors, the only explanation for the achievement gap left is institutional racism. Such conclusions doom our schools to endless lawsuits and preclude successful reforms because they divert us from the real cause of the achievement gap: culture.

Fifth graders in Taipei, Taiwan spend an average of 13 hours a week on homework; their counterparts in Minneapolis spend slightly more than four hours a week on homework.[22] In Asian cultures not having completed one's homework normally results in shame.[23] Completing your homework is positively associated with academic success.[24] Cultural differences provide a complete and satisfactory explanation as to why students in Asian countries do better at math.[25] Culturist explanations can account for some groups doing better than others without resorting to discussions of race. In fact, the existence of multitudes of successful minority students from every background shows that educational success has nothing to do with race. Parameters of culture will be explored and defined throughout this book. At a minimum, though, culture includes the beliefs and practices shared by a group.[26] One cannot claim to take cultural diversity seriously without believing that it may be strong enough to impact educational achievement.

Education is not the only area where we cannot progress until we have frank discussions about cultural values and their impact.[27] Teen pregnancy and crime rates have nothing to do with race. Different rates of such behaviors must, therefore, reflect cultural choices. Drinking a lot and eating fatty foods are often cultural choices. These are enjoyable to members of every race. Race does not cause these actions. The resulting shortened life expectancy cannot be profitably discussed as being due to race. When we condition ourselves to always discuss such issues in terms of race we undermine our ability to address them effectively. People cannot change their race. Whereas discussing race can only result in animosity and helplessness, discussing culture can result in positive reform efforts.

Having only extremely volatile words to express the valuation of one's culture has had a tremendously deleterious effect on the Western nations. Honest discussions of cultural issues degenerate into name-calling. Thus we are left with either hatred or silence. Neither hatred nor silence is conducive to a vital culture. Culturism's overtly being about culture focuses us on important tangible behaviors and problems in ways we can discuss rationally and fruitfully. Being free to discuss culture, as distinct from race, allows us to address many important issues where values, behaviors, and outcomes intersect. The term culturism provides a needed antidote in a country that finds itself unable to discuss diversity and values due to fear of racist implications.

The organization of this book's argument

This chapter has served as an introduction to the meaning, parameters, and potential usefulness of the term culturism. The rest of this book will flesh out the nature, basis, tools, and nuances of culturist understanding. As culturism is not new, the ways in which it has actually manifested itself can be studied. We will look at other types of culturism, but especially work towards an understanding of the nature of Western culturism. These investigations will suggest roles for citizens and social scientists; understanding cultures' general effects in the world will suggest values and policies. By the end of this book you will be able to analyze a broad range of issues and disciplines from a culturist perspective.

Those who say that all restraints on the individual in the name of cultural health are un-American are wrong.[28] From the Puritans to Benevolence Societies to the G.I. Bill of Rights we have nervously tried to forestall the degeneration of our culture. Chapter Two will provide a thumbnail sketch of the meanings and methods we Americans have used to this end. Far from being un-American, the conscious management of our culture is an American tradition. In a very real way, it defines us; the phrase "self-governance" not only applies to individuals, but to communities and the country at large. Our history contains many inspiring examples of culturism in action. Culturism is not an untried or revolutionary idea. Only after seeing this can we reclaim our role as proud American culturists of the traditional stripe.

Culturism is not only an American tradition, but also an ancient and hallowed world tradition. Most all cultures are and have been dedicated to their culturist mission. To understand the cultures involved in our current global conflicts you must understand their ancient heritage. World history also provides many culturist morals. The third chapter will thus explore the role of such phenomena as the recent surge of nations, the rise and fall of cultures, and the psychology of imperialism in world history. Amnesia is as dangerous to cultures as it is to individuals. Without memory we could not be successful individuals and we certainly cannot be successful culturists.

Fully understanding why we must adopt culturism requires a look into anthropology. Western civilization's futuristic orientation often blinds it to the lessons of the past. And yet, much of how the West currently judges itself stems from a contrast with mankind's' supposed peaceful and environmentalist past; the myth of the noble savage is alive and well. The fourth chapter will set the record straight; before modern civilizations the world was much bloodier. Diversity is real. Uncritical tolerance of all human diversity within our borders would entail accepting human sacrifice, selling of child brides, slavery, and gang rape. These are or were human norms. Denouncing these activities domestically means modifying our embrace of diversity and adopting a culturist basis of discrimination. An unflinching look into the bloody and disturbing nature of the average pre-Western culture will also relieve us of the guilt we feel concerning the domestic imposition and assertion of our Western ways.[29]

After surveying the past we will be ready to appreciate how special the Western culture we advocate perpetuating is. Western culture is real, but its characteristics are tricky to nail down because of its decidedly progressive nature. There are, however, strands that make our ancient story coherent. We have striven to liberate ourselves, in fits and spurts, from mental tyranny. We have worked to create a healthy balance of body and mind. Our pantheon of heroes, from Achilles to Martin Luther to George Washington, has been comprised of rebels. We value individualism, self-governance, and rights like no other culture does. The West is also made up of both high and low culture. These are the easy parts to explain. At some level cultural nuances involve inexpressible complexity. But, Chapter Five will illuminate some of the Western characteristics Western culturists love.

Chapter Six will provide the ultimate grounding for culturism. The precedents of culturism in natural history show that culturism does not only reside in the minds of men. Of course, just because nature does something does not mean that humans should. We are different from spiders and apes. But we cannot entirely divorce ourselves from the natural world. Nature can suggest what some of the dynamics of a civilization might be.[30] And it is only when we understand why and how cultures evolved that we can understand their general nature and our responsibilities. Cultures form working units out of otherwise unrelated individuals. They hold and pass on information. The primary function of brains is not to make us radical individual skeptics. We are built to absorb culture. Absorbing a human culture takes long years of nurture. The illuminating lessons a study of natural history can provide for culturists will be presented in Chapter Six.

It has been shown that the Western mind is very bad at putting things into contexts.[31] We ourselves are one of the things we do not put into context. Philosophy, psychology, political science, and the understanding of individuals and communities are inextricably interconnected. Western psychology's heavy emphasis on individualism is not a good basis upon which to create collective mental health. We have social needs. Our acceptance of the idea of absolute individualism has incapacitated our ability to improve the collective mental health of our culture. One way "culturist psychologists" can rectify this situation is by advocating that public space and laws recognize public standards. Creating events that increase our collective understanding of our commonality and creating social organizations are other ways our collective mental health could be improved. As with individuals we must ultimately guide our collective habits and happiness by reminding ourselves of our ideals.

The seventh chapter concerns philosophy and its place in culturism's past and present. Many people are allergic to philosophy because it has become synonymous with abstruse arguments having nothing to do with day-to-day life. This has not always been the case. Plato and Aristotle, for example, were both concerned with man in a social context. Philosophy's focus on abstractions is relatively recent.[32] The most recent sort of philosophical abstraction, post-modern deconstruction, is dangerous. Philosophy has not been included for the purpose of illuminating esoteric nuances. The ideas of abstract rights, abstract individualism, and supposedly universal standards have each had tremendously destructive consequences for the Western world. The absolutist versions of truths leave no room for philosophers to guide us in our efforts to create policies that foster the best approximation of sustainable rights and individualism possible. Philosophy will have a very positive role to play when it returns to its culturist roots and deals with social issues again.

Inevitably, culturism will be narrowly seen as a reaction to multiculturalism. And, to be sure, much of its current significance does come about via its contrast to multiculturalism. Consequently, the penultimate chapter contains a point-by-point comparison of culturism and multiculturalism. Such a comparison can serve as a model for societal discussions concerning the comparative merits and drawbacks of each. As the chapter on philosophy will describe, culturism is not about absolutes. Culturism hopes to help counterbalance our extremes, not replace them. Diversity will always exist in America. But we can choose to emphasize culturism or multiculturalism. Our having accepted multiculturalism as the national dogma necessitates comparing the two isms before many people will be prepared to seriously entertain the culturist point of view.

The tenth and final chapter of this book will detail some culturist policies. As this introduction has stressed, culturism holds that cultural health should be seen to be a legitimate policy concern. Non-Western countries tend do this naturally. The West alone has largely forgotten the perspective that cultures have rights. However, the centrality of rights and individualism to our tradition necessitates our finding a way to pragmatically balance the prerogatives of the individual with the needs of the culture. This effort will be aided by realizing that there are no philosophical absolutes. Your right to be free of eavesdropping is, for example, counterbalanced by our need for reasonable security. Our culture must assert its right to discourage some behaviors. And while many culturists will disagree about what falls inside and outside of our traditions and which policies are justified by our current situations, no one, hopefully, disagrees with the goal of protecting and promoting Western culture in Western lands. Western culture is a great thing and it is our duty to honor and protect it.

One policy is advocated throughout this book: embracing the use of the term "culturism." Using this word will help to reinvigorate our public discourse. The word culturism can remind us of our traditions and our place in the world. It provides a basis of beliefs upon which we can agree and unite. Culturism is a much needed counterbalance to the divisive philosophy of absolute individual rights that has undermined our ability to distinguish right from wrong and advocate values. Culturism can help reverse the sense of division and alienation from our compatriots that multiculturalism fosters in the culture at large. It can remind us that we are all dependent upon each other. Culturism can be the basis upon which we can pressure our politicians to put Western interests first in international negotiations. Politicians' employing culturists policies can, in turn, rejuvenate our sense of place, mission, and pride. On top of all of this, adding culturism to our vocabulary can help to make our culture feel like a culture again.

CHAPTER TWO

CULTURISM IN UNITED STATES HISTORY

Culturism is an American tradition

Many modern American's first reaction to the suggestion of culturism might be to call it "un-American." Many people mistakenly believe that America has always been defined by a dedication to unmitigated individual license and rights. Failures to live up to this commitment are treated as aberrations. In earlier times, however, the view of America was not so individualistic and rights-oriented. Our traditional relationship to our culture has been built on the assumption that America is very special and fragile. This has led us to actively guide and protect our culture against moral threats. This overt culturism has been an American obsession since day one. A quick walk through the history of American culturism will dispel the idea that culturism is un-American.

This quick survey will also help to flesh out what the term culturism denotes. Like most social science topics, culturism cannot be encapsulated easily. Social life being so variegated, the best descriptions of social philosophies often come from lived examples in the historical record. We shall see that culturism has mostly been based on popular movements. Culturist initiatives that find their way into the halls of power usually did not originate there. We will also learn that American culturism has tended to be more persuasive than punitive. Lastly, this chapter will acquaint us with the wide varieties of culturist techniques used by our populace to keep our country safe and strong.

When we use culturism as a tool of analysis, many disparate and contradictory tendencies in America become coherent. For example, many people claim that we have always been a racist nation and then go on to state that American values rest upon a traditional appreciation for diversity. Logically, of course, these two assertions cannot go together. Culturism can resolve the seeming contradictions in these extreme claims. Culturism provides a consistent and coherent thematic schema that ties together what might otherwise seem to be unrelated eras in American history. The culturist framework provides us with a coherent and consistent common-sense understanding and appreciation of our culture.

America has always seen itself as being on a mission. We have traditionally considered ourselves the keepers of a holy flame of freedom. One conceptual model, American exceptionalism, notes that our vision of our unique value has often been framed in contradistinction to the corruption of Europe and the rest of the world.[33] The Old World and, by extension, all traditional societies made characteristic mistakes to which we were to be the first exception. We hoped to bring this improved society to fruition by applying our traditional mores and reason. But we realized all along that avoiding the mistakes of other cultures would not be easy. If the claims of America's culture being special are true, our culturist mission can be rationally justified. The veracity of that claim will be investigated in other parts of this book. For now we will explore the many culturist manifestations of American's belief in our delicate and special nature.

The Puritans were culturists

The Puritans did not come to this country for unqualified religious freedom. That misunderstanding results from a poor grasp of the basics of history and from a conflation of modern and historical concepts of freedom. People who think that the Puritans were purely dedicated to religious and social freedom have forgotten about the Salem witch trials and about the problems depicted in Hawthorne's *The Scarlet Letter*. The Puritans, in fact, came here in order to be able to be stricter in their enforcement of religious precepts than any group in the history of the world had ever been. Puritans were not dedicated to individual liberty and rights.

The Puritans were strict because they were on a mission from God to create and maintain a "City Upon a Hill."[34] They were determined to serve as a model for the rest of the world by providing a highly visible example of excellence. Herein lay the roots of America's American exceptionalism view of itself as a special place that merits perpetuation. Our very reason for existing was to show the Europeans how *real* Christians governed themselves. Many Americans still find it hard to doubt that our versions of democracy and freedom provide *the* model of excellence for the rest of the world. Unlike modern manifestations of this belief, however, our culturism originally held that the best way for us to influence the world was through collectively exemplifying excellence in morals and behavior domestically.

As staunch culturists, Puritans realized that the upholding of their brand of civilization could not be achieved via giving people license to follow whatever inclinations they had. Like all cultures, theirs was based on presuppositions. Their Christian identity envisioned men as being tempted in a fallen world. Puritans thought excellence required self-control, and that self-control required communal control. Towards these ends Puritans utilized extreme measures. Culturist considerations justified, for example, that the penalties for adultery could include death, whippings, fines, branding, being made to wear the letter 'A', and standing in the gallows with a rope around one's neck.[35] Puritans were not squeamish about the methods they used to keep their culture strong. We moderns can agree that their methods were too harsh.

However, Puritans would, in turn, remind us that insistence that all behavior is purely private is also extreme. What we consider purely private matters today often have public implications. For example, Puritans would acknowledge that our choice of mates is a private matter. But once you decide to marry, your decisions have ramifications for your spouse and offspring. Your decisions are no longer purely private. Puritans realized that your family's affairs also influence the wider community. Puritan matrimonial aspirants had to publish their marriage contracts. Marriage was a public act. It would create a building block for the community. You and your family were not separate from society; families were seen to be the stuff of which society is made.

If a husband did not provide, the Puritan community could divorce and punish him. Children who were not being given proper education and guidance were taken away from their parents. This was seen as a responsibility of the community. "For the Puritan mind it was not possible to segregate a man's spiritual life from his communal life."[36] Indeed, if a person dresses in provocative clothes, gambles or abandons his wife and children it does affect the strength and nature of the community. Apart from watching television, few activities can truly be said to only involve the individual. Even watching television has public import if you have not first taken care of your responsibilities. Though we should not return to Puritanical levels of strictness, acknowledging that private actions affect society helps us to understand culturist values.

We tend to consider all infringements on the individual to be imbued with punitive, irrational, and despotic motivations. But such culturist acts were intended for the betterment of individuals as well as the community. Puritans understood that people are not angels and do not always do healthy things with their liberties. Furthermore, they understood that it is harder to be a good Christian in a community filled with sinners than to be a good Christian when surrounded by saints. Modern non-Christian culturists can appreciate the parallel contention that children surrounded by crimes and drugs are more likely to fall prey to criminal lifestyles. Enforcing community standards was always seen as being better for the individuals involved. The Puritans' culturism was not just meant to be punitive. It was intended as a classic "win – win" situation.

Some of the culturist solutions and values the Puritans established still receive public approval. With honest reflection most people appreciate that many individual choices have public results. Approval of the practice, started by the Puritans, of removing children from abusive homes reflects an understanding that communities should protect the young. Being overly dogmatic about the division of the private sphere from public control can be dangerous. People that cannot resist driving while drunk need to be controlled. Their public actions can destroy their lives and other's. The culture has a moral obligation to restrain drunk drivers. But these protections need not negate all the prerogatives of individuals. Culturism seeks to guide, not replace individualism.

Puritans were, despite appearances to the contrary, strong believers in liberty. They would defend your liberty to engage in any type of healthy activity you desired. You could be a doctor or a blacksmith. You would be encouraged to ether help the poor or be an artist. They would recognize, though, that your very ability to engage in these endeavors depends upon responsible behavior. Few personal inclinations can be pursued without health, financial independence, and being able to call upon a social network that will supports your endeavors. Community support can help you realize your dreams and, ultimately, maintain relative independence from others. Communities underlay all successful attempts by individuals to fulfill their potential. Healthy endeavors strengthen your ability and the community's ability to help you achieve your potential.

The terms "liberty" and "license" have had very distinct and important meanings for much of our history. Liberty involves the freedom to act in responsible ways. License, by contrast, involves the freedom to act in ways that might be legal, but hurt you personally, those immediately involved with you or the community at large. Without appreciating the distinction between license and liberty one cannot fully understand culturist values.[37] Much of our inability to recognize our past culturism stems from the atrophying of the conceptual framework the distinction between these words provides. The distinction between liberty and license was a commonplace for much of America's culturist history and informed much Puritan thought.[38] Without this framework we lose much of the ability to distinguish right from wrong.

Puritans prohibited license because it robs you of your liberty. True liberty requires control over your impulsive bodily desires. One will not master any craft or achieve success without restraining his passions. Drinking, gambling, and having mistresses were not seen as real examples of liberty. These were seen as forms of slavery to passions. They lead to illness, indebtedness, and distrust. Engaging in this sort of behavior for twenty years would greatly limit the choices available to you. Someone who spends their high school years indulging their passions will have far fewer options upon graduation than one who disciplines themselves. Laws against heroin use are not meant to curb people's freedom, but to allow them to avoid the trap of addiction. Anti-smoking laws provide a subtler example stemming from our Puritan legacy. Puritans deemed someone controlled by immediate passions a slave to them. Such were the wages of license. Being able to control one's passions and focus on long term plans were central to the Puritans' definition of liberty.[39]

Ultimately, the Puritans were not only interested in the practical, communal or individual benefits of culturism. They wanted to be a beacon of light to illuminate the backwards Europeans. Thus the Puritan's missionary zeal was fueled by a disdain for what the rest of the world and history had to offer. But they did not work purely out of disgust. They were inspired by the vision of providing a beautiful vision of the potential of man to posterity. Being an inspiring example of cultural perfection was a dominant aspect of their self-image. But Puritan accomplishments did not result from pride. Rather than arrogance, their mission motivated close scrutiny of their individual and collective imperfections. They realized that communal success would not magically result from self-satisfied individuals indulging in sloth. In Puritan culturism, individual excellence was based on seeing continuity between individual, communal, and world salvation. The Puritans were altruists who were willing to work hard because they believed in the potential of mankind.

The Puritans considered service to the human race to be a way to both better the world and achieve spiritual worth.[40] Thinking selfishly, we may protest that we do not wish to be a part of a community of saints. Our vision of ourselves as independent individuals with individual rights means that we do not have to consider a social or global perspective. We need never consider the interests of our society. Puritans knew they had no choice. They knew their culture was in danger. Starvation was not that far behind them and lawless frontiers surrounded them. The success that they helped inaugurate makes it possible for us to not think so much about our dependence on a healthy economy. We think we can take its existence for granted. As we prize our freedom to have both liberties and license, we should not embrace the extreme culturism the Puritans adopted. Yet we would do well to realize that we can not sustain real liberty based only on license either individually or collectively.

The Puritans deserve to be regarded as our culturist role models

Puritans deserve to be regarded as our culturist founding fathers. "Puritanism provided the moral and religious background of fully 75 percent of the people who declared their independence in 1776"; possibly "85 or 90 percent would not be an extravagant estimate."[41] Ben Franklin noted in his autobiography that the two most commonly owned and read books during his time were the Bible and John Bunyan's Puritan classic, *The Pilgrim's Progress*. The Puritans' influence on our formation is undeniable.

Our national penchant for self-scrutiny in moral terms provides evidence of the longevity of the Puritan strain in our culture. America has done many things we feel shame over. But many cultures would take pride in the same behaviors. Empires have not, historically, been ashamed of their power. Herein we see some truth in the theme of American exceptionalism. Even if using your power for unmitigated self-enrichment is the historical norm, we take exception to that tradition. Americans tend to feel guilty for having taken the land from the Native Americans. We are sorry for enslaving Africans. We do not celebrate dropping the atomic bomb on Japan. We would readily apologize for any hurt we might have caused other nations while being the reigning superpower. The idea that we should not only do good unto others, but also have a guilty conscience while doing it, reflects our Puritan nature.

Puritans wrote voluminous diaries searching for imperfections that might lurk in their characters. When they found imperfections they did not take them lightly. Puritans were full of anticipatory self-damnation for sins not yet committed in the name of their angry and unforgiving understanding of God. They spent half their lives looking for imperfections and the other half making up for them. Our positive characteristic of freely criticizing our society and government reflects this Puritan trait. The Puritans were at war with their consciences.[42] Ironically and instructively, their self-berating values resulted in their being generally excellent people. Our government's being relatively benign and corruption free results directly from the Puritan tradition of self-scrutiny for sin.

Good reasons support American's traditionally seeing the Puritans as central to our self-image as opposed to what were perceived to be the more racist and less educated Southern regions of our country.[43] Much of what makes America worth debating results from our being a superpower. The Puritans occupied the Northern parts of the future United States where, not coincidentally, industry flourished. Though agriculture helped and was a big business, our superpower status does not result from agriculture. Our economic dominance comes from industry, finance, media, science, and invention. All of these result from having an educated populace who consistently tries to improve themselves and their world. Though the South likely provides much of our contemporary spirit of independence; the North remains the source of our spirit of progress and economic power.

The only substantial region of the United States that could claim independence from Northern domination is the Southwest. Yet history and tradition tie it to the North. These two regions are united by the fact that neither had a history of slavery, both fostered strong Progressive movements, and both were financially successful due to the predominance of non-agricultural industries. California and the Northeast often vote in ways that distinguish them from their Southern and Midwestern compatriots. The family resemblance cannot be missed. California rivals the northeast's claim to economic and cultural leadership. But the Northeast predating the Southwest's establishment by a couple of hundred years necessitates its being acknowledged as the elder sibling in this rivalry.

Lastly, the Puritans can be legitimately claimed as culturist heroes on practical grounds. They are inspirational. The Puritans built Harvard seventeen years after they arrived in American and half of their original population had starved to death. They created the Mayflower compact and thus revering them deepens our identification with democracy. Taking pride in our having a meritocracy due to their healthy obsession with rooting out corruption will serve us well in the future. America and, by extension, American culturism being practical, we should choose the best role models possible. We should recognize and celebrate the Puritans as our culturist founding fathers.

Political science and culturism

Individualists who use American history as a guarantee against all community standards and duty nearly always do so based upon Jefferson's writing that all men are endowed with "unalienable rights" in our Declaration of Independence.[44] They forget that Jefferson was widely known for being a radical due to his tremendous faith in the basic goodness of the individual. His views were traditionally positioned as being on the opposite end of a spectrum from the cynical Alexander Hamilton. In the fifteenth of the Federalist papers Hamilton asked, "Why has government been instituted at all? Because the passions of men will not conform to the dictates of reason and justice without constraint."[45]

The justly famous phrase from the Declaration of Independence referenced above is the only one in the document that can be construed as referring to individuals. This document's independence and liberty being for the group is bolstered by there being twenty-two references to bodies of men in the plural.[46] Jefferson would have seen his document as declaring independence not from constraint in general, but merely from the King's will.[47] The collective intent of these terms can be seen in the fact that when Patrick Henry uttered, "Give me liberty, or give me death!" he was referring to the liberty of our country from England, not his personal liberty.[48] The last sentence of the Declaration of Independence summarizes the document. It says that for our collective independence, "we mutually pledge to each other our Lives, our Fortunes and our sacred Honor." The message is one of a collective fate.

Our Constitution's preamble contains the first official words of our new government. The first three words are "We the people." It does not say, "We the individuals." The preamble goes on to say that the government is to "promote the general welfare." That is a culturist goal. It seeks to "secure the blessings of liberty, to ourselves and our posterity." Securing these things requires a collective effort. This goal necessitated our unifying our disparate political fates under one government. Our Constitution was made because we cannot have liberty when separated. The Constitution was not created to affirm the individual as an inviolable sovereign.

The Founders did not spend much time debating the

Bill of Rights because they did not think it applied to the Federal government. Everyone knew that regulating the personal and private concerns of individuals was the job and responsibility of the states.[49] Alexis De Tocqueville said as late as 1835 that in the United States, "it was never intended for a man in a free country to have the right to do anything he liked." Rather, he noted, "[Townships] . . . regulate the minor details of social life and promulgate rules that relate to public health, good order, and the moral welfare of their citizens."[50] The Bill of Rights was not intended to build an impermeable wall between self and society.

Washington, Franklin, Jefferson, and the other Founders had a healthy understanding of the impact culture has on the body politic. The whole concept of checks and balances was created due to an understanding that a lack of public spiritedness was the one thing that was most likely to undermine their new and experimental attempt at a free government. Famously, Jefferson said, "If a nation expects to be ignorant and free in a state of civilization, it expects what never was and never will be." Notice that Jefferson is saying that the individual's mental state is integral to the fate of our nation. Notice also that the freedom he refers to is not at the level of the individual; it is the collective freedom of the nation. The Founders did not see individual attributes as irrelevant to public issues. Ultimately, for revolutionary-era Americans, the common or public good enjoyed preeminence over the interests of the individual.[51]

American culturism must pay an inordinate amount of attention to political science. This is because America's self-image is strongly rooted in the nature of its political system. Many countries' main source of identity does not stem from their citizens having the right to vote. Being a democracy occupies a lot of space in descriptions of America. Many countries would likely consider their art, religion, race or values to be more central to their cultural essence than their political system. Jealously guarding our unique form of republican government should weigh heavily in our collective and individual self-image. Many nations' Constitutions derive from ours. George Washington was not only the first President of the United States: he was the first President in the history of the world. We are still largely identified by our mission to promulgate the idea that men and women can rule themselves without aristocracy, kings, theocracy, martial law, and heavy-handed culturism. The Puritans would tell us that self-governance in the collective sense requires self-governance in the individual. The founding fathers made self-governance, collectively, central to our identity and mission.

This extended treatment of the Founder's views on the legitimacy of the needs of the community was made necessary by the ideological extremity of our age. Requests for restraint on the part of individuals are too often met with belligerent and indignant legal defiance. These emotional and legal protestations are often based on the misconception that the Founders thought our country's strength lay in the protection of licentious abandon without regard for the impact on the public. Such interpretations are new and inaccurate. The Founding Fathers created a government. They were not anarchists.

Manifest destiny, the Alamo and culturism

The lessons of the Texan war for independence and the subsequent Mexican - American War are crucial to an informed culturist perspective. These lessons were also taken to be common sense by earlier generations. They were common sense to the Mexican government. They are common sense in every other culture in the world. Dangerously, we have forgotten the lessons exemplified by these battles. We need to learn these lessons again if we are to be successful culturists. Our success requires that we address a bit of historical revisionism currently budding.

Many people in the United States now assert that the American Southwest was Mexican land. They even say that we "stole" it.[52] It is a bad sign when two nations start to argue about their borders. It also a bad sign when a nation has to argue about the legitimacy of it borders with large numbers the population living within its borders. However, for this reason, the legitimacy of our current borders is not a topic we can shy away from. Division should be avoided by culturists; unity should be fostered. To the extent a country consists of two divided populations, acrimony will be the major feeling and the prognosis for the country poor. To the extent that your people all see themselves as members of the same nation, you will have a commonality that will bind your country through hard times.

Unlike any other major minority in our population, Mexicans can, and sometimes do, claim that our country should not only be divided in opinion, but in fact. This belief cannot result in anything other than hostility and divisiveness. It causes resentment in those on both sides of the claim. We must teach and understand the weakness of this claim if we are to have relative harmony. The claim that we stole the land from Mexico presupposes that they owned it in the first place. Mexico won independence from Spain in 1821. Their claim of ownership is based on their inheriting the land from Spain. Mexico lost Texas in 1836. They lost the vast majority of the remaining Mexican territory to the United States in the war of 1845. Mexico sold us the bottoms of California and Arizona in 1848. Technically they did "own" it. But, they did so only for a very short period.

To fully understand this issue we need to ask what "owning" property means. Spain owned the Western hemisphere because Pope Alexander VI gave it to them in the Treaty of Tordesillas in the late 15th century.[53] Indians who had lived there for millennia would have been surprised to learn that it had actually belonged to a man in a place called Italy. Jefferson bought nearly one third of our territory from Napoleon. That land belonged to the French, then the Spanish, and then the French again, before we bought it. Again, paper being exchanged between people who had never been in this territory would not have convinced the Indians that they were trespassing. When determining what it really means to "own" property a piece of paper is not necessarily the most valid criteria.

When Mexico got independence, the Pope's deed to Spain transferred into the hands of the Mexican government. On paper, they "owned" expansive portions of what later became recognized as being a part of the United States. But the Mexican government knew they did not *really* own it. Spain had never successfully settled these areas. The local Indian population was too fierce to be controlled and did not behave as though anyone other than them owned the areas they occupied. Due to nearly constant civil war, securing all of what we now recognize as Mexico was even difficult for the rotating Mexican governments in Mexico City, let alone lands nearly 700 miles away from their tenuous grip on power.

Demographics are a crucial part of ownership. People were not eager to go out into these unprotected hinterlands full of Indian warriors without protection. The Mexican government knew that saying you own an area you have never settled and is inhabited by a foreign and hostile population, because of a piece of paper, constituted an exercise in self-delusion. As a result Mexico promised land grants to Anglos if they would swear allegiance to Mexico and become Catholic. They were gambling that they could count on the Anglo's loyalty and thus have the loyal population base so crucial to real ownership. This gamble failed.

Anglo-Americans poured in and quickly overwhelmed the tiny local Mexican population. Just before the Texan war for independence there were approximately 25,000 Americans residing in Texas; Anglos outnumbered Mexican Texans ten to one.[54] This was anticipated. What was not anticipated, however, was how deeply culture is lodged in the human psyche. The Anglo population's declarations of loyalty could not instantly turn them into Mexicans. If you moved to a Muslim country, changing your legal status would not mean that you automatically understood the language and value system of the nation. Legal status and cultural affiliation are very different things. Despite legally declaring their intention to learn Spanish, become Catholics and feel allegiance to the government in Mexico City, the Anglo settlers were never really Mexicans.

The Anglo-American settler's culture not matching the legal borders caused strain due to differences in "economics, religious, political and social ideas."[55] The settlers expected a say in their government (not a Mexican tradition), public schools to be built (not a Mexican tradition), freedom of religion (not a Mexican tradition), laws in English (not a Mexican tradition) and protection from Indians (the Mexican Army could not control this area). Telling a people with a foreign culture, institutions and language that you own their land is futile. Realizing the gamble was going sour, Mexico passed a law barring Anglo immigration in 1830.[56] They tried to stem the tide of disloyal Anglos. But, again, demographics are more important than declarations on paper.

The Texans officially won the technical sovereignty that had been theirs all along in 1836. Much of the rest of the previously Mexican "owned" area was ceded following the Mexican-American war of 1845.

Herein lays the claim that it was "stolen." But this claim has two major weaknesses. First of all, it was largely Indian land before Anglos settled it. Secondly, Mexico, represented by the same President Santa Anna who launched the Alamo and lost Texas, subsequently sold the United States the current border regions of Arizona and New Mexico. This acquisition goes by the common name of "the Gadsden Purchase." It seems patently unreasonable to say that the border regions that were sold without a war were also stolen. It would be very strange to say someone stole my computer, but later I sold him my mouse and monitor. In light of Mexico having sold us the border regions just a few years after the treaty that ended the Mexican-American war was adopted, the historical revisionist claim that we stole the land makes very little sense.

This historical epoch contains many important culturist lessons. Cultural demographics have enormous political implications. The Mexican government invited in Anglo settlers because they knew that demographics determine ownership. They showed less savvy in their understanding of the cultural importance of demographics. The American settler experience showed that changing your cultural identity is not simply a matter of a legal procedure. This episode also shows us that it is hard to fill territory with a foreign population and still control it. That war and secession can result from such attempts is the lasting lesson of the Alamo. Those that do not learn the culturist lessons of the past may be condemned to repeat them. Effective culturism requires that we learn these culturist lessons from history. We must remember the Alamo, remember the context in which it happened, and remember the Gadsden Purchase.

Immigration and traditional culturist conundrums

Nativism was the first American mass movement based on fear of immigrants. Particularly, they amplified the longstanding Puritan fear of Catholics. Puritans viewed their fiercely guarded right to follow their consciences as being special via comparing it to the Pope's claim to dictate Catholic doctrine and conscience. Nativists saw allegiance to the monarchical structure of the Catholic Church as incompatible with a belief in democracy. In their era, the 1800s, the Pope ruled one-third of Italy and frequently sided with other monarchs to suppress democratic institutions. Nativists feared that our country was at risk of succumbing to a Papist attempt to subvert democracy.

Culturism's effectiveness requires that it recognize facts as well as ideals. Wherever Catholics started colonies the result has been oligarchy, low levels of education, corruption, poverty, and a poor distribution of wealth. Mexico typifies these characteristics. Had Mexico taken the American Southwest, there is *no* reason to believe that this region would not resemble the rest of Mexico. Catholic countries' high birth rates and narrow dispersal of education are not generally conducive to first-world economies. Bringing in large amounts of Irish and German Catholics in the mid to late 19th century did not cause problems. But that wave of large scale immigration was coupled with a heavy effort to assimilate the newcomers. These efforts resulted from the recognition of the fact that non-Protestant settlements have not created egalitarian, prosperous, and democratic colonies. Nativists were worried that such settlements not only do not create such colonies, but may undermine them.

The political manifestation of the Nativist movement was the Know-Nothing political party. On the basis for maintaining the cultural integrity of our democracy, the Know-Nothings elected six State governors, secured control of nine State legislatures, and had forty-three representatives in Congress. Their presidential candidate, Millard Fillmore, got almost 25 percent of the vote in 1856.[57] Nativist political parties cannot be removed from America's self-image due to being a small fringe group. Catholic participation in the Civil War quelled all fears of their disloyalty and ended the Know-Nothings. When surveying the long history of American culturism we have to recognize that it has not always been enlightened.

Unfortunately, sometimes racism and culturism overlap and thus become hard to distinguish. The 1882 Chinese Exclusion Act suspended all immigration from China for ten years. The Supreme Court upheld this policy in Chae Chan Ping v. U.S. because the Chinese "remained strangers in the land, residing apart by themselves, and adhering to the customs and usages of their own country." Though not differentiated as such, racial considerations likely outweighed cultural considerations when the Court concluded that it seemed, "impossible for them to assimilate."[58] Sometimes racism and culturism overlap and thus what initially appears to be purely racist hides concerns for cultural considerations. A close examination of such cases can help us distinguish between racism and culturism.

Nuances take center stage when making such distinctions. To appreciate them we need to look at the historical setting of Chae Chan Ping v. U.S. One source of the Chinese Exclusion Act was a fear of economic competition. Whites feared that the bare lifestyle of the Chinese was allowing them to undercut normal wages. This may well have been irrational scapegoating. Another factor was that Asians were periodically the victims of mob attacks in California. These mob attacks were certainly irrational. Nevertheless, they were a source of social unrest and danger for the Asian population as well as being disruptive of general civic harmony. The violence accompanying this source of diversity was one of the reasons the Court upheld this act. The Court noted that the record of hostilities created "a well-founded apprehension from the experience of years that a limitation to the immigration of certain classes from China was essential to the peace of the community on the Pacific coast, and possibly to the preservation of our civilization there."[59]

So was the Supreme Court's upholding of the Chinese Exclusion Act an example of unenlightened racism or rational culturism? From one very valid perspective it is wrong to kowtow to the tendencies of mobs when making laws. Abstract morality arguments would definitely argue against acknowledging such behavior. Then again, government has a cultural duty to protect one's civilization from chaos. During the 1992 Rodney King riots in Los Angeles, the black population targeted Korean owned businesses. Muslim youth rioting in France in late 2005 certainly strained the cohesion of that society. While these behaviors do not comport with abstract notions of ethics, it may not be wholly irrational to take the irrational and ugly nature of man into account when making social policy.

Irrational fears fueled irrational civil chaos and disorder in each of these cases. The Supreme Court was certainly neither ignorant of the demands of abstract morality nor the often brutal nature of mankind. Accepting that people will riot for irrational reasons, the Court had to decide if our domestic civil order was more important than the rights of foreign people to immigrate into our country. For most countries that is an easy call. Does a universal right to be in America exist? Does legislating that someone cannot come into your country constitute discrimination against them? We will see that rights, being an outgrowth of a particular cultural outlook and history, only pertain to the countries and cultures that believe in them and can afford them. The Court at this time routinely held that our rights did not apply to alien petitioners in the same way they applied to citizens.[60] Culturism does not affirm universal values or entitlements. In the absence of intolerable oppression in China, the Supreme Court's decision that Americans have a right to tranquility that overrules the right of foreigners to be in our country has legitimacy.

Currently excluding Chinese on the basis of race would be groundless. Chinese immigration no longer results in race riots. Culturism's being able to vindicate one sort of policy in one era and exclude it in another reflects its not being based on the existence of universal absolutes. Historical situations, international treaties, ideological concerns, general social contexts, and the effects on individuals must always be considered when making policy. Trying to end discussions by invoking "culturism" or "rights" as abstract absolutes will lead to inappropriate social policy. In the absence of compelling reasons, Western culturist values should not invoke any ethnic information. To the extent possible, race should be ignored when making policy judgments in the America culture. Being irrelevant to enlightened debate, invoking race offends our traditional vindication of reason. Considering race also sets a dangerous precedent in a multi-ethnic country such as ours. But, as culturism does not affirm universal values, the Court's reasoning did not violate any culturist values prima facie.

Sometimes our reaction to immigration provided examples of optimistic and positive culturism. "The Americanization movement" provides a positive culturist model worth emulating. Americanization was an enormously popular movement that swept America during the first three decades of the 20th century. In 1915, July 4th was dubbed National Americanization Day. On this day the events in more than 107 cities celebrated the naturalized citizen.[61] It was a day of welcoming newly naturalized citizens. Another year, 35 immigrant groups laid wreaths on George Washington's tomb with President

Woodrow Wilson. Businesses provided English and civics courses that would help the immigrants advance in their careers and prepare to pass the naturalization tests required to attain citizenship status. In 1918, seventy thousand immigrants paraded through New York in the garb of their home countries to show their loyalty to and love of America. This was a positive and welcoming event organized by the Americanization movement.

The Americanization movement protected the immigrant for culturist purposes. Between labor strikes, political radicalism, and the oncoming First-world War, Americanizers found reason to worry about the solvency of America. Rather than fear immigration and restrict it, the Americanization movement sought to foster love for America in the hearts of immigrants. Immigrants arriving at Ellis Island were immediately set upon by scammers. People would take give new arrivals incorrect exchange rates when they paid unfair transportation fees. They would then drop them off at a place where exploitation and terrible housing awaited. Immigrants got exploited at work and ripped off when trying to send money back home. No wonder, reasoned the Americanizers, the immigrant often feels bitterness towards his newly adopted homeland. The Americanization movement protected immigrants so that they would know that America was not solely a den of thieves. This was presented as a win – win situation. The immigrants would be helped and the resulting warm feelings would provide stability. American culturism has included large doses of social services and positive messages.

Liberal Americans rightfully take pride in the Progressive movement being amongst their forerunners. Many who feel akin to them do not know about or take pride in the Progressive movement's role in Americanization. They would do well to remember the Progressive Platform of 1912 proposed Federal action "to promote their assimilation, education and advancement."[62] Americanization provides a positive model of tolerance for the progressive minded to emulate. As World War I approached states passed discriminatory laws against immigrants and the calls for additional restrictive immigration laws got louder. Some have noted that this negative agenda seeped into the Americanization movement. To some degree it did. But Americanizers still worked against restricting immigration. The main model was always one of opportunity. Americanizers always inveighed against discriminatory measures and injustice aimed at immigrants. By and large, in an atmosphere of increasing intolerance, the Americanizers kept their faith in the ability of all immigrants to become positive American citizens.

The Americanization movement was one of the largest and longest lived public crusades ever. Possibly no other civic movement involved so many parts of the American society. The Y.M.C.A., industries, private citizens of all stripes, immigrants themselves, Federal and State governments as well as chambers of commerce, schools, myriads of organizations, presidents, and social workers all contributed. Events happened in churches, conferences, in print, and in community centers. While some American culturist movements had been popular and others top-down; the Americanization movement provides the most widely accepted American culturist movement ever. The Americanization movement attests to vibrant history of positive and vibrant culturist civic involvement. Not only those of the progressive ilk, but all Americans, can take pride in this welcoming emanation of our culturist heritage.

Sometimes culturism gives you clear cut answers. The 1882 Federal immigration policy restricted "lunatics, convicts, idiots, prostitutes, and persons likely to become public charges."[63] In the following decades sufferers from tuberculosis and illiterates were added to the list of undesirables. Those who hold universalistic, absolute ethics might argue that importing all the sick peoples of the world into your country is the right thing to do. Culturism would note that such a stance is not universal, extremely eccentric, not (as these acts confirm) of our tradition, and likely unsupportable. On the other hand, not being about universal truths, if the "idiots" had family here we might want to allow them to enter our country. Maintaining our tradition of providing asylum for those facing oppression might dictate accepting a few people who are likely to become public charges. While these acts only offer a little controversy, the 1924 Immigration Act warrants greater consideration.

The 1924 Immigration Act set quotas for immigrants from each nation based on the ethnic population proportions that had existed in 1890. Had this been purely racist, culturists would reject it a priori.

Were race a main factor we would have to look at it with extreme
skepticism. While some proponents of this Act were textbook racists,
we have to remember that this Act mainly targeted whites. It was an
attempt to exclude Southern and Eastern Europeans. It is possible to
see this exclusion of certain types of "whites" as largely culturist. Many
Italian immigrants "brought with them a hostile attitude toward the
law" from Southern Italy and started the mafia.[64] Eastern European
Jews, like "Red" Emma Goldman were leading violent industrial
struggles, supported assassination, and were in favor of the overthrow
of our government. A national string of bombings likely involved
immigrant extremists and their influence.[65] President McKinley's
assassination certainly did. These southern and eastern European
immigrants did not speak English, were poorer and more illiterate
than the population at large. Furthermore they were arriving in
unprecedented numbers. One has to be familiar with the historic
situation to say whether these demographics and cultural traits
justified a legitimate culturist claim for restriction. Culturism is not a
trump card; it needs to be weighed with competing values.

The right of a nation to control immigration in its own interest is
recognized worldwide. But at what point a country with a welcoming
tradition, like America, cuts off immigration to a group due to
potential harm from a minority of their numbers or their cultural
attributes should not be settled by calls to conform to absolutes that
only allow for complete inclusion or exclusion. All or none does not
present us with the wide policy options we need to make intelligent
decisions. One should always consider the impact on your cultural
values, economic solvency, and other demographic indicators. Since
World War I ended European monarchy, many said we were no longer
obliged to continue in our role as a refuge for the oppressed. The
Statue of Liberty remains, however, an important American symbol. It
recalls our immigrant heritage. The statue being associated with the
less photogenic Ellis Island reminds us that it is a symbol of regulated
immigration. How to balance our complementary traditions of
immigration and regulation is a traditional culturist conundrum.

Popular moral culturism

The First and Second Great Awakenings were huge religious

movements that swept America in the 18th and 19th centuries. They were extremely popular returns to faith that sought to address social evils and revitalize society.[66] The Second Great Awakening was even more focused on culturist issues than the first. Ranging from the 1790s into the 1840s, the Second Great Awakening's members advocated ridding society of drunkenness, idleness, Sabbath-breaking, prostitution, war and slavery.[67] Sound familiar? These popular agendas were clearly in line with America's popular puritanical culturist traditions.

Standing six feet two inches with blond hair and ice-blue eyes, Charles Grandison Finney was one of the best known preachers of the Second Great Awakening. In an amazing show of culturist insight concerning the connection between the personal, the social, and the economic, merchants and manufacturers called on his services to try to help combat lawlessness and raucous behavior in the East Coast boomtown of Rochester. He crusaded there for six months. In the end hundreds joined churches and workers became more sober, industrious, and obedient. Finney's fervent emotional appeals to good morals resonated with Americans. Just as moral culturists, called abolitionists, threw us into a Civil War over the sin of slavery, popular culturist revivals have proved efficacious in attacking subtler evils.

The Second Great Awakening greatly increased interest in pre-existing organizations called "Benevolence Societies." These organizations shared a common agenda with those who flocked to the Great Awakening rallies. They also shared America's traditional belief that the Lord is a vital ally in the personal struggle for morality. But instead of solely depending on charismatic preachers, they set up organizations designed to keep our culture from crashing due to an inability to distinguish liberty from license. They relied on teaching and information (instead of born-again awakenings) to explain that personal, social, and economic health depends on virtues. By now you might be noticing that the Benevolence Societies represented a trend. From the Puritans, to the First Great Awakening, to the Second Great Awakening, to abolitionists, to the Americanization movement, popular culturism has been a tradition in American civic life.

Where looting and "mobbism" by gangs of young roughnecks were a problem this generation of culturists set up Sunday Schools.[68]

By 1836 there may have been 120,000 children in Sunday schools because of the Sunday School Union. Between 1850 and 1860 the Tract Society sold and gave away between nine and ten million tracts a year. The American Bible Society had handed out 6 million Bibles by 1849.[69] The Home Missionary Society assisted an annual average of 1000 ministers.[70] At the end of the Civil War, Jay Cooke, the head of the Sunday School Union and railroad financier, gave money to start churches along the Northern Pacific line because he was sure religion meant social stability and greater profit.[71] Traditionally businessmen, politicians, and citizens have recognized the connection between values and collective success.

The Second Great Awakening and Benevolence Societies reveal the depth and breadth of American culturism. But these are only the most famous examples. They were complimented by Catherine Beecher's army of women that went west to civilize the frontier via teaching school.[72] These frontier culturists were not a matter of a single government agency trying to root out corruption. The Great Awakenings, the Benevolence Societies, the teaching and Americanization movements were popular. They came about due to widespread voluntary citizen participation. Like their Puritan forefathers each generation of reformers knew that people often forget the difference between liberty and license. They continued our perennial and necessary culturist focus on the threats that spiritual and cultural corruption represent to self-government and our uniquely free society.

These popular moral crusaders led us to our apocalyptic confrontation over slavery. But even after the Civil War, America's cultural reformers were not out of energy. Before the Civil War ended northern teachers started pouring into the South to teach the soon to be free ex-slaves. Many know that this happened under the direction of the Federal government's Freedmen's Bureau. But most of the thousands of white female teachers were moralistic missionaries sent by grassroots organizations. These women went to teach morals as well as literacy. They wanted to share the outlook that saw diligence as the key to uplift. The Federal government's efforts did successfully create social changes in the South. Unfortunately, they did not improve the white southern culture enough for the changes to last. The message of uplift was not enough in this case. Again, these women who went south to teach were actually called "culturalists."[73] They provide definite proof of the benevolence and existence of culturism in our history.

While popular culturism continued its crusades for temperance, morality, and literacy, another large threat to our moral order rose on the horizon. The emerging industrial revolution was spawning class exploitation, child labor, massive immigration, and environmental degradation. These did not sit well with our self -image as a godly New World that was to set an example for others to follow. It violated our American exceptionalism premise that our country would not suffer from the same ills as Europe. The popular groups that sprouted to attack this new host of evils were called the Progressives. The Progressive movement was not an anomaly. Rather it was a continuation of a tradition of Protestant culturist crusading in America.[74]

The Progressives differed from their predecessors in that they spent more of their energies on regulating society from the top-down than the bottom-up. They took to trust busting, regulating labor exploitation, education, women suffrage, health and safety concerns, environmental issues, and Prohibition by getting laws passed and creating State agencies. They understood that the massive size of the new industrial enterprises meant that they could not be regulated by moral persuasion alone. Corporations, famously, have neither a body to kick nor a soul to damn. Culturist regulations were needed to keep our society decent, humane, and free. Progressive efforts were also distinguished from the culturist efforts that preceded them by reliance upon science and experts. But beneath their dependence on experts and science lay the very Puritan agenda of rooting out corruption.

Progressives taking a more top-down approach than their predecessors did not mean that they were unconcerned with the impact of individual virtue on society. Progressivism, contrary to popular belief, reached its peak of popularity during an era of wealth.[75] They were not only concerned with economic deprivation. They recognized that the moral underpinnings of our character were based upon the individual needing to overcome his evil tendencies to gain wealth and sustenance. Wealth undermines the self-control necessary to sustain personal and social liberty. Progressives often came from old money. They worried that the newly rich would create a plutocracy of greed that would not understand wealthy people's social role as exemplars of virtue in creating a sustainable and prosperous society. Culturism is not just about the morality of the poor and it is not just important in times of poverty.

Progressives, with the spirit of social engineers, also created social institutions. People have battled over what defines so broad a movement. One source of the confusion comes from their deviation from the traditional grass roots nature of our culturism; they worked with government a lot. But they branched out more than they left that tradition. Progressives created an estimated 400 settlement houses. These were homes where immigrants could come and get help, comfort, education, and affiliation. These houses were generally set up to help struggling immigrants adjust to their new cultural surroundings. Progressives also created social organizations to combat the isolating nature of the industrial age. Since youth, in particular, did not have any place to go they created such organizations as The Boy Scouts, Y.M.C.A. / Y.W.C.A., and the P.T.A. These are just a few positive remnants of their grassroots activities. Their community building and interaction show that they did not abandon our long tradition of door-to-door culturism.

After the First-world War was over Progressivism had one last huge culturist victory: Prohibition. Prohibition was the Constitutional Amendment banning alcohol from 1920 to 1933. Those who say that America does not have a tradition of protecting its culture have forgotten about Prohibition. Can a country that made alcohol illegal for thirteen years not have a history of managing its culture? Prohibition is often treated as an anomaly that does not represent a traditional feature of America. The fact that the roots of the temperance (anti-alcohol) movement go back to before the Civil War lays bare the long continuity of volunteer culturist activism in our country. The battle for Prohibition was fought town by town and pamphlet by pamphlet for over a century. Parades, pledge signing campaigns, prayer meetings, and thousands of women singing and demonstrating outside of saloons led to its passage.[76] This amazing culturist act of will involved everyone from poor immigrant women to

Protestant socialites and congressmen. And though America changed its mind on Prohibition, its passage shows the power of culturist community activism. Constitutional Amendments do not happen because insignificant numbers of reformers agitate for a short period of time. Great Awakenings, Benevolence Societies, wars over moral issues like slavery, the Americanization movement, progressivism, and Prohibition were not anomalies. Serious culturism is an American tradition.

Culturism and Schools

All societies have to teach their young about the cultures they will live in. In tribes religion, morals, and rituals were taught via apprenticeship and initiation ceremonies. Without this indoctrination, the tribe's cultural identity and existence would not continue into the next generation. Schools meet this cultural imperative for the modern world. It has been suggested that the fervor with which Puritans educated their youth was fueled by their distance from civilization.[77] For most of our history schools were a local institution spontaneously created by settlers on a voluntary basis. This fact reflects the Protestant propensity for education, but it also reflects the natural socializing function of schools. In time schools have been justified with appeals for everything from bolstering republicanism to the need to communicate with God and from personal transformation to furthering hygiene. But throughout it all schools have been concerned with cultural health.[78]

Horace Mann is known to many as the 'Father of our Public School System." Few know that he took a demotion from the Secretary of the Massachusetts Senate to accept the Secretaryship of the newly formed Massachusetts State Board of Education in 1837. This being a demotion, he deliberated for a month before taking the job. The factor that convinced him that he had to take the position was an anti-Catholic riot. [79] He saw the school system as a mechanism by which our multicultural society could be made more harmonious. He famously considered schools the "balance wheel of society."

Emphasizing the distinctive virtues of the majority culture has been the default method of socialization since public education began. Textbooks used in America when Mann came on the scene featured geography sections that were focused on the distinctiveness of national characteristics. These characteristics were marred by defects. People of Italy were artistic, "but excitable and passionate."[80] Germans were industrious but their "national character is of a military cast."[81] They created these foils to teach American virtue and the connection between virtue and wealth. This time-tested method was deemed the common sense and necessary way of perpetuating our good nation and the morals that sustain it.

This curriculum also meant that non-denominational Protestantism was the basis of curriculum. [82] When, in the mid-1800's our schools started becoming public this meant that public dollars funded forms of Protestant education. This involved individuals, rather than the Church fathers, reading the Bible and students interpreting it for themselves. Catholics resented this practice and the famous Catholic school system began. The fact that Catholics had to leave them to maintain their distinctiveness has been used to show that public schools are discriminatory agents of cultural imperialism. It can also be used to show that diversity interferes with common purpose and national projects. At any rate, both readings confirm that cultures naturally seek to advocate and perpetuate their distinct modes of life via schools.

The progressive educators fundamentally altered the methods of teaching. They sought to adjust the young to the new constantly changing world of industrial society.[83] John Dewey, the leading progressive educational theorist, is famous for individualizing instruction. In an alienating world he thought it important that the child have the experience of being treated as an autonomous and worthy being. Thus he was instrumental in formulating the focus on individual achievement and potential actualization that now dominates schools. But he did so to ensure a "well-balanced, happy and prosperous society" in order that "civilization can go on."[84] Dewey was not trying to liberate the individual at the expense of society. He just realized that success in a progressive society requires that individuals need to be able to take initiative and adapt and that people were being dehumanized. The progressive focus on individuals, rather than tradition, was different, yet it was designed to facilitate youths' adjustment to society.

When the Great Depression hit education was one of the main tools used to stabilize the country. In the spring of 1935 nearly five million youth were out of school and unemployed.[85] The National Youth Administration (NYA) was set up to help them find a place in society. Showing a great sensitivity to the dynamics of culturism, Franklin Delano Roosevelt decentralized the program. Money flowed from the government, but the projects the NYA undertook were decided upon locally. The youth's work helped the local community which made them have pride in it. It also endeared their communities to them. Showing even more culturist wisdom, Roosevelt made sure that nothing was given to the young people without them earning it so that those involved could retain their "self-respect."[86] The NYA provides a great example of the positive potential uses of schools to culturist ends during unusual times.

Another excellent example of schools being a wonderful culturist tool occurred during World War II. As the war dragged on, the need for soldiers was such that we had to start recruiting illiterate men. The Army set up what had to be the world's largest successful intensive literacy program ever: the Special Training Units (STUs).[87] Nearly a quarter million men gained literacy via this program during the two and a half years that it existed. Being both a boon to the individuals involved and a necessity to our nation's survival, the STUs provide a stellar example of a culturist win-win.[88] We need only regret that we had to wait for war to recognize this redemptive culturist power. Schools can also be used in ad hoc ways to remediate needs before emergencies arise.

The G.I. Bill, it is widely known, helped ease the transition back into the economy for soldiers returning from World War II. It is also widely known that this was a culturist triumph. It set the foundation for the post-war economic boom that solidified our status as a superpower. Less prominent in our collective memory is the fact that when the Russians launched the first satellite ever, the Sputnik, we responded with a culturist emphasis on the sciences in the schools. Duty to self and duty to nation dovetailed and helped lay the foundation for our continued economic boom that the G.I. Bill had started. Since our earliest years we have used schools to the traditional end of stabilizing and perpetuating our culture. These goals have also been met by ad hoc educational programs on frontiers, and during technological transformations, economic collapse, war, and peace. Schools are an especially invaluable culturist tool for dynamic republics.

Culturism during wartime

The extreme situation of war highlights vulnerabilities. Wars threaten our very existence. They often cause panic and result in emphasizing national unity. Things that would violate our basic cultural traditions and tenets become acceptable – if not necessary – at such times. Individualism fades in significance and culturist needs takes precedence. In a normally free society the contrast between lax peacetime traditions and constrictive wartime practices cannot be missed. The contrast shows the connection between culturism and security at its starkest. Knowing about the historic record of our society during war provides a necessary guide for successfully navigating such extremes.

National security has been used as a pretext for abusing our traditional liberties. The Federalists used the fear of subversion by radicals who sympathized with the French Revolution to pass the Alien and Sedition Acts of 1798. These gave Federal prosecutors the power to apprehend, remove and restrain "all natives, citizens, denizens, or subjects of the hostile nation or government" above fourteen years of age and not naturalized. But the Federalists only used the act to attack their critics. There was no danger to us from the French Revolution. This law being passed shows that abuses of power in the name of national security is not something to which America has immunity. Knowing this history provides us with an example to object with whenever national security gets used as a convenient pretext for self-serving abuses of power.

Restrictions of freedom in the name of national security are not, however, always unjustified. Abraham Lincoln suspended habeas corpus and locked up agitators, draft disrupters, deserters and demonstrators during the Civil War. As is their intention, people who foment disruption and dissention during a war compromise its effective prosecution. The North's losing the Civil War would have greatly and negatively impacted our future. These points may appear too obvious to merit mention. But acceptance of these assertions is necessary to claim that sometimes during war individual liberties must be compromised. This does not mean that small wars excuse an abandonment of traditional liberties. The seriousness of the threat to our sustainability must be weighed in making such decisions. But the basic lesson is that rights are not absolute. Historical circumstance constitutes a traditional and legitimate qualifier.

At the start of World War I, one - third of the foreign born were from enemy countries. As Germany was our enemy, people naturally turned against all things German. The government also organized over 100,000 patriotic citizens into groups that rifled through the mail of those of suspect loyalty, infiltrated meetings, and recorded speeches at public gatherings.[89] After the war this sort of monitoring stopped. People were pressured into growing vegetables during World War II. These Victory Gardens allowed more food to be shipped to soldiers overseas. Coercion is not in itself bad. These nearly forgotten incident should be remembered when individualists say that even the slightest violations of civil liberties and coercion during war time is un-American and will lead to a permanent loss of civil liberties.

In July of 1915, a U.S. Secret Service agent uncovered German - American plots to bomb an American Steamship and disrupt our munitions production. Fear of such acts inspired the Espionage Act. This law outlawed any "disloyal" or "scurrilous" talk about our form of government. During the War thousands of Germans were interred for charges as light as uttering pro-German statements in public.[90] Charles Schenck's case was the first the Supreme Court heard concerning the legality of the Espionage Act. Schenck had mailed some anti-draft pamphlets to draftees and others. Off the record Justice Oliver Wendell Holmes said that the "squashy sentimentality" of those who did not realize a man's destiny was to fight made him "puke."[91] Holmes believed that society had a right to defend itself. In his opinion, upholding the Espionage Act he said that speech could be restricted when there was a "clear and present danger."

Was the distribution of anti-war literature during the war dangerous? We can now, the war long won, say that it was harmless. We must realize, however, that we can never know if the unfolding of this unpopular war would have been different had thousands of enemy sympathizers and agitators against the draft been free to spread dissent while the war was being waged. Making value judgments without knowing how things might have turned out without the action being considered taking place can be labeled the "Unknown Futures Fallacy". This fallacy tends to make us overly sanguine. In hindsight the outcome always seems ensured. Was it better to be safe or sorry at the time? The Supreme Court made it very clear that freedom of speech is situational, not absolute. Justice Holmes left it for us to do the hard work of figuring out when that speech presents a clear and present danger.

Those who disparage all forms of wartime culturism often point to the racist nature of the internment of Japanese and Americans of Japanese descent during World War II. The memory of our tendency towards irrational racism during war needs to be reiterated, they tell us, to ensure that such a thing never happens again. On this basis, Americans of Japanese descent have demanded and received multiple government apologies and repeated financial awards based on the unwarranted and racist nature of the internment. This rendition of history serves as a weapon against all who would talk of wartime culturist necessities in a realistic manner.

Our having removed British Citizens from the East Coast cities and interred them during the War of 1812 shows that such acts are an American tradition and not necessarily racist. Was the fact that it had been Americans of German descent that plotted to sabotage our steamships and munitions during World War I coincidental? Is it reasonable to suspect that recent immigrants might have more of an attachment to their particular homeland than random Americans? If a tendency to care about your country of origin is natural to all immigrant groups, regardless of race, the internment decisions can be said to reflect cultural, rather than racial, tendencies. If sentiments have an impact on actions, the relocations during war may have been rational.

During the Second World War we upheld our tradition. Germans, Italians, Hungarians, Romanians, Bulgarians, Japanese, and first-generation American citizens were expelled, arrested, and interred. We now know that Japanese had spy rings and tens of thousands of loyalists on the West coast when the war started. Divulging the number and nature of our ships, let alone sabotage, would have hurt our war effort. In the relocation camps many occupants formed pro-Japanese military organizations, terrorized pro-American detainees, and publicly prayed for Japan's victory.[92] But not all did. This fact illustrates that we often have to consider the balance between the sometimes contrasting values of culturism and individualism during wartime. Our having trials to determine loyalty of each of the over 100,000 people involved with full due process before being able to relocated them was unfeasible. Practical as well as ideological considerations must be considered when making culturist policy of any kind, especially during wartime.

Those who would decry all efforts, no matter how small, at curtailing liberties often invoke McCarthyism to stop debate. McCarthyism happened during war time. If you add up American fatalities from Vietnam and Korea alone, you can see that the Cold War resulted in at least 100,000 American fatalities (not to mention the deaths of millions of non-Americans).[93] Documents released at the end of the Cold War affirmed that the Rosenbergs gave atomic secrets to the Russians.[94] Alger Hiss was not the only spy in the State Department.[95] One could dispute that having spies of in the State Department and the Defense Department constituted a present danger because the dangers unfolded slowly. Spying in the State department did, however, constitute a clear danger; having enemy sympathizers in your government during war time compromises your security and endangers the lives of soldiers.

Those who now say that we would have won the Cold War without clearing the State Department and Defense departments of communists should keep the Unknown Futures Fallacy in mind. McCarthyism often gets conflated with the House Un-American Activities Committee's investigation into the Hollywood film industry. As Senator Joseph McCarthy was not in the House of Representatives, he should not be blamed for HUAC. Those accosted in HUAC's chamber did not have a right to cross examine those who accused them or see the evidence against them. HUAC ignored basic legal rights. One can present reasonable arguments for compromising the rights of the accused in positions directly affecting national security. Few would take seriously the contention that bad movies present a "clear and present danger" to America.[96] In a country dedicated to

relatively high levels of free speech Congressmen compromising basic
rights of filmmakers should be taken as a cause for culturist alarm!

During war the relationship of rights to freedom becomes stark.
Cultures cannot survive with absolute license. Violations of speech
for safety tend to be popular. Zoot Suiters exercising their right to
wear flamboyant clothes while material was being rationed in order
that we might fight a war against two fascist governments reveals an
astounding ignorance of culturism. We all need to recognize that
guarantees of rights in a country that has lost a war do not exist.
While the government was within its rights to enforce rationing of
items necessary to the prosecution of the war, having dress codes or
condoning riots would unnecessarily violate our traditions. It would,
again, be hard to sustain that people wearing flashy clothes during a
time of war threatened our security.

Just as attacking groups without cause or due process is wrong,
tarring all attempts to control individuals in the public good as "racist"
is wrong. During wartime individualism must allow considerations
of culturism. During wartime discriminatory culturism sometimes
becomes justifiable. Those who say our victory in World War II was
obviously assured, regardless of whether we relocated Japanese and
Americans of Japanese descent from sensitive military areas, are
falling victim to the Unknown Futures Fallacy. War is a clear and
present danger. Still, we must be leery of the tendency to be overly
heavy-handed during wartime. As usual, history can be our guide
to what is and is not acceptable. We should take heart from the fact
that compromises of rights have been successfully rescinded at the
conclusion of wars. Adhering to absolutist standards of individualism
during wartime could definitely constitute a "clear and present"
danger to all of us.

Culturism, however, is not just for wartime and it is not just practiced
in the face of clear and present physical dangers. We have traditionally
believed that the greatest threats to liberty come from cultural
corruption. A wide variety of means have been utilized to keep license
from compromising our liberty. Legislation, political groundswells,
education, celebrations, the Civil War, speeches, censorship, and
religious appeals have all played their part in sustaining our free and
prosperous nation. Extreme circumstances, such as war, often cause

panic and rash judgments. But our traditional culturism has been overwhelmingly positive. Persuasion has been used much more often than coercion. Outside of times of war, coercion has shown itself to be much less practical than persuasion. Just because not all dangers are clear and present does not mean that we should not be on the lookout for trends that portend declension. Reclaiming our vibrant tradition of culturism provides our best hope for safely steering our country to a positive future.

CHAPTER THREE

CULTURISM IN WORLD HISTORY

Culturism in the world today

Japan is a racist country. You cannot, without marriage, (assuming the reader is not of Japanese descent) become Japanese. If you asked the Japanese why you cannot become Japanese you would receive a stare of incredulity. Have you looked in the mirror lately? When inter-racial marriages occur, the resulting "mixed blood" children are barred from military service. This exclusion will effectively exclude them from many employment opportunities. Koreans and Chinese have the same sorts of rules. This is shocking and outrageous to an American audience. But these countries' policies fall well within the traditional spectrum of culturist behaviors. Our shock that the desires of individuals might not always supersede the right of a people to define themselves racially reveals our lack of worldliness. They have a right and, from their point of view a duty, to maintain the continuity of their culture and heritage.

Korea, China, and Japan are racist. But they see their attitudes as so obvious that they transcend what we would call racism. They believe that their policy reflects an obvious fact of nature: Japanese are Japanese. Since nations first existed their names have not only denoted a culture and a location, but a people. Germany, Philippines, China, Korea, France and Thailand are not only names of countries. They are references to racially defined ethnic groups. Thailand is a land for Thai people. The citizens of China are Chinese, racially and legally. Germany was a place for German people. Western nations should not and could not go back to being racially defined. Beyond race, citizenship has been traditionally based on shared history, hatred of an enemy, and a strong dose of irrationality. Whether we use these unifiers or not, our current rejection and fear of advocating for our commonality makes our nation bizarre. In fact, the individual and decontextualized citizen we champion is, ironically, just a Western concept.

Our sense of nation is special. The United States is among the *least racist nations on earth.* That bears repeating in current intellectual climate. The United States is among the *least racist nations on earth!* I can tell you what a Japanese person looks like. What does an American look like? There is no answer to that question. Though race used to be an important part of our self-definition, we have transcended that limitation. We have created a nation on the more modern culturist premise of common culture and should be proud of that. Yet our denunciation of our racial heritage undermines a traditional mainstay of unity (other than religion, a shared history, and destiny). For our divestiture of race to be a source of strength we must realize that our non-racial characteristics need to fill the void. Otherwise, we will have lost a source of unity and the resulting fragility will not have been addressed.

Muslim countries are not racist. They are however very heavy-handed culturists. Muslim countries are for Muslims. A Muslim woman in America would have the right to use the law of the United States to complain if she felt discriminated against. But it would be disingenuous for her to feign outrage that someone could be discriminated against in general. This, she would well know, is the norm for Islam and most other cultures in the world. If I wanted to drink beer or live a life said to run contrary to the Koran in Islamic countries, I would be jailed and possibly killed. Every American should know that their right to protest and print their outrage concerning transgressions of political ethics does not garner respect in much of the world. Most cultures believe that decency, cohesion, and pride make many behaviors sacrilegious. We should be less shocked and ignorant of international culturism.

But the question is, "Do these societies have the right to define themselves?" Culturism is premised on the idea that cultures do have the right to define themselves. Up until recently, it would have been obvious to Americans that we have that right. However, many currently think that individual rights are a universal aspiration that precludes any distinctions being made between individuals by cultures. Japan's racism or Islamic religious laws are seen as unprecedented outrages against universal rights. Culturism is designed to temper that extremist brand of individualism. In a world where our competitors have control of their cultures, our dedication to anarchy gives us a disadvantage. Nations define themselves. We have traditionally done so via connection with our culture, history, ideals, and destiny.

This survey of culturism in world history will make us better culturists. Basing much of our sense of culturism on race, like Asian countries, would be suicidal and stupid in a multiethnic country such as ours. Adopting the theocratic culturism of the Muslim world would run counter to our progressive nature, core belief systems, and historical commitments. We are hurt by our cultural tendency towards disdain for the past and things outside of our borders. American exceptionalism has its costs. A quick study of world history will help us to understand those costs. Protecting our progressive nature requires that we are not totally blind to the longstanding culturist dynamics.

Birth of deep cultural roots

Cultures are not created easily. They evolve over long histories and through many battles. Great statesmen have to arrive and become luminaries in the cultural coin. Artists have to set the common tone of the people. Battles have to be fought for the culture to have land upon which to thrive. Philosophers must hammer these histories into moral codes. A sense of cultural honor has to take shape. Legends and rites must spread. Institutions must be created to perpetuate these elements of culture. This is not a process that can be willed in a generation.

World Cultures all start with stories. Islam has the Koran. Western Civilization started with the Homeric epics. Our modern universalistic traditions have their roots in the New Testament of the Bible. Hinduism has its Vedas. Asia has its cultural seeds in the works of the triad of Confucius, Buddha, and Lao Tzu. And the myriads of smaller and extinct cultures that have strutted on the world stage have each had their own creation stories to unify them. They are necessary to flourishing cultures. Culturists thereby know that teaching the stories of our civilization is vitally important.

Culturist history's biggest lesson is that history matters. History creates peoples. The virtues and morals of these stories define a people. History sets the agendas for which they will die and so fuels their continuance. It is not a coincidence that all great civilizations have an intimate attachment to their own story and a side of the story they call their own. Friedrich Nietzsche noted that objectively knowing that your culture is just one of many can undermine your attachment to your particular culture. But, rather than detachment, a deeper understanding of the relationship of founding myths and history to cultures can also foster a deeper appreciation and attachment to your cultures story.

Modernism started with science and started the disintegration of our attachment to history. Nietzsche's denigration of myth was borne of his applying scientific criteria to history. Science prides itself on its being able to distinguish "fact" from "fiction." Science prizes that which is new. Old science books are considered out of date and of little value. Our love of science has undermined our appreciation of our founding myths and history. At the same time science has strengthened our belief in universal principles. It has thereby loosened our attachment to the particular (our particular history being the pertinent example for this argument). And, since we are so powerful, our not realizing that our truths are just our own has consequence for the world. It would be a shame if our infatuation with science and its promised future eclipsed our love affair with our history.

The Western story starts with Achilles. He was our main warrior in the battle between the Greeks and the Trojans. But Achilles' honor was slighted by a leader. He moped around wondering what the use of fighting for glory was when it was so easily taken away. When his best friend, and probably lover, was slain by the enemy he rejoined the battle with ferocity. His re-engagement and wrath spelled doom for the enemy Trojans. Significantly, Achilles knew he was going to die in this effort. He had been told that he could either live a long boring life or go out in a blaze of glory avenging his companion's death. He chose the latter.

Achilles embodied individual glory being gotten via struggle as a virtue for the Greeks. To this day Westerners dream of distinguishing fame born of valiant efforts. To the extent that you dream of fame and glory Achilles breathes. Artistic, political, and athletic competition permeated Greek life. Each having a shot at glory, instead of just a King, was the basis upon which they founded the world's first democracy. It was the awareness of their culture's special dedication to their individual explorations and identity that motivated them in their epic battles against the great tyrannical theocracy of Persia.

When Athenian democracy killed Plato's teacher Socrates, he decided that there was a truth beyond that of honor and glory so revered by his culture. Plato used literature to vindicate his teacher and to replace the values that had caused the mob to kill him. Socrates' had followed ethics into a world where there were eternal truths that were higher than those of the State. Socrates was the fallen Achilles in the battle for higher ethics. This development bolstered the right of the individual to question the State on higher grounds. Socrates died for our right to think, and the questioning and probing has characterized all of our progressive eras. Unfortunately Socrates' love of eternal ethics predisposed us to thinking our truths are not just cultural. This mistake blinds us to diversity even today.

Rome adopted the Greek culture. They ingeniously decided that the exiled Trojans that Achilles and the Greeks had defeated were their ancestors. The Trojans and Greeks had the same Gods. Thus the Gods and history of Greece were taken to be Rome's too. The Romans based man's glory more on self-control and practicality than speculation and individual excellence. But inquiry, rationality, and excellence were still esteemed. This adoption shows us that no culture can fully accept another's ways, but kinship between cultures enables understanding. It also reinforces the fact that, just like individuals, cultures want to have pasts in which to ground themselves.

The collapse of Rome brought on the Dark Ages. For one thousand years the Catholic Church dominated all Western thought. Christianity adopted the concept of eternal truths that Socrates and Plato had championed (even though they forgot the source). They also kept the view that individual was important, as Jesus had not just died for the rich and powerful. Christian ethics combined the stable eternal truths that Socrates discovered and the stoic virtue of endurance and duty the Romans championed. All totaled, Europe imposed upon itself a level of mental and physical tyranny that neither the Greeks nor the Romans would have tolerated. That ended when the renaissance brought a rebirth via consciously recovering our memory of the pagan civilizations we had nearly forgotten.

This traditional definition of the renaissance being based on a recovery of our historical memory contains important lessons. Without knowledge of a changing history and our past values we were stuck in a tyranny borne of amnesia. When we do not know that the present values are unstable we are apt to take them for granted and fail interrogate them. Knowing about alternative social arrangements, particularly from one's own history, increases your collective mental flexibility. When we were sure that meekness had always been the only source of Western glory we were stuck. When we discovered that conquering and questioning had been used in the service of finding fame, new venues for virtue were opened. Collectively, understanding the variety in your past provides flexibility.

Science has, in this regard, resulted in another Dark Ages of sorts. Our past has become foreign to us. Science's constantly bearing fruit has exaggerated our Christian tendency to locate our glory in the future. Early Western scientific practitioners were ruthlessly hounded and killed by the Catholic Church. This has caused a further disenchantment with all that is old (including religion). Thus our story and its relevance have been nearly extinguished from our conscious memory. Thus, as history is our guide, we should be aware that stability and flexibility might suffer as a result of this amnesia. Indeed our not questioning individualism and incredulity at culturist values provides a prime example of cultural inflexibility borne of amnesia.

Another culturist lesson to be learned from this retelling of the story of Western Civilization concerns the pervasive nature and depth of cultural tendencies. Though very few folks can tell you much about Achilles, we still embody his fighting spirit that has been our constant secret to dominance. Individual glory and war against our destinies populate our advertisements. The Western world is unique in its constant struggle against the status quo. Status quo is a pejorative for us. We are also programmed to crave his sense of individual glory. We are living Achilles' dream. As the enemy Trojans' chief warrior Hector found out, you can run from Achilles but you will never get away.

We also have a history of disrespecting our governments. Both Socrates and Jesus strove against the arbitrary nature of temporal powers. They believed in eternal and universal truths that transcended the authority of particular governments. Socrates thought you could find this through questioning everything, Jesus thought you could get it by intuitively tuning into the higher truths emanating from God. Neither saw authority as being grounded in this world. Our constant distrust and criticism of our government is a very old, and culturally specific, tradition. Not everyone considers questioning authority a virtue. But we are so programmed in this tendency that we do not even question our knee-jerk impulse to always question temporal and traditional authority.

Herein lies another culturist lesson: if you do not delve deeply into your cultural heritage you are not likely to understand it very well. Our current version of our progenitor's dismissal of authority has left us thinking that moral codes can only constrict us. No one can tell us what is right and wrong. While neither Socrates nor Jesus would have dropped their right to criticize for any man, neither would either have advocated doing anything immoral. They were both notoriously strict moralists. The perversion of our traditional sense of individual truth into a license for debauchery stems directly from the shallowness of our understandings of our own traditions.

Another lesson we shall see, if we venture forth out of the history of Western Civilization, is that our values cannot be taken for granted. Neither Asian nor Muslim cultures value constant striving for glory against the status quo. In Asia questioning your elders and institutions is seen as a failure to have a basic grasp of the world around you. In Islam actions that go against the Koran result in death; individual deviations are not prized. Until recently neither culture was preoccupied with creating a substantially greater tomorrow. The individual striving to make a future that has no resemblance to or relation with the past is a very Western goal. Our culture is not the world's default. If we do not prize and protect our vision it will be replaced by something different.

Nietzsche was, in the long run, wrong. At first seeing that each civilization has its own stories and mores might turn you into a relativist. But once you come to understand that fundamental cultural stories' morals are diverse, your preference for what you know reemerges strengthened. Asian elders do not need your opinion. The Koran's principles cannot be voted upon. We resent their refusal to consider what we think. This sort of encounter with cultures other than our own makes us more grateful than ever that our Greek forefathers came up with the ideas of individual conscience and democracy. We are programmed to love our values and freedoms and do.

Christianity and science, though they battle, do have a common strain. They both claim to expound universal principles. Neither claims to be a product that only applies to the West. Thus our historical ghost sends us out to convert others to what seem to us to be universal principles in a way that other cultures do not. Failing to realize that our values are not universal means we do not have an appropriate feeling of culturist protection towards our own culture. If it is universal it does not require protection. Not realizing our truths are only "self evident" to us, leads us to not respecting other cultures' sovereignty. Understanding that our tendencies are just ours also makes us value our culture's existence more.

Chinese history and culturist pride

Traditionally the Chinese have described their country as the "middle kingdom" or more broadly "the center of the earth." They have had a reason to do so! China has been civilized for five thousand years. For perspective dwell, if you will, upon this equivalency. If you are generous you can say that the United States is four hundred years old. China being five thousand years old is more than ten times older than us. Our telling China how to live is tantamount to a seven year old telling a seventy year old how to live. If the seventy year old is kind he will giggle and be gently patronizing. If the elder continues to be pestered with advice, however, he may rightfully accuse the child of unimaginable insolence.

The seventy year old finds that it self-evident that all men are created unequal. Babies are not equivalent to their parents. Parents are above children. Honor, peace and strength come when a child has the wisdom to respect and obey his parents. Doing your homework shows a more mature understanding than throwing temper tantrums and insisting on your right to do what you want. Rebellious and disrespectful children bring chaos, weakness, and dishonor. China's long history has also told them that this formula of reciprocal duties that works in the family also works for the state and citizen. Continuing the analogy, they would note that a good parent would not tell a child to do anything that was not in that child's best interest. Good citizens obey their government.

Here we see the importance of culture to statecraft. We Westerners admire youth as holding the key to a new future. The Chinese view of the impertinent fifteen year old is not as indulgent as our own. We see some relationship between the child and the parent's interest, but we value our individual conscience above all else. Westerners will only willingly consent to laws they have made for themselves. Asian culture sees much more of a connection between the glory of the family, the country, the culture, and the individual. We need to see that our current ideas about the absolute nature of individual sovereignty, in the face of reasonable arguments to the contrary, results from a poor reading of our own history. Individualism needs to be put in international, as well as historical, perspective.

Chinese group orientation comes as much from an appreciation of their storied history and the historical depth of their cultural precepts as it does from reactionary racism. The Shang dynasty, that spread the system of writing that they still use today, was founded in 1650 BC! Confucianism, Taoism, and Buddhism each date from the 6th century BC. Creations of the Han dynasty of 206 BC to 220 BC include the invention of civil service exams, textbooks on zoology, botany, chemistry and astronomy, and the creation of acupuncture. The Tang dynasty lasted from 618 AD to 907 AD and left a tradition of literature and art as a legacy. The Song lasted from 960 AD to 1279 AD. It added gunpowder, landscape painting, moveable type and porcelain to the list of creations that fill Chinese with pride.

Knowing this we can start to appreciate the pride Chinese feel in their civilization. Would anyone with such an illustrious background not be proud of their forefather's accomplishments? The answer is "Yes." We fail to appreciate our forefather's accomplishments daily. Your accepting the age analogy at the beginning this section (assuming you accepted it) provides an example. While our history is obscure at 1650 BC, the Homeric epic starring Achilles likely dates from 1100 BC. We created democracy in the fifth century BC. Our philosophy and arts from that time are astoundingly beautiful. We also invented the flying buttress cathedral (1200 AD), modern physics (1600 AD) and television (1927 AD)! This is not to take anything away from the glory of the Chinese. It is only to show that you lose a tremendous source of pride and solidarity when you forget your history.

Personal and cultural memory

You may have noticed gaps between the dates of the Chinese dynasties that were listed above. As every civilization, China has had its ups and downs. Historic vision has allowed them to recognize the tendency for their civilization to rise and fall. This pattern has been termed "the Dynastic Cycle." A trick the Chinese have learned is that part of climbing out of the mud of anarchy that characterizes the gaps between dynasties is remembering your past.[97] Our having only gone through this cycle once means we are yet to see it as a dependable pattern.

This is one of the most important culturist lessons the Chinese can teach us.[98] Our one renaissance should teach us the culturist lesson that reconstituting and going forward requires remembering our past. Crawling out of our Dark Ages was done by remembering our Greek and Roman heritage. Caution should be wrought from recognizing that the reason the Dark Ages were called the Dark Ages results from their being a time in which we lost historical consciousness. Our great advances being based on our reconnecting with our past was mentioned before and we get safer every time it is repeated. The Chinese culture has less of a danger of disappearing than ours because they have not forgotten the necessity of historical consciousness to getting rich civilizations out of dark ages.

The Chinese even have culturist heroes to serve as role models for those trying to forestall the ravages of the culturist cycles between golden ages and dark ages. Zhong Huamin was an expert Chinese culturist who worked in the province of Henan towards the end of the Ming Dynasty. He wrote a book on rites and made officials responsible for upholding them in order that he might restrain people's desires.[99] He established porridge stations to feed the poor and tried to get robbers to readopt the civilized life. Thus the importance of collective responsibility, memory, and destiny are represented in the efforts of Chinese heroes.

We have a fundamentally different orientation to culture than the Chinese. We tend to think of historical precedent as stifling and are less likely to evolve heroes that are famous for reminding us of the past and our collective responsibility. The molding of character was the main point of ancient China's education. Ethical teachings stressed the importance of human relations and history. It taught leaders and others what the ideals of their roles were and identified glory with faithful re-enactment of such roles. We tend to measure our greatness in our ability to defy our roles and historical models. We respect and esteem innovators who break the cultural mold. But we should remember that our art before the renaissance was not as innovative as it was after we connected with our past. Connecting to your traditions gives you more ability, not less.

We are mistaken if we think that our visions of greatness are not historically based. Pablo Picasso can only claim greatness due to his levels of innovation against the supposedly stifling academic style that preceded him. Ironically, his desire to be new and exciting reflected the cultural mainstream True greatness is never a private matter. And he probably would have been more innovative had he incorporated the varied styles that preceded him. Our current assumption that glorifying the country leads to a diminution of the importance of the individual is very immature. It assumes that there is no relationship between people and the country of which they are a part. Our valuing individual glory, originality and conscience should not be thought of as being in opposition to our civilization. Our current refusal to measure ourselves against our past is disrespectful, ignorant, and unappreciative. Pride in culture can be a great source of pride and inspiration to the individual. If we studied history we would know this. We are collectively and individually greater and safer when we immerse ourselves in our culture's history.

Culture has consequences

When the Greeks and Romans fell the Catholics took over Europe. By force and persuasion they dominated Europe for a thousand years. In the 16th century Martin Luther (a figure every Westerner must know) led the Protestant reformation in opposition to the Catholic Church's stifling cultural hegemony. His main cultural wedge was the idea that man's salvation is a result of faith. This meant that all the works of the Catholic Church could not save you. The priest could not save you. Only Jesus could save you. You were saved by a personal relationship with God unmediated by institutions. Herein lays the deep root of the Puritan conscience searching for a sign of redemption and individually asking God for forgiveness.

For Protestants to communicate with Jesus and God it was necessary to be able to read the Bible. To do that you needed an education and a Bible printed in your native language. Herein lays the root of the Protestant emphasis on literacy. The Catholic Church responded to Luther's challenge with a two pronged approach called the counter-reformation. Prong number one was an intensification of the war on all non-sanctioned doctrine. This included killing people that translated the Bible into local languages and suppressing science. Prong number two was the creation of beautiful, inspiring works of art meant to bring you back into the fold via an emotional attachment. Michelangelo's art is the prime example. Herein lay the deep roots of the Catholic's rich art and pageantry.

Protestant movements of the North reacted to the Catholic efforts to secure their turf by smashing all art. Furthermore, they spread literacy and translated the Bible into local languages. By translating the Bible into German, Martin Luther is said to have created the modern German language. Gutenberg's printing press was heavily used in this effort. And whereas the Pope jailed Galileo Galilei for his disagreeing with the Pope, the North eagerly printed his smuggled texts and used them to achieve a personal understanding of the lord through science. The Catholic South got art and the Protestant North took literacy and science. Subsequently the two sides warred with each other for centuries. This history demonstrates another culturist tendency: Cultures in opposition differentiate.

Without this historic background one cannot understand the

Puritan's hatred of Catholicism. They wanted to purify their church of all remnants of Catholic artistry, ornamentation, ritual, and hierarchical doctrine. They feared suppression of literacy and the usurping of the personal relationship with God. Protestants wanted to focus purely on a personal relationship with Jesus through private reading. They were super-Protestants reacting to the still fresh schism with the Catholics. The culturist lesson of this paragraph is that you literally cannot understand your own country's particular culture until you understand its deeper historical roots. America has deep roots in the Protestant reformation.

Colonialism was the world's biggest social science experiment. What would happen if you go around the world and plant Catholic and Protestant cultures? The experiment was done and the results are very interesting. Wherever Protestant colonies were started the results included high levels of literacy, clean government, and economic success. Wherever the Catholic Spanish and Portuguese set up colonies authoritarian governments, low literacy levels, and economic disparity manifested. The culturist lesson of this one is perhaps the most important of all: cultures have huge impacts. Value systems are not neutral ornaments that only decorate; they populate minds, promote values and result in differing action, economies, and outcomes.

The importance of culture to a wide range of indexes has been shown to be true over and over. In countries with mixed populations, Protestants, Chinese, and Jew's economic roles are disproportionate to their numbers. Let us be clear: this is due to culture *not* race! Many poorer countries will assert that the reason they are poor is that they were exploited by the Protestant colonies. But recourse to Protestant interference as an explanation only begs the question. Mexico is one hundred years older than the United States. Why is Mexico not exploiting the United States? Why do Jews and Chinese nearly always economically outperform the averages in their host countries? Both cultures stress the value of education.

This section has shown some cultural absolutes. Economic success is a result of cultural norms. Clean government and low crime rates are also largely cultural manifestations. Cultural and individual values reflect deep, deep historical roots. These, in turn, have massive consequences. What we value, however, is totally culturally relative. Catholic cultures have tighter families and better art. Neither culture's aesthetics can be shown to be objectively better or preferable. When cultures divide they differentiate. That is not to say that one heads in a bad direction and the other in a good direction. We can only show that differences occur with major concomitant consequences. Our preference for our culture's ways only reflects the depth of cultural programming. We can only say that we prefer our culture because it is ours and we prefer it. We value progress and dislike theocracy only because, in a real and personal way, our culture's preferences must be our own.

Cultures compete

Social Darwinism holds that cultural and individual competition will result in the earthly extinction of the deficient and the preservation of the efficient. [100] This is a horrific vision. It is also wrong. Unfortunately, reality is actually worse! It is not necessarily the most efficient (or fittest) institutions that take over in the Darwinist paradigm. Cultures which are willing to sacrifice much of their youth to incessant warfare have a good track record. Unfortunately, the horrific nature of Social Darwinism cannot be denied. As with animals, the extinction of cultures happens. We know almost nothing about the Native American tribe on the cover of this book. We cannot objectively say which cultures are better; we can only catalogue those that did not survive. Because extinction is bad thing we should investigate its causes in an effort to avoid it.

Sometimes the mechanism by which one culture supplants another is demographics. We saw the importance of demographics in the case of the Mexican loss of Texas; once the population was Anglo American, the territory would not be loyal to the Mexican government. The Chinese takeover of Tibet makes this even clearer. The Chinese invaded Tibet in 1959. They realized that an occupying army could only temporarily solidify their land gains. To consolidate their rule they told their population that if any Han Chinese (the majority ethnicity) were willing to move there, the government would waive the one family, one child law. Many did so, the propagation started and now the Chinese outnumber the Tibetans in what used to be called Tibet.

Tibetans no longer have the numbers for a successful insurrection. Even if the Tibetans, got "their land" back they would be a minority in it. Were they to establish a democracy, they would lose every election. Not speaking the language of the majority population, their choices are limited to struggling in ghettoes or adapting to the majority Chinese culture. Their culture is greatly endangered and has, to a real extent, gone extinct. The complex vibrant dynamics of their original culture cannot be preserved in disparate small settlements in India or in the person of the Dalai Lama. Without land there is no power to practice one's cultural values. Without retaking their land and repopulating it, the Tibetans' culture has crossed the divide that sends the endangered to extinction.

Spain's successful destruction of the indigenous cultures of the now Catholic Latin American countries provides another example of the vulnerability of cultures. The original colonizers were relatively few in number. Their securing obedience required a complete reprogramming of the culture. They destroyed the structures and burned most of the texts of the indigenous cultures. Anyone caught engaging in the rites of the indigenous religion was killed. And all that did not adopt the Catholic religion were in danger of torture. They did not replace the population, but ruthlessly altered the thought patterns and rituals essential to their cultural continuance.

Cultural continuity requires cultural transmission. Within a few generations all memory of cultural traditions can disappear. What we know of the indigenous religions comes as a result of a few chroniclers and anthropologists. Some cultural practices provide a feint echo of the original, but no one would really know how to recreate these cultures if they wanted to. Latin American Catholics consider Catholicism to be their nations' historic religion. Apart from some idiosyncrasies buried in the local practice of Catholic rites, the indigenous religions are extinct. Cultural extermination via ruthless reprogramming can be very effective.

The popularity of a culture greatly affects its viability. The Catholic conquest of South America was facilitated by local discontent. Conquistadors successfully exploited this discontent by pitting kingdom against kingdom. Hernan Cortes exploited myths that painted him as a savior of the locals from this suffering. Without this cultural idea he may not have conquered. Without a doubt, if there were no Civil War in the Incan empire or dissatisfaction in the Aztecan Empire, the Spanish conquistadores would not have triumphed. Cultural resilience is greatly affected by the level of satisfaction it engenders in the population.

Cultural appreciation was key to our own civilization surviving. The Greeks were fighting for a culture that would allow them to freely follow their individual consciences. The Persians whom they battled against were a theocracy and would not respect individual consciences in making decisions. The Greeks, unlike many modern Westerners, appreciated how rare a cultural flower their culture's high regard for individual conscience was. Nowhere in their world was there anything other than theocratic monarchies. Losing to the Persians would mean the death of the most precious thing in existence: mental freedom. This realization resulted in loyalty that fiercely fought defeat.

The unique features of Greek culture gave them an advantage in battle. The Greek propensity for local rational democratic power sharing was reflected in our style of fighting. Whereas the Persians had to wait for orders from above, the Greeks depended on autonomous fighting units. When isolated they collectively decided upon their plan of action. Self-governance created a more flexible and effective army. Thus democracy was not only able to inspire martial sentiments; it was crucial to Greeks securing the foothold from which our culture later bloomed. Cultures inspire different behaviors in peacetime that lead to different economic results. Cultures also affect cultural security by the wartime behaviors they evoke.

These differential effects can be seen in American history. The settlement of our country was done under the banner of "Manifest Destiny." Americans filled the continent because they felt an ideological imperative to extend the land mass in which freedom operated. Mexico did not occupy the land because it was embroiled in Persian-like, monarchical-style power struggles for authority. America sees it as befitting the nature of man to minimize central power and share it. Our settlement's form reflected this cultural assumption. Our government did not settle and fight for Texas. It was small autonomous groups of settlers who were regulating and fighting autonomously for their autonomy. Again, cultural assumptions affect actions in decisive ways.

Survival of the fittest includes ethics. But ethics and success have a tenuous relationship. Early Christianity's spread was greatly facilitated by its glorification of defensive martyrdom. Islam engenders offensive martyrdom. This value is conducive to outright conquest and the destabilization of enemies. Catholicism's tenets result in high birthrates and high levels of respect for enshrined authority. Cultures exist in the heads of people. One way to make your culture spread is to have enough people to occupy a large area. Asian cultures engender the type of diligence that leads to economic viability, but subdues individual impulses. Western countries' encouragement of individualism has lead to great achievements and progress; it can also justify selfish decadence. Fittest cannot be taken to imply an ethical superiority.

Culturist realpolitik lessons

Whatever the mental content, cultural existence absolutely requires heads and land. Cultures only exist in heads. If no one remembers your culture, it will cease to exist. Heads nearly always require land. No food, no heads, no memories, no culture. Jews have been unique in that their cultural propensity for literacy (heads) has allowed them to become ingrained in other people's land. Still, even their culture is not supernatural; it cannot subsist without earthly resources. Even though Jewish culture spent epochs without its own land, it still required land. Without this level of physical grounding your culture will be relegated to scholars' history books.

Culturism thus requires thinking in realpolitik terms. Cultures are not metaphysical entities built upon bedrock of universal truths. They live in geographic space in the minds of living humans. If other cultures occupy some of your land, your values occupy that much less space. They have moved closer to disappearance. Were there enough land for all the cultures of the world that wanted to live to exist, they would all be here. Were population levels static cultures could stay in their place without contact, but populations grow. There is a scarcity of that which sustains the heads. That means that there is competition between cultures.

Beyond land, cultural survival requires that those heads be filled with the stuff of your cultures. If you do not teach your cultural values with pride they will not inform the world view of the people living on your land. If all Islamic cultures stopped teaching the Koran and started delivering a purely secular curriculum, Islam would cease to exist in three generations. Even if the formerly Islamic people continued to hold vast and heavily populated territories, their culture would cease to exist. Heads stuffed with secular cultural proclivities do nothing for Islam. Once your ideas are not in the heads of a people sustained by the geography you control, they do not exist. Cultures require land, but ultimately exist in human heads.

The lesson to be learned is that if we do not value our culture's distinctions and thus concern ourselves with heads; if we do not propagate its special features that lead to success and thus maintain land; our culture will cease to exist too. It is not the case, as those who advocate a laissez faire attitude towards culture, that secular humanism and democracy are the universal default that those uninstructed tend towards. Many competing models have sustained themselves and many continue to exist. Historians try to appreciate what the Hittite and Tibetan cultures were like, but they cannot make them come alive again. Being overly free with heads and land shows a failure to appreciate that American exceptionalism has its limits. Cultures disappear.

Mistakenly believing our civilization's truths are eternal and universal undermines our determination to guard the land and teach the heads that sustain it. Just after the Cold War America entered a period of triumphalism in which we felt immortal and as though our conquering of the world was a done deal. Our willingness to believe this probably reflected the insulation from war and cultural protection our geographic isolation traditionally gave us. Such arrogance both reflected a love of our culture and a failure to appreciate that diversity is real. The 9-11 terrorist attacks should have woken us from this dogmatic slumber. The history of the world shows that cultures are proud of their heritage, seek to expand, and do not give up easily. There is no universal agreement that Western ways are the best and the future that every culture strives towards.

The Chinese would love to reassert their perceived rightful place as the center of the world. Though they are aggressively expanding their military capacity, they could not overcome us militarily. Theirs would be a soft aggression. Every year our country gets more dependent on theirs. Economic influence translates into the ability to manipulate political systems. Culture follows power. If the countries see that unfettered rights and individualism lead to poor economic results, low educational attainment, and crime they will not be eager to adopt them. Chinese military aggression will likely only involve Asia. Taiwan's independence gets weaker ever year our trade deficit balloons. The impact of our mentioning their human rights abuses also contracts with our economy. Eventually, economic subservience could require that we adopt austerity programs that would threaten our stability. When our economy weakens so does our moral authority and our independence. That would tilt world ideology in an illiberal direction. Reverence for liberty requires responsibility and self-control.

Islam's threat to our way of life is much less subtle and much more immediate. Their cultural precepts decree that they will not stop at our acknowledgement of their superiority. They need us to completely submit or die. They have already shown that their tactic is to destabilize cultures via terror attacks. They also seek to shut down freedom of speech by killing and intimidating politicians, media and intellectuals that disagree with them. Western media and the Pope himself have been put on notice that their speech must conform to Islamic guidelines or result in international crisis. Fending off such attacks has already caused a compromise of rights and civil liberties in Western countries. Success breeds confidence. Those who expect this aggression to diminish are naïve.

Other cultures already know that control of land and heads are weapons of competition. The Catholic churches' challenge to our sovereignty via providing sanctuary to illegal immigrants and support of high birth rates does not only coincidentally increase the lands on which their heads are situated. Sovereign Western states largely originated as an attempt to constrain the power of the universal Catholic church. Mexico is supplying education materials to our students that argue that young American's loyalties should be to institutions south of our border.[101] Islamic nations are setting up mosques and lobbying for greater immigration from Muslim countries. China lobbies for favorable trade deals. We need to know that cultures compete and disappear. We need to know that lands and heads constitute the battlegrounds for cultural survival.

Imperialism and culturism

Cultures that are successful have unity, pride, and a sense of mission and confidence that borders on arrogance. Chinese civilization is a fantastic example of this truism; Islamic civilization is another. Countries that have internal divisions fall apart during war time. Rome did not start its expansion until the patricians and plebian (rich and poor) settled their differences. The crusades were not a sign of internal division. "The agents of imperialism normally believe that they represent a superior power, ideologically as well as materially."[102] Confidence and pride are not immaterial.

British imperialism provides an example of how a righteous sense of mission and entitlement can be conducive to power. At the top of their game, the British felt a sense of nobles oblige - that is an obligation to share their values with the less developed. They practiced what has been called "Gentlemanly Capitalism." The gentlemen that led this were long trained in social and religious values and code of honor that placed duty before self-advancement. They felt, much as many Americans traditionally have, that altruistic communal virtues were a prerequisite for the self-governance they called liberty. They sincerely sought to spread their self-evidently better, rational, mercantile model of civilization. Their mission was based on - not devoid of - values.

The Colonial Secretary declared in 1833 that Britain's aim was to transfer the ". . . spirit of civil liberty and of the forms of social order to which Great Britain is chiefly indebted for the rank she holds among the civilized nations."[103] "Expansion was not simply a necessity without which industrial growth might cease, but a moral duty to the rest of humanity."[104] That is why the British expended so much money and so many lives trying to stop the worldwide slave trade. That is why the British stayed in Africa even though it was a financial drain that could have severely strained Britain economically.[105] They did not want to rule so much as to instill values which they saw as being so essential to liberty, prosperity and self-governance. The British wanted to give the gift of efficient administration to their colonies.

British economic self-interest and the general good were seen to be interchangeable categories. If all of Africa took to industry there would be an increase in areas in which the British business model could be shared. There would be more consumers of British goods. Expansion was not viewed as inherently hostile because the party expanding viewed their culture as a gift. Because their rational industrial culture was advanced, humanitarian principles made the British duty bound to export it. The West was, at this time, very much in love with itself. British folks were in no danger of descending into the abyss of directionlessness. They had built the modern world of the future and were duty bound to share it. They had a benevolent mission of expansion based on their success.

We now snicker at such an idea. Certainly, the British attempts to export their way of life were racism at worst or a reflection of ignorance concerning the dignity of indigenous ways at best. Modern Westerners assert that feelings of cultural pride are born of insufficient respect for the value of other cultures. From this perspective, the British arrogance was unjustified and led to harm, beyond reparation, to the local ways. And the local ways were equally good if not better than the British. Unfortunately, the self-deprecating stance of modern Westerners undercuts our willingness to study our past. This failure is likely both the cause and effect of Europe's fall from a perch of domination. Lack of historical pride is certainly not an attitude that is correlated with success. Our enlightened modern attitude is in danger of passing from charming modesty to harmful self-effacement.

Though it is hard to validate that our culture's enshrining of rational and efficient administration combined with a zeal for progress results in a more satisfactory life, the Western world should still be able to take some real pride in its accomplishments. Air travel, television, radio, penicillin, computers, light bulbs, film, cars, mass transit, and the modern economic system are Western creations. If not the quality, we have facilitated a radical explosion in the quantity of life. Populations have never been close to this high anywhere. However much the countries that were colonized resented Western presence, many are still desirous of our cultural fruits. Many are happy living communally in their traditional squalor and huts. But Western gifts cannot be said to be entirely without merit.

Without the West, most of the world would be living in huts without electricity waiting for the witch doctor to tell them what the thrown bones dictate. Those in more rationally organized civilizations would still largely be huddled defenselessly in huts; captive to the whims of weather and unable to leave the village into which they were born. The life expectancy would still be thirty to forty years long and childbirth would be an extremely dangerous undertaking. In a real very real sense, the Western world's arrogance led to the creation and diffusion of all that is modern.

I am boasting. But it isn't idle. These achievements lend support to the notion that our culture deserves culturist protection and perpetuation. Our invention of methodical industriousness being applied to every problem on this earth is not the default of human consciousness. Tribal reversion into unscientific brutality is rife in the world. Western consciousness is still special and should be cherished as an achievement. Much of the world still lives in a pathetic trap of superstitious darkness, informed by no hope or system of getting hope. The Western enlightenment vision coupled with a belief in action and individual initiative still provides the only hope for many in an otherwise stagnant world.

We also extended our largely Christian value system. In India women were considered of such low value that they had to jump upon their husband's funeral pyres upon their death to keep from being a burden. In some sense our stopping this practice was an advance. Slavery was not as much started as it was ended by the Western world. Stopping slavery was not evil. Nearly all of the tolerance shown by Islamic and other traditional societies is due to the encroachment of Western values. As much as freedom from theocracy cannot be said to be a universally cherished value, it cannot be said to be uniquely evil either. The next chapter will look at just what we did replace, but whether or not it is due to blind prejudice, we should not feel that our modifying cultures to include human rights was a purely cruel and evil imposition.

Ours is still a fantastic vision. Since the ancient Greeks fought the Persians we have been increasingly (sans the Dark Ages) pushing for valuing the relative free conscience of the individual. Ours is a strong and noble history that has benefited a wider scope of the world than any before it. Some may say that our noble sentiments of "the white man's burden" were just window dressing for avarice. But we alone among imperialists have felt a need for window dressing. Other cultures just subjected cultures they were able to dominate to rape, slavery, and destruction without qualms. They were proud of the plunder they achieved. To the extent that one thinks that we should be ashamed of our plunder, they are using Western values. To the extent that we are ashamed of our civilizing mission, the advance of human rights and Western countries' strength are undermined.

Civilizations, barbarians, and Enlightenment

Is the West civilized enough to recognize that our civilization is an earned treasure worth protecting? The Chinese were in the low part of the Dynastic Cycle when the West finally reached them by sea. They, nonetheless, still considered us barbarians. The opium wars happened because we had to get them to buy something from us. Outside of a cultivated enclave of opium addicts, the Chinese declared that they didn't need anything from us barbarians. They would sell to us, but they refused to import our gimmicky products. Even then the trade was unbalanced in their favor; we were bleeding silver. They would not, it seemed to the British, play fairly. Bad policy was needed to enlighten them to teach them about modernity and fair trade. The Chinese were resolute. Even, and perhaps especially, in the worst of times the Chinese are culturist to the max!

What did the Chinese mean when they called us barbarians? Theirs was the common meaning that identifies a barbarian as a person who lives outside of a known civilization. What did that imply? It implied that we did not have enough of a shared history to know who we were. We had no institutions that told us to respect manners and appreciate traditions. We were a band of conquering folks that would never be able to stabilize our gains without the help of those more civilized. Can marauders run a city? No they just rob and leave. If bandits want to stay and rule a country they must take lessons from civilized peoples on statecraft. They had seen this pattern with the Mongols who had come before us.

Translating the Chinese term for barbarian was not hard for us. We had actually emerged from a fairly old and coherent civilization ourselves. The memory of the ancient Greeks fighting against the mental tyranny of the Persians combined with the Christian view gave us morals that unified us and gave us a sense of purpose. Roman law provided us with bureaucratic habits that could maintain enterprises over a long distance. Furthermore, our Roman heritage gave us confidence that we were capable of doing such a thing. Had we not remembered these things we would have hit and run, or hit and been absorbed like the Mongols. Our past provided forefathers whose standards of decorum and memory unified our members. We would not disintegrate. We were unified, on a mission, and capable of united and sustained action; we were civilized.

But our mission was actually more forward looking than backwards looking. Europeans happened to stumble upon scientific concepts and modes of thought that all manners of humans could use to emancipate themselves from ignorance, superstition, and material want. We had discovered these ideas, but there was no reason we could see that others could not apply them. Science, rational business enterprises, and building towards a free democratic republic obviously seemed to be universal goals all would adopt. It had worked at home and we were sure it could work abroad.

Western culture's confidence during its time of greatest expansion was such that we called the creation of our new rational and scientific point of view "the Enlightenment." Not *an* enlightenment, *the* Enlightenment. This modern viewpoint was correctly seen to be a creation that got its favorable estimation in contradistinction to the Dark Ages. Superstition, oppression, and wars over invisible things (religious beliefs) were being replaced by the rational application of man's mind to the problems of this earth. Much of the world still defines progress this way. Our faith in progress and rational principles turned out to be gifts that are still improving the world.

Unfortunately, the Enlightenment program turns out to have some self-destructive aspects. First of all the Enlightenment based much of its work on science. Science sees itself as dealing with universal principles. Thus, the Western ideals of progress and modernism it fought for were not, after a point, seen to be special. This meant that our triumph would be our defeat. Once everyone had adopted science and progress we would cease to have a distinguishing cultural characteristic. One does not need to fight to prove physics equations or show the benefits of a spreadsheet once it has been widely adopted. Success would undermine the sense of distinction so necessary to cultural flourishing.

Secondly, the Enlightenment's cult of progress saw no value in the past. So the Western traditions were only acknowledged in order to be derided as something we had advanced beyond. Thus the Enlightenment unintentionally cut off the branch from which it bloomed. We do not attribute our successes to our unique past. We attribute them to science and the seemingly natural tendency to want to progress. We no longer have a sense of needing to judge ourselves worthy of our Roman and Greek progenitors. We no longer feel a need to sustain our greatness in the name of prior glories. Sadly, individuals in our individual conscience promoting culture no longer feel a need to vindicate the culture that values them. The individual has superseded the culture that gave birth to him. The modern man simply lives, plunders, and dies without connection to a culture or purpose.

And lastly, the universal laws of science do not allow for temporal variation and neither do our scientifically based Enlightenment ethics. Not realizing the Enlightenment is just a temporal creation, we assume that our truths are universal truths; we then use these universal truths to judge our forefathers without historical perspective. When the Western heirs of the Enlightenment see that we had slavery, they do not simultaneously remember that it was universal trait of agricultural civilizations. History shows our denunciation of slavery and wars against slavery are much more noteworthy than our having had slavery. We condemn ourselves for not having adhered to the Enlightenment's universal standard of right and wrong before we invented them. This unjustly increases our disdain for what little of our past we still care to remember.

To the extent that we do not remember our past, the Chinese were right. We will disintegrate into barbarianism. We will not, as the Greeks did, see our culture as unique. We will not cohere and esteem institutions that extend beyond the self-indulgence of raiders. We will not esteem and protect our collective existence. We fulfill our wants, as all pirates do. But consumerism is not something that can unite a civilization. Consumerism does not teach any ennobling or ethical codes. If we do not take pride in our long and deep historical roots, we will disintegrate like all the barbarian raiders that tried to take China before us. Remembering your cultural roots is essential to sustaining a civilization.

Dr. Livingstone I presume

As Henry Stanley, the famous British explorer of uncharted areas of Africa looked over a plain filled with Africans he felt like a god. He imagined that "all the land be redeemed from wildness, the industry and energy of the natives be stimulated, the havoc of the [indigenous] slave-trade stopped, and all the countries round about permeated with the nobler ethics of a higher humanity." Unfortunately, he also noted the facts on the ground, "At present the hands of the people are lifted – murder in their hearts – one against the other."[106] He relished thinking about the African's future industrial success in this rich land; he was sure that his civilizing mission was noble and would be successful.

The shock to British imperialism was that peoples did not readily take to the British system. They had underestimated the power of local pride to arouse men to rebellion. The locals did not want the British culture more than they hated being ruled by foreigners. They used the British rhetoric about self-determination against the British. If all were to be free and have rights of autonomy, why not us? If all are rational, why not treat us as such? Many locals simply chased the British out. But the locals did not then simply try to compete within the vast impersonal marketplace system the British had set up; they were drawn back to organizing themselves based on their traditional cultural values and groupings.

As we have seen, where Catholic nations colonized the results were not as progressive as where Protestant nations settled. Islamic nations are not primarily interested in implementing a democratic market system. Western, post-Enlightenment cultures have a very difficult time understanding that having many tethered wives, enslaving your enemies, and rule by warlords are every bit as normal and satisfying as the world the British were trying to build. We see rational individualistic striving in a rationalized marketplace as the universal goal. Power, lounging, nationalism, violent raids, divergent cultural rites and mores, getting drunk, and many other diverse motives compete with Western Enlightenment ideals.

Developing nations are largely figments of the imagination. They are only nominally nations (effective government, taxation, and border enforcement are lacking). And, furthermore, many are not developing. They are living their stagnant lives on their own traditional terms. To judge them by how far along the Western path to modernism they have come is to fail to see that our values are not everyone's. Of course the phrase "developing nations" represents a certain degree of truth. But it would not be less accurate to see us as a failing tribal culture. We have forgotten the rites of our ancestors and that our particular way of life needs protection and guidance if it is going to continue.

We judge the developing places where European imperialism happened as behind and feel guilty. We assume that our sense of rationality is universal and that our consumerist goals are natural. This understanding does not recognize the depth of diversity. It rests upon the same mindset that wonders why some cultures in America are not making as much economic and educational progress in America and points to racism as the cause. First of all, we find it hard to believe that cultures could want to do anything but rationally pursue gain on a sunny day. Secondly, to the extent that we do recognize diversity we fail to recognize that can have an impact. Diversity exists internationally and domestically and it has consequences. Not all fail to develop competitive markets out of a lack of opportunity.

If we had a presence in these developing countries we assume that our interference must have hindered their natural desire to succeed in rational business pursuits. Ultimately, our Protestant roots lead us to feel guilty. We see our sin everywhere. Our lack of historical vision leaves us unawares that cultures are diverse. We fail to take pride in the fact that we did not purely enjoy our plundering then plunder again and again. We could steal resources from all over the world if we wanted to. Some people say we do. If we do, we do not take pride in it. Where other nations might brag about their plunder, we feel a need to hide our sins. Our conscience and sense of justice are beautiful; but we must remember they are our ideals and not universal. Judging with our strange ideals of helping others, we did at least as much good as mischief.

Rather than being the result of universal truths, our culture developed from particular historic actions. Without the martial spirit of Achilles we would not have beaten the Persians. Socrates taught us to value conscience; Jesus and Martin Luther taught us to value individuals. Roman law and Protestant individualism were essential to our success. These ideals and Enlightenment principles inspired our Founding Fathers. This is our story, not the world's story. As Westerners we must realize that we are better of living in a prosperous and democratic nation than under other's yoke. Without pride; without remembering that we are a noble experiment that can fail; without consciously reinforcing our cultural underpinnings; without a strong economy; without protecting our lands from those who are indifferent or antagonistic to our culture; our civilization's share of heads and land can recede.

CHAPTER FOUR

CULTURISM IN ANTHROPOLOGY

The noble savage

In learning about culturism in United States' history, the phrase American exceptionalism was mentioned. This phrase suggests that America was to be a different kind of country. In the early 1600s, the Puritans sailed to set up a better world than anything the "Old World" (Europe) had to offer. Our already prevalent disdain for the Old World was made worse by the eighteenth century mainstream philosophical movement of Europe and America named the Enlightenment that we discussed in the previous chapter. The most indelible imprint the Enlightenment made on the Western psyche was the idea of progress. Enlightenment thinkers assumed that science was an advance that would replace the superstition-based mental traps of primitive man.

Hating superstition and living in Europe, most of the Enlightenment's disdain was directed at the Catholic Church. Mankind would be better served, the thinking went, by focusing on this world and forgetting the endless preparation for the afterlife on which the Catholic Church asked the masses to focus. The Enlightenment also found royalty to be an irrational institution. After 1000 years of Catholic stagnation, the Enlightenment invented the idea of endless progress. Enlightenment proponents believed that by focusing our scientific and rational thought processes on this world and its institutions we would slowly improve our world until we had an approximation of heaven on earth.

The Swiss-French philosopher and author Jean Jacques Rousseau was the bad boy of the Enlightenment. He had less reverence for our advanced world than his contemporaries. He thought his contemporary Europeans inauthentic. It was in the context of such criticisms that he would contrast modern Europeans with the "noble savage." One of his famous quotes, "Man is born free and everywhere he is in chains" implies that we in the modern civilized world are corrupt. Man in his natural state was much like Adam and Eve in the Garden. They were free and innocent. Despite a lack of science and civilization, the so-called primitives were said to live in a better world: one without artificiality. Rousseau's supporters held that the Western world was a mistake.

Asked about the Native Americans, many American will confirm Rousseau's beliefs. Common opinion holds that Native Americans were peaceful and ecologically-minded. Many Americans would venture to guess that war, hatred, and crimes against humanity were not vices from which natives suffered. Even if they were not angels, Americans would not expect that Native Americans were as ferocious as Stalin, Hitler, or Mao. These are demons of civilization. Many intuitively accept the common sentiment that our civilization is worse than that of the Native Americans we replaced. They might say that our replacing their culture was not progress, but a crime. Many would suggest that generalizing that evaluation to include the imperialist impact of Western Europe in relation to the rest of the world is valid. Europeans came; they saw; they despoiled.

We are no longer entirely sure about the Enlightenment's faith that our way of life and thought have brought about, or will bring about, a better way of life than that of prehistoric man. The suspicion that the simple and natural life of people with no nuclear bombs or freeways was better causes us to question modernity's value. This view accounts for much of our negative assessment of the impact of imperialism. In the words of the famous '60s song, "We paved paradise and put in a parking lot." Having invented both democracy and nearly every technological invention in existence, we might, instead, look around the world with great pride. If Rousseau is right, however, our despoiling of the world should serve as a deep reservoir of collective guilt.

Margaret Mead and culturism

Rousseau's attack on pretensions is appealing to Americans. But while focused on the backwards nature of Europe, American exceptionalism has also had a domestic target. Unlike today, Americans have traditionally regarded Native Americans as backwards and an obstacle in the way of progress. This point of view justified many an injustice perpetuated by Americans of European extraction. Today, by way of contrast, Americans have a largely positive view of Native Americans. The famed anthropologist and author Margaret Mead deserves much of the credit or blame for this. Her 1928 *Coming of Age in Samoa* became the best selling anthropology book ever. It challenged the idea that Western civilization was an advance over so called primitive ones.

Young Margaret Mead did not decide to go to Samoa on her own. Franz Boas, her mentor, sent her to Samoa. Boas meant for Mead's research to be an ideological tool in his fight against his arch-enemy, Charles Darwin's cousin, Francis Galton. Upon reading his cousin Darwin's writing, Galton decided that cultural differences were the result of natural selection working on racial characteristics. Actually believing that Africans had less developed cultures because they had less developed brains; he was among the first scientific racists. In fact, Galton invented the word "eugenics" and became *the* advocate for breeding humans for good (eu) genes (genics).

The eugenics movement was huge in the United States and, to his credit, Boas was determined to prove Galton's horrible and ugly views false. To this end Boas sent his young student, Margaret Mead, to Samoa to see if adolescent angst was universal. If teen angst even happened in this remote part of the world, he reasoned, it would show that genetics determines our behaviors. If something as basic to our experience as teen angst was absent it would show that culture is a more important influence on our behavior than genes. Mead found that adolescence was a time of tranquility in Samoa. Boas had his proof. Culture, not genes, determined behavior.

Mead's dispelling of the stupid concept of racism was a wonderful triumph. However, she went way overboard in selling the gentleness of the Samoans. Her account of Samoa was, as we shall see later, extremely inaccurate. Worse yet, from a culturist perspective, the implication of her inaccurate work had serious unintended consequences. The belief in the pacific and environmental nature of indigenous people gave rise to a form of cultural relativism. Cultural relativism is the belief that you cannot judge one culture by the standards of another. In its pure form this is a fair assessment. But Mead's extremely romantic depiction of the Samoan's gentle ways has resulted in a caveat to our prohibition against judgments; we are committed to not judging any cultures, except our own. And in comparison to the idyllic portrait she painted, we are bound to look horrible.

Mead portrayed the Samoans as a sexually liberated, jealousy-free, peaceful people. If natives could be this peaceful, our not being so was unnatural. All imperfections imply culpability. Her Pollyannaish portrayal of the Samoans convinced us that all of our social pathologies and stressors reflect unique cultural defects in our civilization. We went from a positive American exceptionalism to a negative American exceptionalism. We now hold that our views are not only not superior; but fail miserably in comparison to the blemish free lifestyle of the Samoans and other indigenous peoples. Our culture is exceptional in that it is exceptionally blemished. By this reckoning it is even improper to advance and affirm our own values in our cultural sphere of influence. Multiculturalism is an instantiation of this view; it celebrates all cultures due to their indigenous status. As Western cultures have tried to change them in the past, it gets cast as an intrinsically aggressive and bad culture that should be thwarted due to historic arrogance.

A closer look at anthropology, however, shows us that we may be sanctioning some distasteful practices when we celebrate multiculturalism without qualification; female genital mutilation is just the tip of the iceberg. A survey of world cultures makes us appreciate anew the special qualities of our own. Culturism could be said to have a cultural relativist stance in that it appreciates and understands diversity. We cannot say that other cultures are wrong based on any objective criterion. However, we can say that from a Western perspective they are wrong and so should be excluded from Western lands. Thus an accurate reading of the modern anthropological record can keep us from imperialist notions while it helps us appreciate ourselves. Anthropology's findings ultimately make the boundaries of the Western world and Western culturism much clearer.

First encounter

Cabeza de Vaca was the first European explorer of the United States. In 1529 he was sent on a journey through what later became the United States as a punishment. And, he ended up getting very lost. Of the three hundred men that set out upon that expedition only four made it back alive. The men were separated from each other and reunited again at various parts in their journeys. During their eight years of desperately trying to find their way back home, they became the first Westerners to see Florida, Texas, New Mexico, Arizona and northernmost Mexico.[107] De Vaca provides us with our best account of America before Western influence.

De Vaca was enslaved by various Native American tribes. He was the first to document the fact that not only did Native Americans have slaves, but they were cruel about it. "Not content with frequently buffeting them, striking them with sticks, and pullout out their beards for amusement, they killed three of the six for only going from one house to another."[108] Slaves were kept without clothes and worked so hard that their fingers bled upon being touched. One was killed on account of a dream one of their captures had had. Cabeza de Vaca had to stay with one tribe for over six months. If he were suspected of trying to escape he would have been killed immediately.

In another tribe De Vaca learned that Native Americans were not all feminists. "The men bear no burden. Anything of weight is borne by women and old men, the people least esteemed. The women got only six hours rest out of twenty-four, spending the wee hours heating the ovens to bake roots. They begin digging at day break and hauling wood and water to their houses, etc."[109] They rarely let daughters live. They tossed female infants to the dogs. This was done because marrying them broke the incest taboo and sending them to another tribe would mean the birth of their enemies and slavery. To get a wife you had to buy them from your enemies. The price of a wife was a good bow and two arrows.

Such information might be shocking to modern Americans, but it would not seem strange to an anthropologist. Anthropologists have long been aware that Native Americans and other indigenous peoples were not angels by Western standards. Native Americans from the Pacific coast to Peru had slaves. The Anasazi engaged in widespread cannibalism. The Pawnee tortured and sacrificed children. These features predated the arrival of Western people. As much as we might deplore some of their traditions, they did not ask for our opinion. Furthermore, they would be able to produce evidence by which to condemn us. Western people stole their land and massacred them. Their having customs we find repugnant does not make us angels either.

One group of Native Americans found Cabeza de Vaca's lost group on the verge of starvation. They left with promises to return with food. By the time they had returned some of Cabeza de Vaca's crew had died. Upon seeing this they "lamented for half an hour so loudly they could have been heard a long way off."[110] Thanksgiving stands as a reminder of Native American's importance in the creation of America. The Iroquois are said to have helped our Founding Fathers in their creation of democracy. A Native American woman was very helpful to Lewis and Clark as they crossed America. Native American arts, crafts, and mythology are wonderfully imaginative creations. Though much of their cultural norms were disgusting by Western standards; their cultures' decimation is a tragic loss.

Native Americans, like indigenous peoples everywhere, were flesh and blood humans with all the foibles that involves. And being human implies a great more diversity than we are accustomed to believe in. To view Native Americans or Western civilization as innocent embodiments of virtue blinds us to the real nature of human beings and history.

Western males and war

Among many modern feminists there is a belief that all war is due to the incursion of patriarchy on the normally peaceful female-led population starting in the year 4200 B.C. These warring invaders were Aryan males.[111] This telling of history chalks up all war and evil to these proto-men of Western civilization. Before the so-called Western "patriarchy," the story goes, humans were peaceful and ecologically-minded. This reading of history is a basic tenet of the new-age practitioners of Wiccan Goddess worshippers. Denunciation of Western patriarchy is axiomatic in many women studies departments.[112] Thus this variant of Mead's vision of the pristine indigenous people's has been taught to many future leaders of America.

Because of such intellectual trends it seems counterintuitive for us to learn that the century that featured Hitler, Stalin, and Mao was the most peaceful in the history of the world! In anthropological parlance there are four basic types of social organization: the band, the tribe, the chiefdom, and the state. Whereas states, such as ours, have full blown "wars" bands and tribes raid each other. These raids usually result in the killing of a person or two. Because only a few people die in such raids, many anthropologists have regarded them as only marginally significant. But when you consider the percentage of the population that die in such raids, they are colossal.

The commonly agreed upon statistic indicates that approximately 25 percent of people died violent deaths prior to the emergence of chiefdoms and states.[113] Approximately 1.5 percent of males in the United States and Europe died as a result of warfare during the twentieth century.[114] To equal the pre-state level of 25 percent of our population dying in warfare, seventy million Americans would have had to have died in wars in America in the twentieth century. We are not even close to having that level of bloodiness. In tribes and chiefdoms every male would be involved in wars. In the modern Western world we have specialized armies and the vast majority of males go through their lives without ever engaging in battle.

Prior to Western contact eighty-six percent of Native American tribes were raiding or resisting raids more than once a year.[115] War often results from scarcity caused by overpopulation. Archeologists have found that in times of scarcity the number of arrow heads embedded in skeletons, broken arms from deflecting blows and crushed skulls goes up. Evidence of violent death found in skeletons in California burial sites goes from 5 or 6 percent to 18 percent in lean times.[116] In chiefdoms and states this pattern is very clear and predictable. Agriculture leads to population growth and the destruction of the environment. Wars ensue and the population collapses. This will be discussed later, but indigenous people's failure to be peaceful often resulted from the same short-sightedness that led them to be bad stewards of the environment. But even in flush times people were locked into counterproductive cycles of bloodshed over items as trivial as a lost pig.

The world order launched by Western civilization is the most peaceful ever. Relatively few Westerners know anyone who has been to war. Furthermore, we have created an ethic that is against war. Many cultures, including those of our Viking predecessors, relished war. Peace is a modern creation. Perhaps some readers will think this is hyperbole, but it is clearly supported by archeological and anthropological statistics. Those who think things are bad now underestimate the amount of diversity in the world. Rather than feel guilt for the wars we have had, we should recapture our feeling of pride in having turned against the enjoyment of blood, gore, and war.

Mesoamerican culture

When Western culturists use Western individuals and cultures as sources of pride bias is involved. But it is rational bias. Our civilization is safeguarded when we see it as special; and more likely to be seen as special when bolstered by an appreciation of those who created it. It would be silly for Westerners to expect that the celebration of the founders of and achievements of the Chinese and Muslims would make us prouder of and more invested in our own culture. No civilization, past or present, outside of the West has spent much time extolling other culture's virtues. This common wisdom is also recommended by the fact that there is often wide divergence between the values of the civilizations in question. This divergence can be used as a source of pride for us.

Diego de Landa's *Account of the Things of Yucatan* is an amazing little book. Diego de Landa himself evokes a strange mixture of gratitude and repulsion. On the one hand he collected and arranged data about the history and customs of the Mayan peoples he encountered. His documentation provides our richest source of information on the Mayans. On the other hand he destroyed articles, codices, and monuments that were obstacles to the implantation of Catholic doctrine.[117] In his own mind he saw only one right culture replacing a wrong one. He only collected information on the Mayans in order to better undermine them.

Arriving in 1549, De Landa spent nearly thirty years in the Yucatan, a peninsula in the southeast of what is today Mexico. After learning the Mayan language, he began to travel throughout the peninsula in order to convert the inhabitants. His zeal led to quick promotions. His cruelty and his usurpation of powers of the bishop and the inquisition, however, got him a trial date back in Spain. After being absolved he began writing his accounts of what he had seen during his years abroad. When we look at his description, we sympathize with his feeling that wrong and a right exist.

The Mayans did have government, literature, and a working economy. Every civilization has things to be proud of. Mayans also had slaves. When giving confession to the Yucatan priests the locals never mentioned infidelity with slaves because, "they had the right to make use of their possessions as they wished."[118] This might be seen as the writing of someone who was trying to make the locals look bad for his own purposes. But no one of that era would have been surprised by the existence of slavery and it was found all over Latin America by different conquistadores.[119] Slavery was a normal practice of pre-modern man.

Mayan religious practices were, though, a little more extreme than run-of-the-mill slavery. "The men made sacrifices of their own blood, sometimes cutting into the edges of their ears at intervals all around, and they left them like this as a sign. Sometimes they pierced their cheeks or lower lips, made incisions in other parts of the body, or would pierce their tongues from side to side and run straws through the hole." A person dedicated to the proposition that all cultures have equal worth could still hold their own. Modern multiculturalists could still defend them. Many Western youth now get pierced and geometric shaped tribal tattoos just to show their sympathy with the indigenous.

Of course, they were more hardcore than most of those who have endured the modern tattooing process. De Landa wrote that, "Sometimes they carried out a foul and laborious sacrifice. Those who were performing it assembled in the temple and, standing in a row, each made a hole through his member [genitals] from side to side; they then passed through the greatest quantity of cord they could, and so all were threaded through." We do not stigmatize much anymore. Sadomasochism is accepted as healthy. So even after finding out that they used chords to get blood from their private parts for an idol, multiculturalists could still defend them.

But human sacrifice is not an action that can be reconciled with modern humanism. As a part of their regular sacrifices De Landa wrote, ". . . they took hold of him [the one to be sacrificed] and bound him, as they all danced and watched him." "Then the unholy priest came and wounded the victim, whether man or woman, in the private parts. He drew blood, then came down and with it smeared the face of the demon." In the end the executioner would tear out the living heart and the priest would use the blood to anoint the faces of the idols. This is gruesome stuff. We prize freedom of religion. But culturists would prohibit human sacrifice in the United States as un-Western. Multiculturalist faced with this level of diversity might even recoil.

It gets worse! "Sometimes they performed this sacrifice on the stone on the top step of the temple and then would set the body to roll down the staircase. At the bottom, the officials took the body and flayed it completely except the hands, and feet, then the naked priest wrapped himself in this skin and all the others danced with him. This was an occasion of great solemnity for them. These victims were commonly buried in the courtyard of the temple or, if not, were eaten, being distributed among the chiefs and those they were sufficient for. The hands, feet and heads were for the priests and officials."

These practices were not only specific to the Mayans. The Aztecs were constantly battling their enemies to get bodies for sacrifice. These were called Flower Wars.[120] One reason Cortez defeated the Aztecs was that they sought to take their opponents alive in order to sacrifice them instead of killing them outright.[121] And these sacrifices involved no small loss of life. At the dedication of the main temple to Huitzilopochtli as many as 80,400 captives were sacrificed.[122] After being sacrificed by the priests the happy captor could take the body home, eat it and hang the bones as a sign of prestige.[123] It was normal for certain priests to wear the skins of those sacrificed for twenty days.[124] Diversity includes such behaviors.

If you are not to judge cultures you have to accept human sacrifice and the wearing of the victim's skins and the eating of their bodies. Our worst serial killers are thought mad when they do the same thing. You have to condemn some cultures or stop judging serial killers. Such rites are not acceptable by Western standards. We do not even impose such barbarous fates on convicted serial killers or rapists. If you think that our outlawing "cruel and unusual punishment" is good, you have to denounce widespread premodern practices. Multiculturalists do not announce parameters for their love of diversity. If you denounce sacrificing humans and wearing of their skin, in America, you are a culturist. You have qualified your love of diversity.

In the name of contrition for our crimes, providing esteem to those descended from Mesoamericans and being respectful, multiculturalists must distort history, archeology, and anthropology. From a Western point of view, we can only see the cultures of Mesoamerica as nightmarish. Yes, they built marvelous pyramids. But they were built steep in order that the victim's bodies would roll down them quickly. Praising a mass murderer for his clever apparatus undermines your sense of morality. It is wrong for us to sacrifice the Western culturist perspective on the alter of multiculturalism. We have created an ethical system that decries war waged to gather sacrificial victims. From our perspective human sacrifice should be condemned. We should enhance our pride in those who have fought against such practices by noticing the difference in values.

The depth of diversity

Diversity is not confined to behavior. We cannot really appreciate what it means to enjoy skinning someone for the gods as the Mesoamericans did. Our rational biases might cause us to miss the radical depth of such diversity. Stop and imagine the mind set of the person torturing children to propitiate the Morning Star before killing them as the Pawnee did.[125] Try to imagine what it means to kill sleeping children you come across to pass on your sorrow as some Northwestern Native Americans did.[126] What is the mindset behind the joy of headhunting? To think that these behaviors just represent a misapplication of our detached application of calculating reason is to underestimate the mental diversity implied by these actions.

It has been found that Western dichotomies of mind versus body and natural versus supernatural and the corresponding division between psychiatry, medicine, ethics, and religion rarely hold in other cultures.[127] The creation of these mental styles is done early and is, interestingly, invisible to us. Having children sleep alone in a room communicates messages of autonomy, individuality, and a private world to them. But we just see such action as natural. Asking a child what they want to eat means that individual taste, regardless of magical implications for the tribe, is to be considered.[128] We are usually unaware that such a question is a cultural construct that conveys the importance of individual desire. We finish our preverbal children's sentences for them. In doing so we assume the existence of, and thus mold, a rational pattern of thought in the mind of the child.[129]

Ilongot are headhunters in the South Pacific. Their youth are not assumed to have sense until they have taken a head. For Ilongot names bestow consciousness. The baby is not given a name because, not having sense, a spirit could call it away if it had one.[130] If a child falls, the mother may spit on its head and call it back so that it does not go away. When they can speak they are not thought to have sense yet. So they are directed by threats of death if they do not comply. Even after speaking children are not given names. Rather than the Western inner rational actor Ilongot describe themselves as being guided by the disturbing feelings born of situations.[131] A farmer could, for example, be made dizzy by the vitality of her crops.[132] Their world has many disturbing energies that pull them. The build up of this disturbing energy is released when they take a head. Cultures can have fundamentally different kinds of consciousness.

De Landa thought Mayan thinking patterns were very different. He said their ". . . men do not wish to be guided by the light of reason that he [God] has bestowed upon them, they begin to be tormented in this life and to feel part of the Hell they deserve in the difficult rites they continually perform to the demon god, with lengthy fasts, vigils and abstinence, with unbelievable offerings and gifts of their possession and property, with the constant shedding of their own blood, with severe pain and wounds to their bodies and, what is worse and more serious, with the lives of their fellows and brothers."[133] Anthropology has confirmed De Landa's findings. If nothing else, anthropology asserts that men unmodified by culture do not exist and could not exist.[134]

In many indigenous traditions youth have to go on a quest in which they find spirit guides. This usually involves fasting and often also involves ceremonial mutilation and torture. Kwakiutl youth, like so many other Native American youth, had to spend time with their spirit to be initiated into their society. No one could use each other's names during this period. In the woods the aspirant ate corpses. When they came back they went into frenzy, bit mouths of flesh from those trying to restrain them and ate the bodies of slaves who had been killed for them.[135] Only after being treated with menstrual blood could they start to come back and be a real member of the cannibal order of the Kwakiutl.

In many other cultures menstrual blood is treated as a horror. Yanamamo believe it to be a danger to the whole community. If the woman does not refrain from normal activities subterranean dwarf spirits will transform her into a rock and destroy the whole village.[136] Such attitudes are inculcated. An unconscious and emotionally disturbed space underlies this sort of widespread "logic" that we are not acculturated to. Neither treating menstrual blood as magic, biological or dirty is natural. Others humans are driven by spirits and disturbing feelings to eat dead people or chop heads off. Diversity is such that we would likely vomit soon after starting to cut someone's head off. Our detached logic is not the default mentality of humanity. We should not be surprised that when we neglect conscious socialization bizarre and cruel behaviors appear. Diversity is deep and wide.

Our truths are not self-evident

There is no objective basis upon which to say that one culture is better than another. Were our way of life inherently more satisfying than others, Western culturism would not be needed. The triumph of cultures dedicated to rights, individualism, and progress would be just a matter of waiting for natural practices to occur. Anthropology shows that people are accustomed to endure long suffering before changing directions. In fact, the belief that inefficiency and pain are bad only reflects Western assumptions. Female genital mutilation is not naturally resented by those in the cultures that practice it.

Our existence offers others a choice that can result in a negative evaluation. But such an evaluation is not apparent in the practice without comparison to another culture. Indigenous practices offer us choices. Maintaining our unique values while others simultaneously maintaining their unique values creates the greatest worldwide variety of choices.

The Yanomami live in Venezuela and surrounding parts of the Amazon rainforests. They called themselves "The Fierce People" and fierce they are. They inhale hallucinogens through their noses daily.[137] They raid neighboring villages for purposes of sorcery, murder and food theft often.[138] Approximately thirty-five percent of Yanomami men die in warfare.[139] This puts them, again, only ten percentage points ahead of the usual tribal population. Women wear almost nothing except for sticks that pierce their faces. As mentioned in passing earlier, Yanomami consider menstruating women to be dangerous. And women who leave the areas women are supposed to stay in are considered fair game for gang rape.

One Yanomami woman, Yarima, got married to a visiting Anthropologist. He fell in love with her and felt anxious knowing that she might be raped there (she was). He married her and took her home to New Jersey.[140] Dressed up in Western clothes, she had children and spent long days in the shopping mall like other suburban women. She lived on flattened earth for her first time. Those who see our mall-strolling as an obviously better way of life would be shocked to hear what she ended up doing. She decided to leave her professor husband and go back to the fierce people in the forest that had raped her. Was she insane? No. She found Western life boring. It is not self-evident that our way of life is better.

The previously mentioned Ilongot headhunters of the South Pacific provide another interesting case. Westerners did not find some of these people until well into the 20th century. There are many of them. The Ilongot kept headhunting until the 1970s. The Ilongot life cycled around sad feelings of the heart that could only be quelled by beheading someone. It is hard for the Western mind to understand the joy and lighthearted feeling that comes from cutting off another person's head. After cutting off human heads the Ilongot seek out flowery reeds to wear that signifying lightness and come home singing.[141] Whether or not we get it, cutting off heads remains a joyous spiritual event.

Since headhunting was outlawed many Ilongot have become Christian. This new religion was taken on to relieve the pain created by the inability to hunt heads. The major study of the Ilongot relates that elders prefer not to be reminded of the loss of this tradition as it pains them to know that the young will never know the glory of headhunting.[142] But recently headhunting has had a resurgence.[143] It can be blamed on the centralized government's failures to modernize the local people. But it is also a triumph of the traditional. The local Dayaks recently took the heads of 400 migrants in one raid and said it really felt good.[144] We cannot assume that the Western world provides a more appealing lifestyle.

Female genital mutilation happens in over 25 African countries, among some minorities in Asia, and in immigrant communities in Western countries. Female genital mutilation is listed along with dowry murder, honor killings, and early marriage as harmful traditional practices by the United Nations.[145] It involves cutting out much of the inner vagina and then sewing it shut. The sewing guarantees the girl's virginity before her wedding night and eliminates temptation to stray after it.[146] For healing purposes pastes that include dung are applied to the cut areas and her legs are tied together.[147] Approximately 135 million girls have undergone this process and six thousand a day currently take place.

"Female genital mutilation" is a Western phrase. Without a doubt the indigenous terms for the practice would not imply such condemnation. So called female genital mutilations are often performed by grandmothers who had the operation themselves. To prohibit such an operation means that you are condemning their offspring to being unacceptable women in their communities. Many men *and* women would be against such a ban. Some cultures love headhunting. Others consider rape and drug use to be proper. Some wear each other's skins after sacrifices. Many other practices that are disgusting from a Western perspective are integral to traditional pre-Western cultures. Such practices are problematic for both culturists and multiculturalists.

Culturism holds that dominant cultures should celebrate and

protect themselves. From the Western vantage point, headhunting and female genital mutilation are ugly and reprehensible. Culturists realize, however, that this constitutes a Western bias. As we tend to think our values are universal this realization is hard for us. We love our values. These practices are repugnant to us. But they are only repugnant to us. There are different variants of culturism. Yanomami have a right to their culture. Western culturism is for the Western nations. We are not the world. We can condemn female genital mutilation inside of our borders as this is not a Western practice. But if we wish others to respect our right to define ourselves, we must be willing to respect other's right to define themselves.

Such indigenous practices present different challenges for multiculturalists. Culturists have a hard time tolerating such practices in other countries. Multiculturalists must have an even harder time celebrating them. Those dedicated to celebrating diversity without announcing qualifications must praise human sacrifice, drug use, head hunting, slavery, and female genital mutilation. Usually multiculturalists attempt to surmount this ideological difficulty by either imagining diversity as less wide ranging than it really is or picking and choosing which cultural attributes to celebrate. But once you start to pick and choose which practices you are and are not going to tolerate you are no longer celebrating diversity; you are judging cultures.

Internationally, anthropologists will tell you, promoting "human rights" means promoting the modern Western lifestyle. It is wrong and arrogant for us to tell the Koreans that they cannot prefer Korean values and persons in their laws. When you outlaw headhunting, you outlaw a way of life. To go to the Middle East and insist that they adopt separation of church and state or China and say that they must have democracy is unacceptable. It would be as if they were to come into Western countries and told us to start shooting psychedelics in our noses every day. Cultures are diverse. Culturists appreciate diversity, know that it is their bias that prevents them from doing so when they cannot, and do not advocate forcing foreign cultures to adopt variants of Western values.

Cortes told a Mesoamerican king that he must "Give up your sacrifices and cease to eat the flesh of your neighbors and practice

sodomy and the other evil things you do."[148] He wanted to leave a
cross, but his comrades thought it too early to leave a cross in their
possession. They feared that the locals might do something degrading
to it. They probably would have. It was rude for Cortes to suggest
leaving his symbol in their world. It was a crime for Cortes to destroy
the Aztecan culture. If a culture wants to follow another's lead, it
should be purely voluntary. The impetus for cultural changes can and
should only come from within the cultures that live them.

We are special!!!

Some cultures have practices that are morally repugnant to us.
Native Americans of the West coast used to allow rival chiefs to land
boats on their slaves to display their wealth. This would kill the
slaves. Having slaves, killing them, and (traditionally) conspicuous
consumption are all things that leave a bad taste in our mouths. But
within the framework of the Native's logic, one had to do such things
or suffer ignominy. Telling them that they could no longer do such
things would strip their lives of meaning. Basic truths are culturally
bounded.

Western style ideals of justice are not universal. For example
when a member of one Northwest Native American tribe died, they
did not mourn. Instead they would go out and make someone else
mourn. Famed anthropologist Ruth Benedict wrote about this taking
place when a female of a tribe died. No one knew how she died.
Having left and not come back, she could have still been alive. Such
logic chopping was not important. They were sad that she was gone.
As custom dictated the men went searched until they found some
strangers sleeping. They killed everyone including two children. They
had transferred their sad feeling to someone else. They felt good
about what they had done.[149]

These Native Americans of New Mexico were not unusual in their
feeling great joy at killing others. The sense of solemnity over having
taken a life was not included in the proceedings. There was no sense
of the sanctity of the individual life. In one Native American culture,
while parading around with the victim's scalp women would come out
dressed as clowns and there would be much dancing.[150] Our media
would be quick to condemn any community they found still practicing

such customs. Our somber and careful approach to the taking of a life is not the universal norm. If you want individual human lives you must support Western nations and values.

There is no universal idea of justice. Western Justice exists, but other senses of right and wrong exist independently. Knowing about both Western and other standards of appropriateness is useful. If we want to judge the Puritans, for example, we can condemn them for their witch burnings. But we must realize that our condemnation is invoking Western, not universal, standards. The Jalé of New Guinea regularly had festivals where they ate those they had killed in war. They would close the eyes, mouth, and nose with bat bones to keep the spirits in and then eat.[151] When we compare the Puritans, using Western standards, to the diverse spectrum of possibilities that exist, their transgressions seem pretty tame.

We should be conscious of when we should be judging by Western standards and when we should not. It is appropriate to judge the Puritans by Western standards – they were Western. It is not appropriate to judge the Jalé by Western standards. Cannibalism is a very widespread phenomenon. We choose not to eat human flesh. That does not mean that others should not. We do not believe souls escape through the nose and mouth. What others believe is not our business. But we can take pride that, according to Western values, we amongst the most agreeable people ever. Seeing that there are various standards should not lead us to abandon our standards. From our vantage point increasing our affiliation with our mores does more for our causes and maintains an area in which we are comfortable with our surroundings.

Using a pluralistic system of values helps us understand who we are. When antebellum Southerners killed their slaves it was a bad thing. Why? What was the ethic that the act violated? It was bad because we respect the individual and their lives. North pacific Native Americans killed their slaves to impress rival chiefs. Use of the death penalty is not a time for parties with clowns for us. Unless we knew about the diversity of cultures that exist we might not realize that our way of life is special. It is very distinctive to say that we are a culture that considers the taking of a human life significant and solemn.

We judge the killing of children to displace mourning more harshly than Puritan witch killing. Why? In the example given, the children killed to escape mourning had nothing to do with the supposed death being mourned. The Puritans killed for a bad reason, but at least the supposed crimes were attributed to those who were killed. We are a culture that believes in the value of individual life and a sense of justice based on rational attributions concerning individual culpability. Again, we learn what is special about us when we realize that alternatives exist.

Marind-anim are located in Melanesia. They believe that semen is essential to human growth. To ensure a woman's fertility, therefore, as many as ten members of the husband's lineage have sexual intercourse with her in the course of an evening. If there are more men on her husband's side, they continue the next night. This has led to severe pelvic inflammatory disease and infertility in their women. Even if one does not wish to judge such a tradition, it would eventually lead to the culture's extinction. Rather than alter this custom, Marind-anim took to shopping for children and raiding other villages to obtain children before the government outlawed their tradition of repeated intercourse.[152]

We would have probably questioned the assumption that gang rapes lead to fertility rather than buy children from others. We scrutinize our own culture for defects. Our using the scientific method to find fulfill our secular goals of life, liberty, and the pursuit of happiness is a wonderful Western contraption. The West does and should judge itself by Western standards. We have a coherent value system (coherence is important to us). We should apply our standard to ourselves in order that we might improve (improvement is important to us). But just as it is fair and necessary to blame ourselves for our violations of our ethics; it is also fair and necessary to give ourselves credit for having created our ethical system.

We are special in that we have chosen our values. The extent to which we really do things out of an application of rational standards is debatable. Halloween does not make sense. We hide Easter eggs because we hide Easter eggs. There are historical precedents, but that is not why we do it. Much of our culture is not chosen. Love of peace is just assumed to be a virtue. We do not experiment with headhunting to confirm our hypothesis. But we instinctively know that we cannot choose to love headhunting, but the experiment would so violate our ethics that we do not perform it. But within limits we consider questioning our culture to be a virtue. We may not be continuously doing so at a deep level. But to the extent that we consider rational self-scrutiny a virtue we are special.

It is fine and fun to have public holidays that do not make sense. They are a big part of what builds collective memories and identities that support cultural viability. But our public policy, reflecting our unique cultural tradition, should be decided upon rationally. The goal that they should seek to accomplish is securing the blessings of liberty to our selves and our posterity. These are decidedly Western goals. Our goals are ours and should be celebrated for this reason. Western policies best protect our values when they reflect the fact that our beliefs are not the universal default; when recognizing that our belief system is special.

Diversity, culpability and responsibility

Dr. Hector García was the founder of the influential Latino rights organization, the G. I. Forum. Among other incidents, Dr. García was motivated to start this organization by his visiting Mexican citizens living in America's southern states. Films of these encounters show dirty half-naked children playing outside of shanty homes.[153] These Mexican children were filthy, diseased, illiterate, and neglected by local officials. He spent much of his life trying to get the American government to pay attention to this situation. Within his organization there was also an admission that the Mexicans themselves were responsible for their situation.[154] Culpability estimations have to hinge on your reading of anthropology.

The common view that such poverty can only be the result of oppression is based on the idea that American levels of attainment and aspirations are the norm. This is not true. An anthropologist found a community in Eastern Kentucky that was at least as badly off (by Western standards) as that for whom Dr. García had worked. The children in this community were covered in big sores from malnutrition and filth.[155] No one in this community ever brushed their teeth or used toilet paper.[156] They smelled and were diseased. All the anthropologist's kind efforts to bring youth out of this community misfired. The youth saw no point in changing their clothes, learning or leaving their community.[157]

Were the lifestyles of these communities the fault of the United States? Yes and no. Yes, because these communities were within the borders of the United States. But on the other hand, if this is close to what the default level of human mentality is, it certainly is not a case of inflicted harm. In fact, looked at from the long perspective of human history, the existence of the United States provides the only reason either group could have a dream of a better type of life. Before blame is assigned we should always acknowledge that it is a blessing that there is a Western world to lift people up. The United States was not at fault for the state of these communities. That was a natural state of affairs. But the United States might have had responsibility to address these situations.

The government of the United States definitely should have done something to assimilate the community found in Kentucky, but the may not have had a responsibility towards the community Dr. García found. Girls in the Kentucky community had sexual intercourse starting at the age of six. They did not think that there was anything wrong with this.[158] Many women in Mexico are stunned to find out that it is a crime for their husbands to beat them. They just feel that beatings are a part of a woman's lot in life.[159] Both communities' practices are repugnant to modern Western sensibilities. But cultures are not necessarily reflective about their behavior. Neither community appealed Western ethicists for definitions of right and wrong. On what basis can a culturist state that there is a responsibility to enforce norms on one community and not another?

The Kentucky community consisted of English speaking Americans with loyalties to no other country. The residents Dr. García found were on American soil, but they were clearly Mexican. They did not speak any English at all. They were in the United States as a part of a guest worker program. It is not our place to tell other cultures how to live. Our drive and determination to achieve cleanliness and advancement are not the universal default. If people are more comfortable in sheds, that is their business. If they wish to pursue Western-style rights and goals, that is their own concern. Within our borders we have an obligation to make sure that our basic norms are aspired towards. All things considered though, because the "Mexican" community was within our borders their assimilation probably was our responsibility. But their being on the border geographically and culturally makes it less certain that they were our responsibility than the community in Kentucky was.

This is not racism. This is culturism. Culture is not created by race. Making any sort of human accept the dominant culture's way of life takes conscious effort. Language was the only factor making the Spanish-speaking group harder to assimilate than the English speaking group. It is the job of the government to monitor the cultural assumptions of the people within its border because no people are naturally reflective. If a white woman is raised in a community where people think it is okay to beat women, her whiteness will not afford her any protection. She will assimilate the dominant mores of the cultural milieu she finds herself in. It is because culture is not built into people generically or into their race that Western values require active protection and propagation.

Progressive agendas

Self-scrutiny is healthy for Western cultures. Doubt in our basic competence is not. Our doubt in our greatness and the progress we have brought the world gets reflected in the silence that follows the question, "Who are we to judge?" Within our sphere of influence we *are* very competent to judge. The archeological and anthropological scholarship is overwhelming in our favor of saying we are competent at implementing our values. We have created a world where a person is freer from terror (a Western goal). We have created a world where the Western goals of life, liberty, and attaining property are protected. We have done so by discouraging sloth, violence, sexual assault, irrationality, and many other natural propensities of man.

Modern anthropology does not use the word "primitive" as it implies too much judgment. This prohibition is upheld despite the clear evidence that some levels of social organization necessarily come after others.[160] Such judgments would run counter to anthropology's determination to be as objective as possible. As a science, this practice makes sense for anthropology. You cannot appreciate the values of people you have already judged as wanting. Judging a culture in which you are a guest could also cause your invitation to be revoked. These professional uses of cultural relativism have their uses. However, the general public's judging by Western standards within Western countries is not only appropriate, it is necessary.

Judging ourselves by our standards is integral to our culture. Science is the basis of our vision of progress. Science is based on doing experiments and judging the results. Judging based on rational criteria is not the default behavior of mankind. Decisions being made on the basis of divination and shamanistic spirit journeys remain widespread. We are the first culture dedicated to constantly improving the world via scientifically applying our powers. We must, however, recognize this propensity as special. Rather than consciously advancing, it is the natural default of cultures to be conservative; even when this involves a lot of pain.

Protecting our culture means consciously judging. If you wanted to methodically investigate which facets of your culture were consciously chosen and which are ruts, you would not start by looking at matters that your culture already consciously questions. The cultural facets that are "self-evident" and beyond questioning are more likely to be widely accepted falsehoods. Culturism holds that the inviolability of individualism as instantiated in rights at the expense of the culture is one area where we have ceased to utilize our critical faculties. The unqualified acceptance of any and all behaviors in the name of celebrating diversity is another. Our resulting inability to judge behaviors within our borders provides another example.

Our government's deference to Native Americans generating revenue from the traditionally condemned practice of gambling reflects our misreading of the Anthropological record. Gambling was previously relegated to Las Vegas, which thereby earned the moniker "Sin City." Challenging this revenue source brings up the touchy issue of how we destroyed their intrinsically worthy way of life and corrupted it with our malevolent influence. We would certainly be hypocrites to tell them about morality! As cultural relativists would argue, we should respect their culture. But they should also respect ours. When Mead's influence gets applied domestically we get multiculturalism. Multiculturalism robs us of the authority to protect our culture.

We cannot assume that our way of life is intrinsically preferable.

Given a choice, many people choose killing and drugs as hobbies. To encourage unqualified diversity is to condone and advocate more than variations of rational lifestyles. Our celebration of individual rights and self-governance only represents one potential cultural proclivity. Denouncing certain behaviors is a part of promulgating our unique way of life. The criminal justice system cannot celebrate diversity as anthropologists understand it. It is anthropologically ignorant to think that the ways of an English gentleman are what the result of never judging behavior will naturally lead to.

Some cultures have died out because people no longer saw themselves as worth the hassle of sustaining.[161] Roman culture has been thought to be an example of this.[162] The Soviet Union failed to stay united due to popular discontent with its ideals. It did not die out due to not working; people were fed. Many cultures continue even though they do not "work." Ideas are not just matters of idle debate. Our having adopted the multiculturalist creed that our culture is not special may be dangerous. If we inculcate the idea that your culture is inherently evil in comparison with others for a couple of generations we may find people unwilling and unable to defend our progressive and peace loving civilization from internal degeneration or external attack.

Our technology has allowed the world population to flourish. Due to Western technology our life expectancy is nearly twice that any primitive tribe ever attained and triple what many achieved. Our civilization has lowered worldwide bloodshed, enslavement, and brutal male dominance that used to be (and still is in much of the world) the status quo. We invented democracy and rights. Other cultures having rights within their countries largely results from pressure we exert as a successful country. The best tactic for those who wish to see a world with rights created is to make sure that a strong progressive culture is living within our borders. If that involves telling Native Americans that encouraging the irrational, addictive, and bankrupting habit of gambling in our culture must stop, we can present clear culturist reasons for doing so.

Environmentalism

Humans have been and are an environmental disaster. Moderns also feel guilty because they assume that have been taught that indigenous peoples were environmentalists and we are not. At sometime in their lives most Americans were taught that Native Americans used every part of each animal they killed out of respect for the sacredness of nature. Alas, in this section Western civilization cannot be vindicated. We, as all other populations, have had a huge negative impact on the environment. But the best hope for turning this around lies in applying Western science to the problems we face. In the meantime, the naïve belief that indigenous were great environmental stewards does not help; it undermines our sense of efficacy.

Native Americans were not careful to preserve the environment at a cost to themselves. Eighty percent of the large animals in South America and seventy three percent of those in North America were wiped out between the time the Native Americans got to the Western hemisphere and when the Europeans arrived.[163] It is not possible to tell which extinctions were due to climate changes. But the animals having survived for hundreds of thousands of years and then disappearing after the arrival of Native Americans on the continent lends credence to the common sense conjecture that human action must have contributed to the extinctions.[164]

The Anasazi and their neighbors occupied much of what are now the states of Arizona, Utah, Colorado, and New Mexico. Because of forests a dense population was able to survive there. Because of dense populations, the forests were not able to survive there. The areas the Anasazi occupied now provide that look of barren expanse that serves as a background in cowboy movies. That barrenness is due the natives having deforested the area.[165] When they had undermined their ability to feed themselves they descended into warfare and cannibalism. By the time Columbus arrived in the New World, the area had its present look and was filled with abandoned archeological sites.

Humans are not primarily the rational analyzers of their situations Westerners take them to be. We, as we shall study later, are built to absorb and practice a culture. If you were going to see evidence of people being able to control their fates as a collective, it would be on islands. On islands people know the extent of resources available. They can see that there is no vast expanse of unused resources to exploit beyond what is visible. On Easter Island the civilization's response to the deforestation that eventually killed them was building taller versions of the statues they are famous for.[166] Again, by the time the first Westerner got there the population consisted of very few people obsessed with cannibalism.[167]

The Maoris of New Zealand drove a dozen species of large birds to extinction six centuries before the first Westerner got there.[168] The heavily forested Middle East was turned into a desert by agriculturists well before the Western expansion.[169] The Mayans likely undermined themselves ecologically.[170] Much of the drive to colonize the world was driven by the Europeans having destroyed their own ecosystem.[171] To the extent that they can, people usually multiply and undermine their ecosystems. This is followed by collapse and warfare. This is, sadly, as near universal for the human species as we can establish.

Modern man only destroys more than his predecessors because he can. Facing that honestly (not idealizing the past) is the only hope we have. Much of the West's self-definition centers on our ideal of ourselves as a scientific culture. The destruction of the ozone was halted by monitoring and a rational reaction that no indigenous culture would or could have done. The West is also defined by not just blindly accepting traditional ways. As such, we are very adaptable. During World War II we became an environmental nation. We grew a large percentage of our vegetables in Victory Gardens. We recycled materials as never before or since. We did so because that was what was needed for the war effort. Had the culture of the inhabitants of Easter Island adopted this sort of critical self-analysis and action, they might still be here.

Westerners erroneously believe that indigenous peoples were wise environmental conservators. It is also, however, widely known that Indians killed buffalo by stampeding them off of cliffs and then spearing the top layers. Simultaneously holding these two views bolsters this chapter's contention that integrating facts is not a human priority. Because of our scientific bent, if any culture has the wherewithal to think and adapt their way out of our environmental crisis it is the West. Abandoning our engagement with the Western tradition of scientific engagement with the world out of a false sense of comparative guilt is dangerous. Now is the time for Westerners to recommit themselves to our efficacious culture. Human sacrifice will not solve anything.

Back to the garden

Margaret Mead's celebrity outside of the academic anthropology community had tremendous cultural impact. A basic hippie counterculture tenet was that we needed to go back to nature. The chorus of the 1960s hit song "Woodstock" concluded, "And we've got to get our selves back to the garden." Pure Rousseau. Pure Mead. The multicultural fallacy that native cultures were noble and good and that we are corrupt has now permeated much of our culture. If the disaffected youth were aware of how special what they take for granted is and how horrible the alternatives are they would likely stop getting tribal tattoos and battle to maintain the Western lifestyle. Anthropology and archeology show us just how far the Western world has come.

The full historical record shows that Mead's peaceful Samoans were nearly always at war until European enforced peace.[172] Between 1830 and 1832 one Samoan village had 197 battles.[173] From 1865 to 1871 11.7 percent of the adult male population of a group of islands was killed in war.[174] This round of protracted warring was started because the wrong person blew a conch shell! The losers in Samoan wars had their food supplies and villages burned. In one war hundreds of men and women were thrown into a fire and many small boys were cooked and eaten. Those slain on the battlefield had their heads chopped off and carried away in triumph to be shown to the chief.[175]

Derek Freeman did a methodical follow-up investigation of the Samoans in the 1960s. What he found is more representative of what modern anthropologists would expect. Samoa's assault rate in the mid 1960s was about five times higher than that of the United States.[176] Their rate of rapes was twice that of the United States in 1966. This figure does not include "surreptitious" rapes. In this category of rape the male inserts his fingers into the female's vagina to break her hymen. This is done either by sneaking into her bed at night and doing it while she is sleeping or by knocking her out during the daytime via a blow to the sternum before inserting the fingers.

Surreptitious rape has symbolic significance. At their weddings the female is disrobed in front of the assembled guests. The groom-to-be sticks his fingers into her vagina and breaks her hymen in order to ensure that she is a virgin. If there is no blood her female relatives fall upon her shouting insults and beat her with stones, disfiguring, and possibly killing her. Mead mentions this in her books, but minimizes the impact of such attacks![177] The real meaning of surreptitious rape is that the girl must now either elope with the fellow that broke her hymen or face this unbearable fate on her wedding day. If you include this type of rape the Samoan's rape rate was over five times that of the United States of 1966.[178]

Those who are unaware of anthropology take the Western sense of life to be the universal default. This fallacy is manifest in our determination not to discriminate based upon creed or religion. Naiveté about the range of diversity is apparent when people do not realize that some cultures might be more inclined to value a life of study than others. Mankind is as apt to value macho wife beating, headhunting, killing for God, and shamanistic trances, as he is to value fair play and rational pursuits. Cultures are not only more diverse than we imagine, they are more diverse than we *can* imagine.

The indigenous Samoan way of life might be very satisfying. Our ethical problems with it are purely based on cultural bias. There is no way for us to prove our way of life is better than their traditional way of life. It is not our place to do so. However, cultural programming is such that we Westerners cannot but believe that rape and genocide are bad things. That means that our living in a world that does not include these values would be unpleasant for us. In this diverse world, our partiality to Western culture makes it important that we protect and promote a space where our particular culture can thrive.

CHAPTER FIVE

WESTERN CULTURE

Western Civilization exists

The phrase, "a nation of nations" contains a logical error. This assertion is meant to indicate that the United States has no traditional or dominant culture. It is an assertion that America is, at its core, a cultureless blank slate. The logical flaw results from the fact that not having a culture would make us unique as a nation.[179] No other nation would make the claim that they are a nation without a core culture. If nothing else, the fact that this claim could be made should prove to people that we have a unique culture. You cannot assert that we are a "nation of nations" without simultaneously saying that we have a special and particular national culture.

One reason for this confusion is that we, falsely, take our culture to be the universal default for humanity. But as we saw in the previous chapter, many diverse ways of life and value systems have thrived. Our culture is but one of many. Our culture neither makes decisions based on shamanistic journeys nor wears the skins of sacrificial victims. We consider the first as irrational and the second grotesque. These judgments come so naturally to us that we do not see them as culturally specific. But in the age of suicide bombings, it should be apparent to us that not every culture shares our values.

Islamic culture, for example, does not hold that the rights to wear and say what you want are self-evident. Much of the Muslim world sees it as moral to kill women who dishonor their families. Killing to impose religious uniformity is something Muslim cultures celebrate and their governments support. Even when we had a considerable economic and technological advantage over China, the Chinese did not think freedom of speech, religion, and assembly worth adopting. Now that our dominance over them has diminished we should not assume that they will suddenly join us as an enclave of unfettered individualism.

Much confusion over our version of life being universal is born of the fact that the demands of large states create pressures to adopt some common institutions. Governments and schools are a part of all countries. But both the Aztecs and NAZI Germany were states. Similarity in institutions still leaves room for quite a bit of diversity. Furthermore, history shows us that nations not only come into being, but dissolve. Nowadays states are dissolving based on claims of cultural distinctions. Statewide claims of hegemony that exist are very often very thin. Many states are more aspirations than realities. It is questionable how much control Afghanistan's government has outside of the capitol city of Kabul. Western style enforcement of values, peace, and rights do not represent eternal truths. They have only existed for a little time, under certain conditions, in some areas.

Rights, as we understand them, currently exist in Western Europe, Australia, New Zealand, the United States, and Canada. These areas are the core areas of Western values. Democracy and rights have tenuous grips in Latin America and Eastern Europe. These areas may become more Western with time. They may revert to their more traditional modes of existence. Tribal and religious intolerance, irrationality, and crude oppression hold sway over much of the rest of the world. Some areas outside of the Western core areas are thriving. Many perceive the Western core areas as not doing so well. Asia sees this as an affirmation of their right to dominate us. Much of Islam sees this as signifying an opportunity to destroy us.

Our toleration of subcultures and dissent makes us unique. Much of the world suppresses dissent. We allow little "nations" inside of our nation. Much of the world does not value diversity and so does not like having diversity in their part of the world. They are heavy-handed culturists. Islamic states do not take kindly to apostates. China does not like protesters. Nigeria does not tolerate either. The traditional reactions to those whose behavior deviated from the norms in any way have been exile, exorcism, and death. Our level of tolerance and protection for diversity are not universally endorsed virtues. Ignorance of this fact is not inconsequential. We trade our sense of mission for a sense of apathy when we fail to realize just how distinctive the West is.

Deep and subtle cultural distinctions

Part of what makes any definition of a culture so difficult is its subtlety. The distinctive pieces that go into making up a whole culture are not the culture itself. Even as cultures disintegrate or assimilate other culture's contraptions, they retain a distinct ineffable essence. The institutions of a culture are not the entirety of that culture. There is a sensibility that permeates cultures that transcends these institutions. Cultural essences are not easy to delineate in simple catch phrases. None of the cultural attributes listed in the rest of this chapter will convey the totality of Western culture's essence.

One way to get an inkling of the differences between cultures is by imagining their various founders in conversation with each other. Think of the difficulties that would emerge in a conversation between Socrates and Mohammed. Socrates' Socratic Method of constant questioning wouldn't get far with this violent apostle of revealed faith. Islam is violently opposed to questioning its fundamentals. We do not understand fatwas. But putting a price on someone's head for printing dissenting views is not foreign to Islamic cultures. Socrates, as one of us, believed that defending the right to rationally philosophize on every subject was the best way to attain truth. Communication would have been dangerous and impossible.

Christianity does, of course, have revealed truths. But even within our revealed tradition there are very distinctive characteristics. Jesus refused to let Peter use the sword against his Roman captors. Muhammad killed hundreds for not converting. Muhammad was a warrior. He was wounded in battle and did not retire. You would have to have had an army to get Muhammad on a cross! Jesus valued the lives of even the fallen and the lowliest dissenters amongst us. He would not strike back at his enemies. Jesus did not even, in a very deep sense, consider them his enemies. Were Jesus and Muhammad to have met we must wonder what the result would have been.

Confucius and Jesus would have also had difficulty with each other. Jesus' insistence upon individual conscience and defiance of authority and tradition would have seemed anarchistic to Confucius. Our cultural icons are often rebels. Achilles, Jesus, Luther, and Shakespeare were all great in contradistinction to the traditional norms they faced. Ours is not a culture that celebrates faithful recreation of the previous generation's values. We do not seek harmony with the nature of the world or the ways of our ancestors. Confucius would have calmly praised the traditional virtues of the past while Jesus would be busy condemning the so called leaders of our society and doing so from personal revelation.

Imagine a conversation between Henry Ford and the Yucatan Mayans! Their bloodletting and human sacrifice would have horrified him. Along with our constant rebellion against the past a view of human efficacy pervades our world view. We believe in the rational use of our powers to efficaciously reach our goals. Ford might have appreciated the technical aspects of the Mayan assembly line methods used in their human sacrifice. Beyond that he would have seen their killing people to propitiate supernatural forces as a waste of human potential for improving the world. Similarly, the Mayan men might have seen his aversion to killing for Gods as unmanly. Real men fast, get drunk, and kill.

The very modes of our conversations reveal much about us. Plato's use of debate showed a love of controversy that would have been unwelcome to Confucius. In ancient Asian philosophy books, questions are rare and are not confrontational.[180] When the wise master gives his answer one is to be satisfied. Continued interrogation would be seen as disrespectful to his age and wisdom as well as destructive of the very harmonious state being sought. Western discourse ends in stalemate after reveling in the clashing of ideas. Harmony is not the goal. We would not vie for a uniform stagnancy. It is in our love of unearthing the tranquility of the past via progress that our rebellious and rational tendencies meet.

Much of the subtleties of a culture lay at a level below the words we use. "Teacher" does not have the same resonance in Western, Asian, and Islamic cultures. An entire worldview informs the use of the word. We use the term as a job title more than a term of veneration. Teacher does not connote religious authority in our world view. Relational names are found in most cultures. But what it means to be a father in every culture varies greatly. "Father" has a familiarity and sense of equality in Western thought. This list of differing interpretations of common words could be extended indefinitely. The point is that there are pre-verbal assumptions that form a world view that the upcoming list of Western attributes will only skirt.

A culture is as much a matter of temperament as a matter of tightly delineated rules. Just because these worldview differences are subtle does not mean that they are not important. Our sensibility has led to the West being the creators of dreams for the future. It is that visionary quality that has inspired others to want to join us. Others often see the products and not the world view it is predicated upon. We ourselves make the same mistake when we consider it a coincidence that our culture has generated so many spectacular inventors. Our competitive and anti-historical sensibility sees acceptance of differences as par for the course. We unite in our willingness to have differences. Our failure to notice that this large, but subtle cultural trait does not extend to others, is one of the reasons we are failing as culturists.

Protestant Work Ethic

Perhaps more than any other Western country, America's culture has been informed by a strong streak of rabid Protestantism. Our ideals of independence, our ability to sustain a democracy, our sense of mission, our entire culture has a Protestant feel. Though people might now chafe at the declaration, America has historically been an overwhelmingly Protestant nation. In fact we started off as extreme Protestants. This attribute lies behind much of our distinctiveness from other Western nations.

Our economic success famously results from the Protestant Work Ethic. The relation of this ethic to economic success was first formulated by Max Weber in his 1904 book, *The Protestant Ethic and the Spirit of Capitalism.* His explanatory schema has withstood the test of time. As one economist recently put it, "The correlation between the growth of economic institutions and the growth of Protestantism seems inescapable."[181]

Weber's relatively short book is essential reading for American culturists. That is because, unlike most modern social scientists, he takes belief systems to be a primary explanatory factor. He relates the doctrines that several brands of Protestantism hold in common in great detail. The fact that this culturist reading of historic causality has been supported in so many ways provides strong backing for the concept of culturism. It also provides a beautiful analysis of the presuppositions of our sensibilities.

Weber traces the Protestant work ethic back to Calvin's idea of predestination. Predestination is the idea that it has already been decided who will and who will not go to heaven. There not being a lot of room (only 144,000 will go) creates deep fear. To alleviate this fear early Protestants constantly looked for signs of redemption.

One major sign that God has chosen you is your having received a "calling." Martin Luther, Protestantism's most famous creator, invented the idea of calling. It is somewhat analogous to having a mission. A calling might be seen in your having a talent. God gave you that talent because he has a mission for you. You have been chosen! But if you neglect that mission, you might have been mistaken in thinking that God chose you. You do not have the spirit so a mistake might have been made. You must pursue that mission with relentless vigor to confirm that God has a positive plan for you.

Callings are not given to you for selfish purposes. If you see a community need you might have seen your calling. God made that community need apparent to you so that you can solve it. The need might present a business opportunity. If you saw an opportunity and made a fortune it was a sign that god had favored you. If you were poor it was a sign that God abandoned you. Your talent could not be hidden from the world. A role in society undertaken for purely private reasons could not be considered a calling in any proper sense. Weber called the Puritans "worldly ascetics." They applied themselves to their worldly callings with religious devotion in order to fulfill public needs.

This work ethic often resulted in great wealth. But wealth was not its goal. Rational hard work was an end, a form of devotion to God, in itself. Those who are saved devote themselves to constant worship via work in the name of God. In other cultures, Weber notes, work is a necessary evil. He specifically notes that in Catholic cultures people work in order to be able to stop working. Puritanism viewed work itself as redemptive. For Puritans constant work showed that you had the spirit of one who was chosen. The resulting wealth was actually viewed with suspicion. It was likely to lead to ungodly leisure and sloth. For this reason profit was to be plowed into positive endeavors rather than being allowed to sit idly.

Work, in the Puritan worldview, is life. All other activities become distractions. Sleep should be minimized. Sport can be indulged in only if it increases health so that one may increase their dedication to work. Benjamin Franklin promulgated a secular version of this work ethic. He would get to work before others and leave later than they did to show he was worthy. Franklin, sought to be worthy of credit instead of salvation, but in terms of the need to prove oneself as virtuous, the sentiment was the same. As with the Puritans, Franklin did not work for money. His work was a mission. Dedication and work were signs of virtue.

America's Puritan origins are still quite visible in our society. The Puritan's constant expunging of sin has led us to having one of the least corrupt nations around. We would be outraged if we had to bribe an official to get mail sent or your papers processed. These are commonplaces of other nations that our constant surveillance for corruption has dislodged. We still work longer hours and take shorter holidays than other countries.[182] Even now, Americans derive more of our self-worth from our work than people do in other nations.[183] Though we may not all be Protestants in belief, we are Protestant in ethics. Despite ourselves we remain a relatively Puritan nation.

Literacy is an element of Protestantism that Weber does not deem distinct enough to emphasize. But within seventeen years of arriving in America the Puritans had created Harvard. Recall that Protestantism was been traditionally defined by its opposition to the Pope and the Catholic Church determining your salvation. No one intervenes between you and God in Protestantism. As mentioned in an earlier chapter, if no institutions or persons intermediates between you and God, literacy is necessary. You must have personal access to the word of God. In 1647 there were already laws passed in Massachusetts and Connecticut ordering all towns to maintain teaching institutions.[184] Literacy is also a distinctive characteristic of the Protestant ethic informed American culture.

Mind over matter

Our work ethic ties in well with the modern culturist vision of adult responsibility. Though we are still an overwhelmingly Protestant country, Protestant religion is a more difficult fit in the modern world than the Protestant Work Ethic. It is a difficult fit because less and less of us believe in religion. And to the extent that we do we increasingly want a personal and permissive God, that fits in with our own beliefs and needs (this is the height of individualism). It is also a difficult fit because advertisers have capitalized on the 1960's counterculture's determination to escape from so-called "repressive morality." We are told more and more that sex is the goal of life and that all assertions to the contrary are hypocrisy.

Even without invoking faith, Protestant morality has deep secular roots in the Western tradition to guide us. Plato was the first person in the West to conceptualize the psyche as a battle between appetite and reason. He said that reason should rule appetite using the will because ideas are loftier than appetite. The appetite creates drive and motivation, but it cannot create direction. The will is the way that you control your direction. Reason should be the guide. If appetite alone guided you would be an insensible beast. Without any appetite you would not have a reason to get out of bed. Not everyone could control their appetites to the point of only having Platonic relationships. Ultimately, though, people were improved by striving towards the ideal by having their reason control their appetites.

Christianity built upon Plato's vision that reason should rule over appetite. Christ, however, exaggerated Plato's value judgments. Jesus said that if you look at a woman with lust in your heart you have committed an abomination of the spirit. Plato accepted that few could conform to his level of asceticism and created a place in his system for men made of different metal; only a select few would be expected to conform to relatively strict levels of asceticism. Catholics established priests to embody this ideal of pure chastity. Puritans believed that all could be made perfect in Christ's image and that no sex would happen outside of marriage. And so the puritanical sexual ethic -that modern society gets so much of its identity rebelling against - was born.

Sigmund Freud provided much of the current sexual revolution's language of "repression" and "libido." Freud said the animal impulses of sex and aggression, which he named the "id," lay just below the surface of all noble acts. Freud renamed Plato's concept of appetite, detailed its contents, and gave it more importance. Arts that snicker at the thinness of this veneer of the rationality that hides animal appetites are not alerting us to new concepts. This has been a topic of discussion since Plato. Freud was very conservative. He agreed with Plato that channeling this energy towards positive things made civilization possible. He considered sublimation of lust to productive work a good thing. Freud harped on this psychic configuration because he thought being aware of the id would allow us to more consciously control it and thus avoid neurosis.

Media has confirmed Freud's contention that we need to be aware of this dynamic. Media outlets have discovered that lusts are attractive on a primal level. As such they use carnal images to get viewers. Since there is very little conscious control of media, like a human without rationality, they are ruled by titillation. In the real world, however, blind indulgence in lust necessarily involves complications. Media being make-believe, does not portray pregnancy or STDs that give people pause when considering giving in to their appetites. The media uses the pervasiveness of secularism as an excuse to avoid responsibility in its programming. But it still can be, and should be, judged by rational standards. Culturist media decisions need to be made with an eye on social reality and knowledge of the importance of putting reason over appetite to achieve success.

Protestant morality made for a much more realistic interface with reality than uninhibited indulgence does. If we cannot agree on the acceptance of religious reasons by which to order our relationship between body and soul we need not abandon reason. We have an ancient tradition of recognizing that we share bodily impulses with animals and that our ability to think is what makes us special. Behaving like a pig is fun, but it does not ennoble you. Furthermore, relying on reason will allow you to feed yourself in respectable ways. This will further allow you to have your children spend longer in school and develop their uniquely human mental potential. Ultimately we can all agree that society and personal success are only possible when reason controls the appetite.

Secularists would say that we should never go back to seeing the body as evil. Most Christians would not disagree with this. Social mores sometimes advance. But rejecting the body-as-evil paradigm does not mean that we have no common ground for morality. Secular culturists will recognize the importance of values generally, and putting the mind over the body particularly, in our economic and social success. Christians naturally understand that the soul is more sacred than the body. They have an old language to discuss the need to control the body. Actually, all Westerners do. And we all very much need to reinvigorate our tradition of seeing the soul or reason as elevated. Culturist understanding can unite Christians and secular progressives as both can celebrate our Western tradition of honoring the mind over the body.

The meaning of our story

Our Protestant sense of identity has become more and more secularized in the public sphere. Privately we are still an overwhelmingly Christian nation. But whereas we had once seen ourselves as the shining example of a perfect Christian nation, we have come to see our selves as the shining example of what a perfect nation could be, whether Christian or not. The leap was not difficult. Puritans sought to be released from the bondage of passions and sin. We now see ourselves as battling evil in other forms. Understanding our mission is an important part of recovering our cultural focus.

Liberty, rights, opportunity, progressive outlooks, and democracy comprise much of what perfection looks like to us. We must see that this is not just an American thing. This pantheon's roots in the Greek battle against the Persians unite our history with the whole of Western history and the rest of the West. The Greeks fought against Persian theocratic monarchical tyranny. The victory at Salamis of the individualistic, self-governing Greeks marked the first successful assertion of these values on earth. Greek's very success in this context has been attributed to the fact that the Persians were lead in battle by a removed king on high.[185] As befit our early vision of liberty, we fought in flexible autonomous groups. The longevity of this vision bolsters its claim to being worthwhile and sustainable.

The original Protestants also fought for freedom from theocratic tyranny. This time the enemy was not the Persians, but the Pope. The Pope's claim to represent God on earth meant that his interpretations of the Bible were final and irrefutable. As such, he was an adversary to free thought. The church spent a lot of time seeking out and destroying heretics. A Pope personally saw to Galileo's life sentence. Popes killed people who translated the Bible into vernacular languages because it undermined Catholic monopoly on thought.

Martin Luther, again, is a hero in the struggle for freedom of thought. His claim that only Jesus can save you still constitutes the common denominator of all Protestants. This truth was radical because implied that neither the Pope nor any other worldly power could save you. In order for you to know what Jesus wants you need to be able to read the Bible yourself. To this end Luther defied the Pope by translating the Latin Bible into German. Protestants thereafter have prized literacy and eschewed authoritative leaders. The Protestant relationship to Jesus requires listening to an inner conversation. Our Puritan forefathers came to this land because the Anglican Church, though it had broken from the Catholic hierarchy still thought of itself as an authority that lorded supreme over the parish.

Our Revolutionary War continued our eons long battle for self-governance. The Founding Fathers could not justify a war for independence based on the need for cultural autonomy. We, by and large, shared the same culture as the British. We were both populated by English speaking, white, Protestants. We fought to obtain the rights that our English heritage entitled us to. We wanted to be self-governing and not slaves to the whims of a monarch. Greeks, Protestants, Puritans, and the Founding Fathers were all dedicated to the sentiment of Jefferson's mission statement, "I have sworn upon the alter of God eternal hostility against every form of tyranny over the mind of man."[186] Western history's luminaries are largely freedom fighters.

The Civil War was another war bent on expanding English rights. Believe it or not, the South also saw itself as protecting freedom. They believed that enslavement of one segment of society was necessary for the freedom of the other segment. This was, after all, the way it had been in Greece. It was the traditional agricultural economic arrangement and philosophy. The radical Northern States' vision of absolute freedom for all was seen to be a radical departure from time tested truths. These visions of freedom were incompatible. But they were both visions of freedom. The newer and better version won.

Science also has also been seen as a force for liberation. It is a weapon in Jefferson's eternal war against all things tyrannical to the human mind. The Protestant northern European countries were welcoming to the scientists that the Catholics persecuted. They were partially welcomed because the Northern Protestants felt camaraderie with them due to their status as escapees from Catholic oppression. Science also was welcomed as a tool in the mission to better understand God's mind via exploring the world he had created. Later, the Enlightenment scientists saw science as a tool for creating a future that would free us from the enslaving bonds of nature and tradition. Science has long been seen as a tool in our ancient mission of freedom from bondage.

The turn of the twentieth century political movement, called Progressivism was another effort to purge sin from our midst as we created a bold new free world. Our creation of a new and improved future was, as always, partially created to strengthen our contrast to Europe. Our aversion to the class system and landed nobility of the Old World translated into a determination to avoid the class conflict and oppression that had accompanied the European industrial revolution. Individual's fates were not supposed to be decided by the accident of birth on our soil. But Progressivism was the result of our traditional drive towards creating a perfect world. This made it synonymous with the spirit of Manifest Destiny that pushed us into the geographic frontier in an attempt to expand the area embracing freedom. We embrace new technologies, progressivism, and our manifest destiny due to their potentials as quasi-divine redeemers of the world.

World War I was to make the world safe for democracy. Here again we see the belief America has in its ability to be a universal harbinger of a new world. But we went reluctantly. That is because much of our feeling of self-worth has come in our consciously contrasting ourselves with the sin and depravity of the Old World. This was the same understanding concerning liberty's cultural specificity and precarious nature that made us reluctant to take immigrants from traditionally less free parts of Europe. Appreciating the rarity and cultural specificity of freedom made us highly ambivalent about getting mixed up with the cultural problems of the Old World. Their wars were born of history-laden rivalries that mired people in the strictures of the past. Their fighting for royalty offended our sense of modernism.

Our greatest war was World War II. That is because its contrasts spoke to us as a black and white depiction of good and evil. Tyranny and evil were never more clearly illustrated for us than in the forms Germany and Japan manifest. The value of our dedication to freedom was seen in stark relief during this war. It was the battle of Salamis all over again. The sons of the Greeks were up against the ideological descendants of the Persians. Americans understood our historical mission better during that the Second World War than at any time since the Revolutionary War. Again, a generation of Americans put their lives on the line to reaffirm our principles.

The Cold War, the Korean War, and Vietnamese War were also fought over the ideal of liberty. Yet these were aberrations from our traditional mission as they were attempts to defend our values abroad. The Puritans had only sought to lead by example. George Washington warned that we should protect our liberties by avoiding foreign entanglements and alliances. Our one prior experience that could be seen as an attempt at exporting our values would be the Spanish-American War. Yet that war was largely seen as defensive effort to drive Spanish oppression out of our hemisphere. We would not have gone to the Philippines to spread freedom had we not been chastising the Spanish for being in our hemisphere. Still the foreign nature of these wars did not invalidate the continuity of theme in the mission.

The Civil Rights movement is revered because it speaks so clearly to us about the nobility of our heritage. Like World War II, it was a classic story of oppression contrasted with liberty. Martin Luther King knew that connecting with this traditional understanding would be essential to his triumph. He consistently harkened back to our national creeds of liberty, equality, and opportunity for all. America's story's resonating with the black struggle for rights and freedom explains why the many historical allusions to it in his speeches are so moving to us; it also explains his success. The Civil Rights Movement was a

Western success. King reminded us of the responsibilities bestowed upon us by our historic mission to combat tyranny.

Our belief in our historical role of spreading liberty has been a source of unity for us since the time of the ancient Greeks. This theme unites the Protestants and scientists who took on the superstition and tyranny of the Pope. Our very founding was a blow against the irrational tyrannies of Europe. Our Westward expansion, embrace of technology, and involvement in World Wars have all been understood to be part of our identity as harbingers of liberty. The Civil Rights Movement sought to make our traditional values a reality for all of us. The Cold War was a war against enslavement. Even our current wars in the Middle East have been promoted as extensions of our tradition of missionary idealism in the name of liberty. Americans recoil at tyranny. We all feel this strand of our ancient heritage in our bones.

Separation of church and state

Another cultural attribute that separates us from all our historical predecessors and much of the present world is our enshrinement of the separation of Church and state. More than any other decision this has allowed us to respect and honor the pagan past as a part of our story. But it should also remind us of America's particularity. The first part of this phrase is Protestant. The phrase is "Church" and State. It is not the separation of the religious institution of your choice and state. And it isn't separation of mosque and state. It isn't even separation of cathedral and state. The phraseology reflects our historic Protestantism.

The assumed Protestant nature of our nation has traditionally been seen as integral to the freedom that the Founding Fathers were creating. In Catholicism the Pope is the ultimate power. He is not elected. Your individual conscience is not the ultimate authority. At some level Catholicism is incompatible with freedom of conscience. This is a reason that, until very recently, none of the European Catholic colonies have become democratic whereas all of the Protestant colonies have. This is a reason that none of the Catholic colonies have achieved wealth, whereas all of the Protestant ones have. Independence of thought and salvation based on merit is a powerful ideology. The use of the word "Church" is an important base of freedom for us.

So in one way the Founding Fathers were making a consciously culturist decision when they specified that churches were going to be separated from the State. In another sense, the Founders just had no need to include other religious places of worship in their analogy. Wars between Catholics and Protestants had plagued Europe for hundreds of years before America was founded. We understood that we were the offspring of a country (Britain) that was Protestant. We understood that our traditional sense of ourselves was that of a Protestant nation that was escaping Catholic tyranny. That was a widely shared source of common identity for us. Mentioning Mosques, Synagogues, Cathedrals, and Hindu temples would have been silly and meaningless additions in their historical context.

Culturist distinctions between religions based on the distance they put between the religion and government is not blind prejudice or insignificant. Muhammad was not only the prophet of the Muslim religion; he was the political head of Medina and later Mecca. The word of God and the word of the State were one under his rule. Islam and democracy do not have a good history of mixing because Islam means submission to God. Democracy requires free debate based on individual conscience. In most Muslim countries the government enforces the death penalty against those that violate the sanctity of the Koran's decrees in word or deed. God and his commandments do not go up for a vote after a lengthy debate.

Cultures travel. In 2004 a 'Dutch-Moroccan' killed a film maker named Theo van Gogh because he had made a film criticizing Islam. The Muslim (whose name is being purposely omitted) shot Van Gogh six times, cut his throat, and then impaled to his chest a five-page note threatening other public figures. Imagine the chill on film making. Would you feel safe making a documentary on the abuses of Islam in the Netherlands? You can see how quickly a small minority of Islamic folks can corrupt a free republic.

This Muslim who killed Van Gogh was not a fringe person who did not represent the mainstream of Islamic thought. The publishing of cartoons that did not conform to religious orthodoxy set of a firestorm of protest across the Muslim world. Muslims rioted because they said we were not respecting their culture. It was clear that they did not understand or respect our culture. Freedom of the press is integral to our sense of public life. The Muslim who murdered Van Gogh demonstrated an incompatibility between being a Muslim and a European. His belief in the strictures of the Koran did not diminish his belief in the freedom of speech; it completely destroyed it. It is not clear that separation of Mosque and State is a possibility.

Our culture's survival might well depend on understanding the peculiarity of our cultural traditions. To the extent that our valuing the separation of Church and state is essential to our identity, protecting it is also. Whereas foreign governments should be encouraged to invest in profit making enterprises in America, funding the building of mosques is a culturally aggressive act that may well undermine our separation of Church and state. Culturism recognizes that we have a duty to protect our cultural viability. Much of our nation's establishment was the result of a Protestant effort to avoid theocracy. Our unique and vital traditional commitments mandate that we are vigilant defenders of the separation of Church and state.

Opportunity and diversity

America has long been called the "Land of Opportunity." Judging from immigration patterns, the entire Western world now deserves the moniker. One aspect of this reputation refers to the economic opportunities. But wealthy countries like Saudi Arabia and Japan will not let you in because they practice heavy-handed culturism. The necessary compliment to the economic underpinning of our being called the Land of Opportunity refers to our soft culturism. We welcome people from all over the world and give them unheard of freedom and opportunity. This opportunity is predicated on our openness as well as our maintaining a first-world economy.

Tribes, bands, and chiefdoms did not feature a wide arrange of roles to choose from. There was, as we saw, an amazing amount of diversity between tribes. But within the tribes anthropologists do not need a lot of time or paper to describe all of the opportunities available to men or women. Basically, men hunt and women gather. Agricultural states are often identified by sharp hierarchy in jobs. Most people are peasant farmers in such societies. Their opportunities are stable, predictable, and thus also easily describable. Those that are not peasants are usually members of the priestly elite, army or royal family. These roles are also stable for generations.

Western industrial societies virtually defy description. We have so many different types of identities and roles to choose from that it is dizzying. Our schools try desperately to give everyone a taste of all the possibilities so that they can decide what they want to be when they grow up. But even if they succeed, modern Americans no longer spend their entire lives within one profession. Fluidity of trends and identities are one of our most consistent and characteristic features. But explaining diversity would not help a prospective immigrant asking what will be expected of them in America. We can only say that there are opportunities.

Women's roles in America embody our direction, hope, and essence. In old world cultures women's roles are tightly prescribed. They rarely have opportunities outside of the home. The further back you go the worse it gets. Women's changing roles perfectly mirror our entire progressive trajectory. In the United States women can be whatever they want. Women have more rights in America than any nation in the world. They have gotten these rights through struggle. Young educated women's salaries have surpassed males in big cities.[187] Women's opportunities embody self-creation, choice, and our culture's sentiment of freedom. Again, having a culture means some things run counter to that culture, having values means some behaviors are counter to those values. Women who wear burkas and other forms of traditional garbs go against our entire progressive history. Their contrast with American women shows that we do have a culture to assimilate into. Our unique culture is progressive, modern, and fluid.

The possibilities open to Americans provide more diversity than ancient heritages do. Our economy provides the backbone of our ability to be diverse. These possibilities are not available by virtue of a mystical decree. People in other countries do not have many opportunities. People need to eat. This shortage of wealth often prevents people from going to school. People without educations can only do jobs that can be learned quickly. Even if you have an education, in many societies very few non-agricultural jobs exist. People without money cannot buy homes, take up expensive hobbies, and travel.

Having a diversity of industrial and post-industrial economic sectors is a prerequisite for our diverse opportunities.

Our economic opportunities and diversity were created, as previously mentioned, by our Protestant cultural tendencies. Sobriety, hard work, thrift, and a focus on education paved the way to our industrial might. Continued wealth will also require maintaining these cultural habits. Uneducated people with high birth rates are neither conducive to the creation nor the maintenance of first-world economies. If they were, the poor countries of the world would be rich as their populations have children early and low rates of education. Modern economies are built upon mind power more than manpower. From computers to vehicle manufacturing, the highly educated are the modern creators of wealth.

Poverty feeds upon itself. A lack of educational opportunity leads to poverty which leads to a lack of educational opportunities. The original and continuing separation of rich from poor countries can be traced to cultural values. Women are praised to the extent that they have a lot of babies early in some countries. Women, therefore, do not go to college. In these countries women both raise children and toil in manual labor. Only a strong economy could afford to keep the resulting large populations out of the work force for the amount of time required for a solid education. When people have no economic opportunities, children become their source of wealth.

Lack of opportunity might be seen then to be the cause of people having poor educations. Yet even within countries that can afford such a luxury, not all cultural groups show equal propensities to take advantage of these opportunities. Even in first-world countries, some cultural groups show a drop out rate that cannot be reconciled with a determination to be educated. Of all the groups that immigrated in the late 19th century only Jews considerably raised their economic level via public schools.[188] As a result they have contributed more to the economy than their numbers alone would predict. In making culturist judgment we should always keep in mind that we are trying to maintain a first-world economy. No magic was involved in creating our economy. A widely shared Protestant-style cultural focus on being educated, having smaller families, and getting ahead are necessary for our maintaining our status as a land of opportunity.[189]

Individualism

Individualism is one of the defining characteristics of Western culture. It so thoroughly pervades our worldview that we do not notice it unless we spend a lot of time in other countries. Marriage partners are chosen by your family in much of the world. Islamic countries have decided what people will believe before they are born. In pre-historic cultures there was one set of skills for men and another for women. You did not use your mind to devise a life plan. Those who messed up the patterns of ritual invited evil curses upon their people. People do not seek to stand out of the crowd in such situations. People in the Old World are given strong cultural hints as to what their roles should be. Western individualism means having as few strictures put on your behaviors as possible.

As previously mentioned, our constellation of cultural heroes is largely populated by rebels. Achilles, Socrates, Jesus, Martin Luther, the Founding Fathers, and Martin Luther King all questioned and fought against the given conditions of their society. In other cultures ambition is channeled into epitomizing the dictates of your religious station. Extreme piety is the ultimate virtue. Whereas other cultures hate those who defy ancient traditions, we love rebels even when they have no cause. We consider traditions to be stifling and unnecessary constrictions. We do not expect you to follow your parent's ways. We celebrate trendsetters. Western individualism means forging your own path.

Like all cultural ideals, individualism is manifest in behaviors. In other cultures people live with their parents until they are married and only then move out with their parent's permission and financial support. In America you are kicked out at eighteen. Whatever happens to you is your own fate. If you are still at home at twenty five, you are considered a loser and no one will marry you. This is a very specific cultural trait. We have small nucleated families because people go off to college to define themselves when they are young. Those who do not go off to college need to move out in order to "get a life." Western individualism means standing on your own two feet.

Individualism has been our traditional approach to approximating a meritocracy. Some cultures do not have any mechanism for getting the right people into the right positions. Kings have largely been selected based on the basis of their being their father's son. In America it is not uncommon for the father and son to have radically different economic circumstances. Our cultural value system has created a people that are brutally self-centered when it comes to economics. Whereas other cultures naturally help family members, we hate nepotism. Much of our economic strength derives from the fact that very few Americans get political or economic positions they have not earned. Western individualism means earning what you get.

Socrates was killed for questioning too much. His student, Plato, wrote the only completely preserved body of work by any Greek author in an effort to vindicate Socrates. Greeks had, again, fought for self-governance against the Persians. This self-governance included a right to kill dissenters. After Socrates' unfair death, we had a new level of conscientiousness about killing individuals without good reason. Our love of the individual comes out of a very particular history. Western individualism is secured by our being conscious of belonging to a culture that has struggled to allow the individual to deviate.

Individualism went into occultation when the Catholics took over Europe from Rome. Catholic peasants were not encouraged to think differently. The Protestants revolted, again, to assert that your salvation is the result of an intimate relationship with God. This matter is so personal and of such importance that no institution is seen to have the right to intervene in it. As such the government and individual conscience are divorced in Western counties. You can find God or not in your own way according to the dictates of your conscience. It should not mean that you turn your liberty into license. Western freedom assumes a culture in which we will strive to better ourselves in the absence of interference. Western individualism was designed with the assumption that you would strive to better yourself.

Rights, liberty, self-governance, and responsibility

Outside of the West, cultures have dwarfed the individual. Persia dispensed of the peons in its army as their god-anointed ruler saw fit. Catholics routinely set dissenters on fire after torturing them. Even today, most cultures keep the individual on a very short leash. China's government exercises the right to imprison and kill anyone whom they like. In Muslim countries contradicting rules set down hundreds of years ago is punishable with death. Understanding that individual human's liberty is a very precious and delicate commodity should inform our sense of right and wrong.

Rights have traditionally been regarded as protection from government-imposed cultural impositions. These are called negative rights. Our Bill of Rights is an enumeration of negative rights. The government cannot interfere in your speech, religion or right to peacefully petition the government. The government cannot break into your house without a warrant. Positive rights refer to your being entitled to something. This new idea is manifest in the idea that you have the right to services such as healthcare, unemployment benefits, and an education. The strong assertion of positive rights is a new development in our continuing experiment with self-governance.

Traditionally, not even negative rights have been asserted strongly. The distinction between license and liberty, as we have seen, was widely acknowledged in early American history. You were free to do good actions that led to your betterment (liberty) but not to engage in behaviors that were harmful to yourself or others (license). Restricting your right to sin was not seen as an infringement of your freedom. Such restrictions were necessary to the success of our experiment in free government. Lust for power would cause people to become kings. Lust for drink would undermine people's economic ability to support themselves. Being able to remain free requires that your whole culture knows the difference between liberty and license.

The faith that we could understand this distinction was based on the hope that people would remember the battle between the body and the spirit that Plato, Jesus, and Freud meditated upon. True liberty was something you earned by resisting enslaving passions. As liberty was spiritual, the only way in which the government could help you was by removing obstacles. Creating an environment where you would not be led into temptation was done to enhance your liberty. But in the end, Protestant-style, your salvation had to result from an inner struggle. If you avoided drink and sex, and devoted yourself to righteous activities in a disciplined way, you would be able to guide your own destiny. This was the path to true liberty. Ultimately this was a personal struggle.

Our foray into anthropology showed us that those who have no guidance are not, by default, forward-looking ambitious rational people. Impoverished groups warring with other groups for ridiculous reasons happens. Self-government has come to mean next to no government control of individual behaviors. Remaining free without guidance requires that we have an even stronger internal understanding that wealth, rights, liberty, and self-governance cannot be sustained by debauchery alone. The ultimate check on self-governance comes from economic reality. If you indulge in too much license you will suffer economic deprivation. The government must be aware of the moral message it sends when it severs this check on license. Individually and collectively we must recognize that we need to be worthy of our liberty.

High culture and culture

A traditional function of culture (in the artistic sense) is that it unites people. For most of man's history he has been in tribes with common rituals and common beliefs. Tribes had distinctive markings and languages that reminded them of which group they belonged to. When writing was created it allowed these shared cultural attributes to be spread over a larger area. Monuments, text, and art all informed the culture's inhabitants of a shared legacy and destiny. Widely dispersed collective concerns, countries, and civilizations were thereby made possible. We have an immense amount of cultural artifacts to serve this purpose.

Culture is often taken to be synonymous with high culture. In this sense, to be cultured is to be familiar with the classics of your culture. Culturism is only incidentally concerned with this definition of culture. Culturism concerns the management and protection of dominant cultures writ large. High culture is certainly an aspect of this. But to the extent that your ideas only reach a tiny elite minority, they are not affecting the culture at large. Popular culture is a sphere successful attempts at culturism cannot ignore.

With the purpose of culture in mind the television show "I Love Lucy" could serve as an effective a source of common identity as William Shakespeare's plays. In fact, at first glance "I Love Lucy" may seem a superior basis upon which to base your cultural cohesion. "I Love Lucy" is accessible to a wider audience. After a long day of exhausting work, more people watch situation comedies than struggle through Shakespeare's works. If Shakespeare were aired during prime time he would be ignored. Most everybody can and does love Lucy.

Shakespeare, however, is a preferable source of cultural unity. Knowing about "I Love Lucy" only binds you with traditions going back sixty years. It does not convey the longevity of our culture. Furthermore, it is, sorry to say, specific to one generation. Young Americans are more likely to know about "Buffy the Vampire Slayer" than Lucy. Shakespeare is a cultural artifact that can unite all living generations. Because Shakespeare is English using him ties us to another Western country. Plato is, by this criterion, superior to Shakespeare because he ties us to Western civilization in its entirety.

Another difference between our Lucy and Shakespeare is in the esteem they generate. Hamlet is even understood to be a product of unequaled genius by those who have not read it or seen it performed. Thus it engenders veneration. No great concern would be expended to sustain the culture that brought us "I Love Lucy." It is important that we remember and celebrate Homer, Herodotus, Plato, Jesus, Saint Augustine, Michelangelo, and Shakespeare along with our military and popular leaders. A nation's sense of its value is undermined when citizens do not believe that their culture is special. Our culture has achieved unparalleled levels of artistic excellence.

The excellence of these icons sets the stage for a stronger Western future. A sense of excellence is a prerequisite to accomplishment. We cannot all agree upon standards of greatness. But the only thing worse than not having any agreed upon standards is having no standards at all. The absence of standards means that you will put anything into your body and soul. You are what you consume. A culture that has no connection to excellence will not strive for excellence. If you do not strive for excellence you will not create it.

High culture can provide our society's secular members icons to represent the ideal that some things are higher than others. Puritan excellence was predicated on avoiding all unprofitable actions and influences to an extreme. We are not as neurotic as the Puritans were. We need not scorn "I Love Lucy" because it is too trivial for us. Fun is a big part of our modern economy. Fun is appealing. We are probably more likely to defend our culture because we do not want the fun to end as we are to do so out of a sense of duty. Yet it is ennobling for us to remember, via Shakespeare, the Bible or Plato, that some endeavors profit one's soul more than others.

Conscience

One of the most beautiful aspects of America is our belief in right and wrong. Unlike more chauvinistic cultures, we have a sense of conscience that we wrestle with. Are you for the death penalty or against it? Are you against abortions or for them? Which sides are right? Should an independent counsel look into the President's fund raising? Americans argue passionately about these issues. It is useful for us to occasionally take a break from this fighting over issues and appreciate the forest comprised by the trees and congratulate each other for taking part in ethical debates.

One such debate flared when the Smithsonian proposed to commemorate the 50th anniversary of the bombing of Hiroshima and Nagasaki. Many were still uncertain whether the bombings were justified. Couldn't we have bombed an island instead? Wasn't there any way that we could have minimized the bloodshed? Did the Japanese really deserve such devastation? Were we just using the Japanese to warn the Russians? How much of the impetus to drop the bombs was due to expedience and how much was due to morality? Could the total lives lost have been reduced by a land invasion? What a wonderful country we are to have agonized and fought over this issue.

The Japanese do not share the same sense of soul scouring. During the war they raped and pillaged and lied without conscience. They tortured prisoners of war. After the war they refused to acknowledge these crimes. They said that the seventy thousand women they had abducted and transported to military bases for constant gang raping were paid in room and board! Their textbooks and presidents still do not mention their crimes. If the Japanese would have had the bomb they would have dropped it with glee. They certainly would not have had a national debate over whether dropping the bombs were right fifty years after the fact.

What of Vietnam? What about what we did to the Nicaraguans? What about the Philippines? Yes we did some harm in those nations.

But each time we found it necessary to have moral justifications for our actions. In each of these wars our soldier's public mission was to go across the ocean to a strange land and defend stranger's freedoms with their lives. What could be nobler? Korea was a near perfect parallel to Vietnam and it has rightfully resulted in gratitude. Just because we lost in Vietnam does not mean that the impulse was not noble. We were not involved in any of these situations to indulge in the joy of plunder and violence.

When we have felt that we have done harm we have apologized. After we went to Vietnam to save them from communism we allowed those who felt persecuted to come to America. The Philippines were promised and given freedom after fifty years of training for independence. President Ronald Reagan was so afraid that his questionable actions in Nicaragua might unleash vocal principled opposition he went to imaginative lengths to keep our involvement from being traceable. And when we found out about it we had Congressional hearings because we believe that truth and justice are integral to the American way. We gave a paid apology to Japanese in that had been in relocation camps regardless of their loyalty during wartime.

The Japanese have given no compensation to Americans tortured in death camps. They have not compensated their Asian rape camp victims. Most nations have gone to war for conquest, slaves, and booty. The Japanese and Germans did not start World War II to liberate anyone. The list of countries fighting for reasons other than the ruler's aggrandizement, revenge, and money is very small. It is not unusual that we have sometimes acted in self-interest. That we have tried to justify it in moral terms when we have is strange. Having repeatedly gone to war to save other people is bizarre. We are amongst the most altruistic cultures ever.

We may be conscientious to a fault. Even when we are dealing with deranged mass murderers, we give the perpetrators many expensive rights. As good Puritans, the West is easily manipulated by guilt. We feel guilty for the wealth we have created. We feel badly when we give preferential treatment to our own country's needs. Multiculturalism was born out of repentance for the sin of pride and desire to be fair to others. Having a conscience is good. But when it leads to a constant focus on one's faults it has gone too far. We have, and should be proud of having, a strong sense of conscience. The Puritans and the Founding Fathers would like that about us.

Our past and our future

Multiculturalism is wrong about our not having a core culture. We have a very strong and specific culture. A look at a broader sweep of cultures makes this obvious. We value liberty and rights beyond what any current or historical culture ever has. Our culture has very deep roots. Philosophically they are built around self-creation and self-governance. Current Western values are heavily influenced by their Protestant roots. And from Greece to the industrial revolution our emphasis on self-improvement has helped our culture become an engine of creation. Ours is a culture in which people are expected to create themselves anew each generation. Our heroes are heroes because they embody this virtue.

The New World is not just a factual name. It is descriptive. Our disdain for the past is a long standing tradition. Traditionally America has not liked to be confused with the Old World (of any continent). The Puritans set out to create a new vision for the world. Our Founding Fathers created a new form of government. George Washington rallied against foreign entanglements because they got us caught up in squabbles over backwards traditions. We tried to stay out of the World Wars as they represented the silliness of people that had not shed tradition. America has always consciously shunned the past and worked to create a future that looked nothing that had gone before. When multiculturalists romanticize the past they cut against the grain of our futurist identity.

Cultures permeate all levels of society. The New World does not just mean the country is involved in a process of renewing itself; our individual identities are formed around the concept that anyone can be anything they want. Individual responsibility has been the bedrock upon which our ideal of the self-made man has rested. Old World colonies provided support to generations of recently arrived immigrants. But the idea that your ultimate goal was to be defined by the roots of an ancient tradition is anathema to our ways. Encouraging individuals to seek find their identity by conforming to a stereotype of

what their ancestors did is not the way to create futurists. In the Old
World, the accident of your birth pigeonholed you for life. Not here.
We are a frontier culture. Individuals doing things that their parents
never dreamed of doing is in our blood. This sense of what success
means unites our culture.

One solid piece of evidence that we have a specific culture is the
stellar cast of cultural heroes we have. They all embody aspects of our
cultural sensibility. Rational struggle and creation are at the heart of
each of them. There is a direct line between Socrates' questioning of
the State and Luther's defiance of the Pope. The Puritans, Benjamin
Franklin, and Thomas Edison all hated to waste time. Achilles
and Oscar Wilde both railed against the limits of their situations.
Shakespeare and Picasso are both known for breaking down limits.
Washington and Lincoln's moderation in victory are distinctive. Ours
is a creative and realistic struggle to be free. Our heroes are rational
innovators. They are thinkers. They struggle out of discontent with
limits. Our cultural icons are unlike those of any other culture.

Surpassing precedent is one thing that all of these creators share.
It is a virtue, but also dangerous. The past and our understanding of
it are essential to our successfully continuing to live up the mandate
to pass on our experiment in rational self-governance to posterity.
Ignorance of history keeps us from knowing how rare and precious
our experiment is. Ignorance of history keeps us from understanding
the responsibilities that liberty entails. Ignorance of history has cut us
loose from the mooring provided by elevating the mind over the body.
Ignorance of history has led us to romanticize the past. Ignorance
of history cuts us off from those who would be our inspirations.
Ignorance of history has robbed us of understanding the nature
of our progressive mission. Ignorance of history has kept us from
knowing who we are.

If Western culture ceased to exist the world would be thrown into
a much more traditional mode. Theocratic and race-based countries
would be free to perpetuate themselves without regard to freedom of
the individual, freedom of consciousness or the sense of rights that
the Western cultures hold dear. Technology would continue to roll out
of cultures that are conducive to this sort of creation. But the humane
nature of the world would be undercut. The world of free expression

and opportunity our culture considers nearly synonymous with life itself would be severely limited. Diversity exists and the Dark Ages happened. The ability to dissent might be diminished or destroyed.

Our experimental and idealistic culture is a very fragile thing. Western culture lacks the racial or theological sources of unity that have defined most other cultures. We have freedom and a separation of Church and state instead. All we have to unify us is a shared understanding of our culture and its values. If we forget that it is our duty to strive to vindicate these values, they will lose ground. Less sensitive, heavy-handed cultures that do not mind indiscriminant killing of individuals have advantages in battle. Our advantage is in our ability to adapt and recreate ourselves. Our ability to change rapidly also means that we can easily go in bad directions. Going in the right direction requires that we remember our mission and traditions.

CHAPTER SIX

CULTURISM IN NATURE

Caution

This chapter is going to show how cultures work and become conscious entities in nature. Understanding this process will facilitate our becoming more effective culturists. Crude and one-sided comparisons of human and animal behavior have been used to justify atrocities and often simply reflect the politics of the hour.[190] Caution is warranted. To say we should form a highly regimented caste system because ants do would be absurd. To recommend monarchy because it is what bees do would result in disaster. Having females kill their mates and eat them during copulation because some spiders do would be highly objectionable.

We have to be discerning when generalizing from other species' behaviors to our own. Basic zoology tells us which animals we are more and less like. It would be absurd for us to expect zebra behaviors to fall somewhere in the spectrum of bird behaviors. It would be less absurd for us to expect finches' spectrum of behaviors to overlap with those of the parakeet. Furthermore we must not forget that the spectrum of types of behaviors a species may exhibit happens in the context of a particular environment. Primates, for example, who spend much of their lives in trees tend to be smaller. We should not divorce insights taken from the animal world from their contexts.

Forays into nature are justified more by revealing guidelines than specific recommendations. Humans are special in that we need not mechanically follow nature's commands. Females can make babies and males cannot. That does not mean that all women must do this and nothing else. Neither can we, however, completely disregard the requirements of the natural world. If no one makes, raises or protects the young our longevity will be compromised. Anyone who thinks that we can completely ignore the natural world has forgotten about the birds and the bees.

Looking into nature will show us the good, as well as the bad and ugly potentials of our species. Being aware of such dynamics allows us to be aware of when we are going in a direction that is not sustainable. Kibbutzim tried to eradicate family partiality. It was doomed to failure by our basic psychological make-up. The Soviet Union tried to eradicate competition from the human spirit. A lot of death and frustration could have been avoided if Karl Marx had studied ethology (animal behavior). Being ignorant of our basic nature is does not shield us from it. Ignorance will not help us avoid excesses.

Culturism in nature

"The goal of research is to produce a validated model that both organizes and best interprets an expanding body of data"[191] Culturism is meant to be an organizing principle for a vast array of data. One can use it as a model by which to organize the disparate facts found in every branch of the social sciences. But this model must be based on actual facts or it will simply deserve to be treated as fiction. Culturism is shown to not be fiction by its being an effective organizer of factual data. Ultimately, showing that it holds in the natural sciences as well as the soft is meant to establish its objective existence. As such it can be confirmed as "validated model" with which to interpret situations.

Many are under the impression that hard sciences do not evoke a frame of reference when announcing facts. But facts are not just facts. When we are looking for the properties of wood, it is necessary to consider the parameters of our investigation. Are we purely interested in listing elements? Are we concerned with wood's rate of combustion? We might be looking at its function within an ecosystem. Then again, its place in the national economy might be the question at hand. Investigating "wood" is always done at some chosen level of inquiry.

Nature presents us a meaningless diversity unless we choose to look for patterns. Lists of incidents and examples could substantiate any pattern one wished to contrive. But this investigation will be done with an eye to verify culturism and hazard applications. Culturism assumes individuals exist in groups. Neither gestation time, mating structures nor patterns of food sharing can be understood without reference to the contexts in which they happen. Animal behaviors only make sense when seen as adaptations to the social and natural conditions they are ensconced in.[192] It is not, therefore, strange that we find actual patterns when we look at nature for applications to culturism.

Group selection

Evolution is a fact. This is beyond dispute. Disputes do still rage, however, over what the mechanisms that direct it are. Is the gene pool mostly changed via sexual selection (females mating with the biggest) or natural selection (mutations that survive in nature being passed on)? Do behavior changes lead to genetic types being conserved more often than genetic changes lead to behavioral innovations? In reality evolution includes various mechanisms and they work in different proportions within different communities in differing circumstances. In general those qualities that increase the viability of a species will do better than those that do not.

For our purposes the debates over whether genetic survival is a function of individual or group success are a priority. The struggle for survival has been popularly portrayed as a struggle of individuals against individuals. During the 1960's and 70's natural selection was found to be efficiently modeled at an individual level.[193] "Selfish genes" were deemed to be the raison d' arte of evolutionary struggle. Chickens struggled to have their genes passed on. But at a deeper level, chickens were just mechanisms for genes to copy themselves. A chicken was humorously said to be a way for an egg to copy itself. This was an individualistic, reductivist model.

This explanation ran into trouble because of the prevalence of altruism in the animal world. Some animals put their lives in jeopardy by warning others of approaching predators. Animals will sacrifice themselves (and their genes) to save their fellows. A purely individualistic struggle for gene perpetuation would not allow personal genocide. Furthermore, many social insects are sterile. What were these little guys thinking? Don't they know that it is not the struggle for *other's* survival that they were supposed to be involved in? Individual models of evolution had to account for such behaviors.

Mathematical models were employed to explain away this problem. Your willingness to sacrifice yourself was discovered to be proportional to your genetic relatedness to those you were benefiting.[194] Thus the concept of "kin selection" was born. An animal sacrificing itself to warn a group is said to pass on many genes that are like his. The animal that warns the others may die. But if three siblings who each share fifty percent of his same genes survive, his genes will have done the selfish thing after all. His warning only deceptively seems to be concerned with the other.[195] In fact, mathematical models showed, his sacrifice is selfish from the gene's point of view.

This explanation does an unsatisfactory job of rescuing the individual as the focus of gene transmission. Even if one accepts the mathematical model used to justify the altruistic animals actions, you still have to acknowledge that the individual is not the mechanism by which genes are passed on. The individual died. The genetically selfish thing to do was to sacrifice himself for the group! That means that the fates of the genes rise or fall with that of the group. Genetic selection, by this model's logic, is happening at the group level. The animal that sacrifices himself must, then, really be concerned with the group.

"Group selection" means that groups rise or fall, pass on their genes or fail to, based upon whether or not their *collective* behaviors lead to successful birthing and rearing of offspring. As with the molecular and economic analysis of wood, several models may be true simultaneously. Models, again, should be favored if they both organize and interpret an expanding body of data well. In many parts of the natural world, dog-eat-dog individualism is an inaccurate model. Group selection is attractive because it accounts for nature as it actually appears, as an aggregate. It accounts for the many situations in which the individualistic selection model seems inadequate.

Groups are a prevalent feature of the natural world. No animal is an island. All interact with their environment. Many insects, fish, birds, and mammals gather in groups for protection, the ability to have division of labor and to better manipulate their environment. No solitary ant could build an anthill and isolation is emotionally hard on gregarious animals.[196] The nature of pregnancy requires that nearly all living species need to come together to cooperate at some point in their lives. And the more recent the appearance of the species the more likely it is that raising the child will require cooperation.

Successful models help us understand the world and our place in it. To know where we belong in nature it is helpful to know that two types of animal groups exist. Anonymous groups are those in which the members do not know each other individually. Fish swarm and bird flock together to confuse predators. They may know their mate or offspring temporarily, but have no personal relationship with other group members. Individualized groups are those in which the animals know other group members. As sure as we recognize people outside of our family, we are a part of the category of individuated group animals. Knowing what characteristics all animals in individuated groups share will tell us about ourselves.

Belong to an individuating category of animals means, first of all, that we should take a group selection / culturist approach to understanding our behaviors. Individualistic "survival of the fittest" models are inappropriate for us. To be sure, we have our individual struggles for survival. But ultimately, we rise or fall as our group does. We recognize others and have dependable relationships with them. In our niche natural selection is kinder than we have been led to believe. Nature favors individualized groups where members altruistically care about each other. The cruel "war of all against all" model does not provide a fulfilling explanation for our category of species.

Individual organisms

The boundary between the group and the individual is fuzzy in nature. Slime molds are everyone's favorite example of this. They are made up of individual amoebas that spend much of their lifecycle as individuals. But when food becomes scarce they join together to create a slime mold – a larger organism. Some amoebas become stalk material. Others become spores. Those that become stalk do not propagate. They sacrifice their chance at reproduction so that those who become spores can reproduce. Lifted aloft by the stalk, spores can ride the winds to areas where, hopefully, more food can be found.

Lots of lessons are to be derived from this. You might object that humans are so different from slime molds that no parallels can be found. However, upon reflection you will recognize that we also see groups as meaningful sometimes and unimportant at others. Not coincidentally, we also tend to ignore the group when things are going well for us and cling to it when things are not going well. It was during the Great Depression that we realized that the government had a role in managing the economy. We should not feel guilty about our only realizing the importance of others when we are in trouble; it is natural.

Furthermore, we can take moral direction from these amoebas. They are willing to altruistically sacrifice for the common good, because they realize that the group's interest and their own are contiguous. Each of the amoebas has the same genetic make-up (as kin selection folk would point out). Though Western society is no longer defined by a genetic stock (slime mold part pun intended), we have a common interest in the perpetuation of Western culture. If you identify with that culturist statement (especially when we are attacked), your genetic progeny and cultural con-specifics will be blessed by the continuation of our culture. Without altruistic sacrifice in times of war our culture would be doomed.

Kin selection folk would say that all having an identical genetic identity shows that slime mold amoebas are not really altruistic. In effect, the slime mold does not exist. We see a bunch of individuals that have come together that just *appear* to have formed a larger being with differentiated parts for the good of the whole. Genes are just trying to get copies of their genes passed along. The slime mold is an unimportant illusion resulting from the coordinated acts of genetically selfish individuals. While groups are sometimes obvious, they would say, they are not real. But we are not hallucinating when we see slime molds form. And, fortunately slime molds are not the only example of group behavior we have.

Entire bee colonies change from foraging in a less nutritious area of flowers to a more nutritious one in minutes. When bees return from foraging they do what is called a "waggle dance" and unload their pollen. How emphatically they dance and how quickly they unload their nectar conveys how much pollen gold they have struck. Individually they cannot know whether theirs was the best or worst find; they have no point of comparison. The hive compares and follows the one with more energy and nectar en masse. So the group can make decisions that the individual bees could not make on their own. Their group is a source of added intelligence. The group is a reality.

Slime molds and bee colonies adapt to their environment as a group. They also illustrate that nature works on different levels simultaneously. As kin selection folk will tell you the individual does what he thinks right. But at the same time, that often involves being part of a group. Purely collectivist political philosophies ignore the reality of the individual and are not sensitive to changing situations. That is a bad extreme. On the other hand, extreme individualism results in the negation of social reality. It robs us of potential social intelligence and may make collective adaptation harder. For optimal survival value, we should avoid extremes in either direction. We are individuals that need groups for survival.

Fitting in

We live our lives within social systems. This is painful to Western ears. We think that we are "self-made" individuals. But our place in the animal kingdom belies the fact that our existence requires a community. Large primates nearly all live in communities and we are large primates. The only exceptions to this rule, orangutans, live in trees. We are ground dwelling primates. And even orangutans come together for mating purposes and have social bonds with their offspring. Our natural state, as a species, is social.

With apologies to Western creed, rank gradations are ubiquitous in the animal kingdom.[197] Absolute equality is a nice thought, but not reality. In nature some animals rule over others. The struggle for rank tends to be more of a male thing, but it is widespread even amongst females. Having a boss is not only a human thing. Those at the "top rungs of the pecking order" tend to have access to the better foods and more females. The sad corresponding fact is that the losers in the hierarchical struggle have less access to quality foods and females. They get the dregs.

Though many may be gloomy about the fact that nature is not communist, there are warm and fuzzy tendencies embedded into this system. In a lot of animals, the battle for primacy tends to be stupid and brutal. Animals with antlers simply bang their heads into each other to see who is top dog.[198] "Alpha male" is the term given to the animal in the dominant leadership position in the group. In primates, becoming the alpha male is as much a matter of being liked as it is of head banging. Male baboons get to the top by a combination of fighting and coalition building. But staying at the top is more a matter of psychological intimidation and social skills.[199] If a baboon is brutal he will often be righteously hated and overthrown.[200]

Even amongst our most bloodthirsty of relatives, the chimpanzees, physical strength is only one factor in determining dominance. The ability to make coalitions with males *and* females is at least as important as the ability to dominate physically.[201] Frans de Waal carefully described how one alpha chimpanzee doubled the time he spent with females when his status was under attack.[202] When they abandoned him, his reign seemed to be over. His subsequent recapturing of the alpha male position was due to strategic coalitions and female support. His reinstatement happened despite the fact that he could no longer dominate physically.

As we elders would hope, age and experience are respected in the rest of the primate world. Alpha males often rule due to their seniority. That they do so is largely a function of their having long lasting relationships and knowledge. When baboons go through treeless areas they form a circle. Females with infants are brought into the center of the formation.[203] Then an elder male is often sent out alone to scout for predators. This is the most dangerous position.[204] Why do they send him out? He has more experience searching for predators; he can spot them better. Due to their wealth of experience old baboons are very necessary even when they pass their physical prime.[205]

Impartiality is a key to being a good alpha male. Arbitration reduces discord. One might think that apes would support their relatives, friends, and allies. This is indeed true for most members of an ape society. But a successful alpha male follows different rules. He is involved in restoring peace more than in aiding his friends.

Maintaining order in primate communities requires that the government impartially applies rules. Successful cooperation in a socially aware group requires a sense of fair play. Herein we see a guideline to social stability that America's Founding Fathers would appreciate. We primates have a sense of fairness.

When alpha male chimps do take sides they often support the weaker against the stronger.[206] One reason for this is, undoubtedly, that there are more poor than rich in every tribe. But this political assessment on the part of the chimp reflects a consciousness that transcends brute power. It recognizes that unfair dominance will result in resentment. That is it recognizes a psychological truth. Apes are shrewd as well as instinctual. The two are not mutually exclusive. We share this psychological characteristic. We know that the powerful joining the powerful against the weaker will invite resentment and political instability.

Dominance hierarchies are not things we should have a negative reflex to. Our Western aversion to them is like having an aversion to wind blowing. In nature they are devices for turning aggression and competition into peaceful, stable, and cooperative social systems.[207] Social scientists should note that males have a need for dominance. They will always be a constant jockeying that butts against equality. If such tendencies are not channeled by society, they may get out of control. Furthermore, staying on top is not just a matter of physical dominance. Allies and being seen to be impartial are necessary. Social dominance is social.

The evolution of learning

Looking at the evolution of culture is instructive. Once upon a time, there was no culture. We organisms adapted to our surroundings by spinning genetic mutations. Microscopic organisms still prefer this method. Within their small genomes, every mutation is very significant. Furthermore, their reproduction happens at a very fast clip. Toxins increase the rate of mutation. One of the mutations will prove to be immune to the toxin, survive and reproduce. Within hours a resistant population will have been generated. This process of overcoming toxins results in antibiotics and pesticides losing their effectiveness after a while.

This method of "learning" also happens in populations of larger organisms. But it is a painful way to learn to adapt. The black plague was brought to an end by its having successfully killed everyone that did not have a natural immunity to it. The still reproducing population was able to live amidst the disease and reproduce. Within a small group, hoping genetic variation will enable them to face an environmental hazard provides a less practicable defense. Our personal genomes cannot mutate; the offspring are the only mutants. The individual gets no comfort from this form of collective learning. Only large populations can gain survival through genetic variation.

Small organisms have short lifecycles. Their whole population can mutate within hours. Elephants can live to be over seventy years old. By the time the elephant genome has adapted to its environment, the immediate situation will have changed again. Worse yet, the more complicated a genome gets the less important a single beneficial mutation tends to be. The odds of a small herd of elephants mutating their way out of an environmental hazard in time are infinitesimal. Fortunately, evolution came up with a better source of avoiding lion attacks than genetic mutation: behavioral choice.

Behavioral choices started early on in evolution. Amoebas make choices. Motile amoebas have two propeller-like appendages. These allow them to move towards areas of nutritious chemicals. To facilitate the process the amoeba has a small amount of memory. It compares the concentration of nutrition in the water before and after its action. That is how it decides whether it is going in the right direction or whether it needs to try another direction. So they have a goal and go for it. But is this a choice? Is this mental? Or is it just as unconscious as water "choosing" to separate from oil? This is a tough call.

The behavioral options of the amoeba are hardwired. It cannot decide to try another sort of food or go on a diet. It is nearly as accurate to say "The nutritious chemical attracts the amoeba" as it is to say "The amoeba swims towards the nutritious compounds." But flexibility is always a matter of degree. Do you choose to be scared of the horror film or does the horror film scare you? Do males choose to be attracted to beautiful women, or do beautiful women attract them? We have a choice of what to eat and when to eat it. Eating is hardwired. The "mental state" of hunger is not chosen.

The difference between us and the amoeba is not strictly in whether or not we have a choice, but in the amount of choices we have. Amoeba must swim towards certain chemical compounds. If chimps cannot find a monkey to eat, they can eat termites. They know that certain sorts of leaves are edible. They have options. Thus when the seasons change, they can survive. And every time the environment changes, those who have been able to survive have added another option to their species repertoire. Birds have fewer options than we do. Their options are by and large predetermined. The bigger animal's brains are, the more behavioral options they have.

Eventually open systems evolved in which organisms are able to learn about the environment they are in and adjust their behavior to it.[208] This expensive hardware requires big brains. Being able to recognize prey and catch it or recognize predators and avoid them requires a lot of information in a complex world. This requires flexibility as the stimuli that should elicit escape behaviors vary from region to region. Programming the exact predators and responses into brains would take up too much space and be inflexible. Thus brains created heuristics or general rules to live by. Rather than just being afraid of their particular predators, animals are generally afraid of large objects that move towards them at rapid speeds. Other heuristics tells the animal generally when the chase has ended and when to turn and fight.

The complexity of heuristics reflects the long evolutionary path through which they were refined. Beings were originally mechanisms dedicated to finding a chemical. Eyes that could differentiate colors you can run through and those that represent solid objects evolved. Animals learned to eat meat. The meat learned to run away. The predator got faster. Only those animals that ran away from sound at a distance survived. Hair trigger heuristics that made prey afraid of all sudden loud noises evolved. Henceforth, only those animals that could sneak up on their prey survived. And so the dance of survival created senses, abilities, complex arrays of options to consider, and rules of thumb by which to make reasonable decisions.

Psychology in nature

To many the heading "psychology in nature" may seem problematic. They will take it as self-evident that amoebas do not think. Putting us in the same discussion as chimpanzees presents less of a stretch. Still, the objections for comparing us to other animals are immediately obvious. Comparisons need to be approached with an appreciation of our unique levels of freedom of cognition. We are different and should celebrate that. But before the nature and range of our differences with other species can be appreciated, we need to see the ways in which we are similar.

The evolutionary approach to psychology explains much of our behavior satisfactorily. Successful gene propagation explains much of the dance of love. Men can impregnate many women. Spreading their genes is best achieved by having as many partners as possible. Women cannot increase their fertility by having multiple partners. Females maximizing the amount of children they have who reach maturity gets best facilitated by screening the quality of, not increasing the quantity of, their sexual partners. Thus, before sex, it pays off evolutionarily for them to seek evidence of an ability to provide and willingness to stick around. They do so.

Evolutionary psychology's predictions for humans have been confirmed. Women are attracted to men that have status. That is because status is correlated with access to the resources needed to feed offspring. Women also seek expensive rings, in our culture, as a sign of fidelity and the ability to provide for their offspring before having sex. Men's programming keeps them seeking fresh sexual partners. Thus evolutionary psychology successfully explains why the overwhelming majority of pornography caters to men. Men wan partners, women want promises. Thus, out of evolutionary prerogatives, emerges the dance of romance.

Women actually prefer the smells of men with high status![209] Men who lost their jobs lose most of their testosterone.[210] Their smells change. We should not feel bad. We are not alone. Chimps who lose their status also lose testosterone. When men fight for status, it is not always done with the awareness that there might be a deep biological reason for their striving. Freud recognized this connection. But many of us do not think "I must get a promotion so that I can get more women and leave more progeny." The drive to achievement just seems natural to us. It is.

Men are programmed to find fertile and genetically healthy women stimulating. Youth, symmetry, and good skin are evidence of these traits.[211] Men find these traits attractive. Seeing these reproductively promising characteristics results in the chemical oxytocin being released in our brains. This, in turn, facilitates social interaction and induces bonding between mating partners.[212] We are not always aware that we are working in evolutionarily beneficial ways. Poor families' best shot at resources is to have their pretty daughter marry up. Poor families spend more time with their female children. The way for rich families to maintain their wealth is through their boy's achievement. Rich families spend more time with their males.[213] A more evolutionarily appropriate strategy could not be chosen were we consciously designing them.

What does marrying up mean anyhow? Again, heuristics are important. Programming different indicators for status for every possible cultural arrangement we might ever encounter would be impossible. Instead women are attracted to, and men strive towards, the culturally approved determinants of status. In some societies status is conferred on men who make money. Other societies reward bravery in battle and hunting. If you cannot make money in our society you still have hope. Perhaps you can be the leader of a punk rock band. Your status will increase the circle of friends you can draw upon for favors. And perhaps it will translate into money. At any rate, the females in your tribe will be attracted to you; they also have a status seeking heuristic.

Culture is evidence of human thought. The level at which we think is radically different than that of any other animal in existence. At some level you cannot compare us with any other animal. We have differential modes of survival and proving ourselves that chimpanzees could, literally, never dream of. But there are evolutionary programs running underneath the conscious levels of control we exert on the world. Strongly identifying with musical, sports, and other groups and seeking status in niches are embedded heuristics. Ignorance of such dynamics does not make us less able to manipulate such variables. Being aware of our evolutionary imperatives does not degrade us, it makes us more conscious.

Growth

Heuristics saved a lot of construction costs. A brain that had, again, a gene that coded for knowing about every possible situation would be overly complicated and large. Furthermore, it would not be adaptable. If climate changes forced a new predator into your region, the brain would have no gene to recognize it. Rules of thumb work better. These heuristics work best if they are general and specifics are learned after birth. Thus the bird can show you how to eat and to eat long tubular things. But, in a specific environment, mother can show you what sorts of tubular things and where they are located. Thus learning was born.

To facilitate this learning behavior nature created childhood. Children of many species are born unequipped to make it in the real world. Moms fill the gap. Anyone can lay an egg and leave it. But being a mother requires a lengthy dedication. To facilitate that devotion, love was born. And, beautifully enough, love *is* one of the characteristics that distinguishes smarter animals. When you destroy love's place in your culture you undermine the bonds that allow children the time and security they need to develop their potentials.

Pregnant women are not good providers. Children do not know how to hunt. Mother and child do not make a sustainable unit. In nature their abandonment often leads to death. Kids that survived had responsible fathers. Love facilitates this. A general sense of responsibility for the children in your community would help. But the connection between training youth and survival would have been so obvious that it would not need a strong emotion to enforce it. A child who gets no economic support or guidance from the community will not survive or thrive. If someone shows junior the tools of the trade, he can live to help in the hunt. The state has taken much of this responsibility in the West, but family is important.

Play is a rich source of learning.[214] The child learns to read faces. We, as other mammals, express emotions such as sadness and anger with our facial expressions. The range of expressions and their meanings are innate. All humans smile, laugh and cry. But how much teasing we can get away with and how to charm and deceive with these built in tools needs to be learned in social situations. We also learn who we are in social situations. All of us come with dispositions. Some learn that they are weak. Their best defense lies in making friends. Some will learn that we are strong. They will practice bullying and bluffing. Youth is a time for finding out where you fit in the social order. We learn who in our immediate social world we can trust and who lies a lot. In play you not only learn to hunt, protect, and evade; you learn to get along in a complex social world.

To a limited extent, animals also learn through imitation. Birds refine their songs through imitation. More impressively, some chimpanzees choose and clean sticks in order to get termites to eat. Not all do. Other chimpanzees break nuts open with rocks. Not all do. These behaviors are not hardwired. They can be said to be, in a rudimentary sense, cultural. They are regionally distinct behaviors. A lot can be done with imitation. In 1952 Macaques on Koshima Island were given sweet potatoes. The following year a young female started washing them in the fresh water stream. Others saw this and eventually they all learned the behavior.[215] But years later some of them were still washing the sweet potatoes in the salt water ocean! Imitative learning is a painfully inefficient combination of watching and trial and error.

Only humans engage in active teaching. We not only have extended childhoods and doting moms, we have teachers. Dolphin mothers dissuade their young from going near boats. A baboon dad will break up a fight that has gotten too rough. But they do not teach novel behaviors to their young. The slight variations that occur between groups result from imitation. Birds pick up the local accent by imitation. Chimps learn to get termites with a stick by imitation. We actively teach. This unique cultural feature can only exist become we come hardwired to learn. Without direct guidance, kids pick up the language and cultural traits of those around them. Again, as with what we have discussed before, it is not efficient for us to have too many specifics built into this system. We come hardwired to adopt variants of cultural tropes. But after we have absorbed the basics we also have the ability to consciously transmit and absorb advanced information in a way that other animals cannot. This ability has made us extremely adaptive. Being hardwired to learn has been *the* ingredient that has led to our taking over the world.

Territory

To understand behavior we have to look at its meaning with its complex social web. We have all seen male animals ramming each other. The Ugandan kob (a species of antelope), for example, displays the typical dynamics. They meet on the stomping ground and head butt. The males compete for central territory and the females flirt with the winners. The females will, in fact, only be sexually responsive to the winning male. Central properties bring more female kobs than perimeter properties. Nature has seen to it that what the male strives for and what the female prizes coincide. [216] This is what nature wants. Animals that win such fights have, on average, larger antlers and more offspring. The species thus gets grander. Those who lose, move to the perimeter. There they are picked off by predators.

Competition between members of the same social group is not bloody. There are signals whereby one animal acknowledges the superiority of the other. Wolves, for example, roll on their backs and urinate a bit. Such concession behaviors immediately stop the fighting. The struggle for survival within groups is largely a matter of struggle for mates, not battle to the death. Animals do not have aggressive combat with other species either. They may hunt them, but this killing does not involve the aggressive emotions; hunting is not done from anger. Deadly aggressive fighting happens between different groups of the same species. Moral behavior within groups is often used to facilitate immoral behavior between groups. This contrasts strongly with the notion of universal morality. The operating heuristic is cooperation within groups and struggle between groups.

Marking is more often used to maintain territory than actual combat. Extreme colors announce an extremely aggressive and territorial fish. Corral fish are so bright because they live in an area of limited resources and must mark their territory.[217] Ants are constantly licking each other for purposes of identification. In howling monkeys males of different troops utter warning cries. They may sound ferocious, but intimidation keeps the competitors at bay. Smell is another common method of marking territory. Dogs leave smell markers all over their territory. Rats also use smell. They love their young. They are kind to each other. They teach each other where food sources are and how to avoid poisons. But if you take their young out, clean them and rub them with another scent they will then ruthlessly kill their relative as they would any other invader.

Nature's large ubiquitous array of territorial markers serves to minimize violent confrontation. A territorial neighbor is not usually a threat. They stay on their side of the boundaries and you stay on yours. Birds recognize the songs of their neighbors. They are often neutral to the songs of their neighbors, but react aggressively to a stranger's song.[218] The net effect of a well-established spatial system is a reduction of antagonistic behavior to low levels and innocuous forms.[219] If all goes well strangers and neighbors will respect the borders and violent confrontations will not be necessary. Good fences keep battles to the death at bay.

The threshold value of fight-eliciting stimuli is at its lowest where the animal feels safest.[220] Translated that means animals will fight anything that dares get near the middle of its territory. Furthermore, the closer to his core area an animal is the more likely he is to win the fight. Invading someone else's turf is not a good idea. If a neighbor wanders into the middle of another's territory, the local will chase it out. As the pursuit crosses over into the neighbor's territory the animal being chased increasingly gains confidence and a willingness to turn and fight. Meanwhile as the pursuer gets farther from his core area his motivation wanes. Close to his home range the animal being pursued will turn and chase the chaser back. Eventually, they will come to equilibrium at equidistance between their respective territorial centers. The boundary reestablished, they can go back to their normal lives.

Environmental economic logic underlies explains these behaviors. Fighting is bad for both sides. The core area has the highest concentration of predictable resources. It makes sense that we should defend it violently. Peripheral areas can remain contested core areas cannot.[221] The home territory size must be big enough to feed those in it and provide a cushion of safety. If the core area were to get too large it would expose the animals to unnecessary danger as they infringed on other animal's territory and take great effort to defend. Territorial boundaries strike a balance at the need / safety ratio. This formula seems to apply widely in nature.[222] Still great variation exists. It is nice that not all of nature follows the ways of our closest relatives:

chimpanzees.

Chimpanzees are highly territorial. Even in captivity, male chimps patrol their borders. Males regularly go on border patrols. Patrolling chimps destroyed enemy nests they came across. Genocide is known to happen.[223] In the time that Jane Goodall lived with chimpanzees she saw four chimpanzee populations wiped out by war. The winners of such struggles kill the enemy infants and males and claim the vacant territory and females in it for themselves.[224] Feminists have often wondered why we do not compare ourselves with Bonobos. They are just as genetically related to us as regular chimps and are more peaceful. The reason for comparing ourselves to chimpanzees is because of how similar we are. "Lethal raids" are common to both of our species. Humans and chimpanzees are the only animals in which gangs of males expand their territory by deliberately exterminating neighboring males.

Chimps are not kind to strangers. Bringing foreigners into an existing zoo group is very dangerous. They value the lives of those outside their group much less than those within them.[225] The males of different communities kill each other through highly coordinated actions against single males of other communities. They stalk, run down, and swiftly overwhelm victims, who are beaten so viciously that they either die on the spot or have no hope of recovery. This is calculated murder. It is not the dispassionate aggression seen between different species in a hunt. One attacker pins down the victim while the other angrily bite, hit, and pound him.[226] They twist off limbs, remove fingernails and literally drink the blood pouring from wounds until the victims stop moving. They return weeks later to check on the outcome.

When chimp communities split, the out-group is "de-humanized." Chimps that had previously played and groomed together, reconciled after squabbles, shared meat and lived in harmony become enemies. Former friends drink each other's blood. Old elders are no longer respected. Any association with the enemy becomes grounds for attack. The distinctions are socially constructed. Well-known individuals can become enemies if they happen to hang out with the wrong crowd or live in the wrong area.[227] Groups unite in battle. So long as individuals feel a common purpose, they suppress negative feelings between individuals and clusters within their brood. But as soon as the common purpose is gone, tensions rise to the surface. Young males eye the position of the alpha male again. Unity and hatred are greatly modulated by the group context.

These group tendencies have important implications for our understanding of the nexus of culture and nature. Breaking into enemy groups can only indirectly be a result of genetic influences. We see groups forming and defending territory. But chimpanzee females leave at maturation and join another group. Fifty percent of the genes you are passing on are those of your enemy. The groups fighting each other are very similar genetically. Which gene pool gets passes on does not depend on which group wins. Selfish genes can only partially explain these groups' existence. Breaking off into groups favors the survival of those within the new groups because it reduces the strain on the environment for both of them. Genetic similarity means this benefit is conferred at the level of the individuals involved, not their genes![228] Their collective activity protects each of them. It is to the advantage of an individual to identify with a group.

Thus territory and group marking provide a scaffold that explains the value of culture. Culture bonds us to a group and differentiates us from other groups. This analysis establishes that culture a real force in nature. It is not an arbitrary creation like other sources of value. Culturism does not claim to be the prettiest source of values; but it has been shown herein to fulfill a necessary function. In nature it pays the group and the individuals in that group to be a part of a unified group. If a group splinters under attack it will lose its territory and likely be annihilated. When your neighbors raid, the defense of your group and territory must be loud, distinctive, and intimidating. You must back up your alpha male. And in the animal world the threat of another group attacking you is never remote. Survival dictates that in a world where unified attacks work you must be unified and attached to your group. Thus was the need for having social and cultural worlds born.

Culture, the limits of natural selection, and learning

The key to the evolution of language may be found in grooming. Primates spend a huge amount of their time grooming each other.

This is their way of touching base, making alliances, and mending hurt feelings. It is the flipside to their jockeying for power. After a male has mounted an unsuccessful attempt at toppling the alpha male, he will have to make-up with him. He does this by prostrating himself in front of the alpha male as men do in the presence of kings. He may kiss his hand as Catholics do to the Pope. In either case, he will inevitably end up nervously grooming the alpha male he previously sought to topple for exaggerated amounts of time. He re-establishes fealty. Grooming the alpha male and your strongest allies provides the keys to primate social stability.

Primates that live in bigger groups have larger brains. One famous theory as to why language originated postulates that it allowed larger groups to emerge.[229] Primates have distinct enough faces that humans can recognize familial relationships between them from photographs. Chimpanzees clearly recognize each other as individuals. Chimps can also express emotions with their faces. So grooming can be supplemented with gossipy looks and grunts about who can and cannot be trusted. But doing so requires a group size in which face to face contact is possible. Language allows you to keep tabs on people that are out of your visual range. Birds that sing socially live in dense forests where visual contact is difficult. They are keeping in touch auditorily. The same environmental pressure may have increased our primate progenitor's vocalizations.

Language would allow large groups to have stable hierarchies. The alpha male could be feared or loved from a distance. Language is a social act. This hypothesis would explain our infatuation with gossip. Reputation being very important and honor being so important seems to hint at a verbal analogue to an older system. People guard their reputations fiercely. Being called a liar is met with more indignation than it would rationally warrant. With a defense of reputation, your dependability or lack there of can be spread far and wide. "Everyone knows that he rewards people that follow him." "Everyone knows that you had better not cross so and so." Everyone can be a large group. Larger groups have had an edge when competing against other groups.

But before we go overboard, let us remember how much gets done without language. Dad goes to work. Moms raise the kids. The kids play and learn. Long and complex relationships are established. Wars happen. Generations live together and grow old together. And, in primates, some learn to make tools. Territories are demarcated and defended. Communities were maintained. Political hierarchies, chiefs, and a sense of justice and adjudication happen. All of these activities happen in species that do not have language. Revenge and love predate man. Not only can chimpanzees do all these things; rats, for the most part, can too. With that in mind we can appreciate that the ratio between what is instinctual and what language allows can become clearer.

Language allows larger groups, but for most of time human groups have not been very large. But just as opposing thumbs do not only help you grip, language generated unintended capabilities. Though functioning to facilitate the unity of large groups and allowing them to unite and differentiate, language allows us to actively teach instead of just imitating. We are special in that we supplement passive imitation with active teaching. But new abilities in nature supplement rather than replace older ones. Efficiency dictates keeping the same old brain mechanisms that created the basic structures of society. For efficiency, rather than genetically priming humans for the millions of unique traits that a specific tribal life might require, the old heuristics of imitating those around you (especially those who are successful) would provide a simple yet successful enough guide to transmit culturally successful behaviors. Innovations were very rare in tribal society. But when one came up, it could reasonably diffuse and stabilize via imitation.[230]

Language is a means by which we pass on our culture and its attainments. Its original purpose is not to facilitate skeptical inquiry into the nature of truth. We are programmed to accept our cultures. The previous statement's validation can be seen in the likelihood that you probably accepted it as you read it and moved on. Cultures where people fought over truths would soon disintegrate, collapse, and get eliminated. Furthermore, think of the difficulty scientific scrutiny entails. Unity would not happen if each generation had to be convinced of the rationality of accepting the programming of their culture. Conserving unity and the accumulated knowledge of your community is achieved more efficiently by just giving youth the heuristic predisposition to absorb their cultures without question. That this happens can be confirmed by the fact that people perpetuate the most bizarre cultural practices and beliefs imaginable. There is scientific research that substantiates our gullibility.[231] But we can move on to the next topic much quicker if you will just take my word for it!!

The nature of societies

Cultures teach people how to interact. Language facilitates this aspect of culture. Language not being formed for the purpose of thinking can be seen in man's lack of inventiveness and adaptation. Throat and girth harnesses choke horses and reduce the amount that they can carry. Nevertheless, they were used for nearly two thousand years.[232] Greeks and Romans used them. It is not the case that people that fail to upgrade their technology are unintelligent. The mind just is not designed for consciously scrutinizing and improving the world. This is an approach to the world that has to be taught. Even then, though the many may be willing to adopt the new creations, only a few will create them. Most people just accept the values and learn the behaviors of the culture they are in without a lot of reflection.

We tend to think that cultures strive upward. Our confusing our culture with man at all times and in all places reflects, again, man's propensity for taking what he encounters for granted. Some social forms include a larger population than others. Cultures that include small populations are classified as bands and tribes. Chiefdoms and states include larger populations. But size is not progress. It is not the case that this is the natural direction of the universe. Bands have often lived unperturbed next to states for eons without seeing a need to adopt this form of governance. And just as sometimes bands become states, states also return to being organized as bands. "Advance" happens as much as a result of pressure from the environment as it does a conscious decision to complicate life.

To a large extent, cultures and levels of organization are independent. The economic underpinnings of culture are not indicators of the types of cultural arrangements your society will have.[233] States have had widely varying cultures from each other; bands have too. And yet it is not the case that the cultural forms are irrelevant. Some cultures will aggressively pursue slaves for sacrifice. Some cultures will expect you to have several wives. Some conscript for the army. Others stagnate peacefully and build monarchies. At every level of organization a variety of cultural patterns will suffice to perpetuate society. The resulting societies will have distinctive impacts on their environment, neighbors, and citizen's lives. Cultures are not economically determined or unimportant.

Nevertheless, there are some discernable patterns that accompany larger societies. Smaller societies have greater specificity concerning your participation and duties; The taboos they ascribe to their participants are much more detailed. Because you are Bill's brother, who was the son of Bob and stepped on the root of the sacred bon-bon tree Jim got hurt. Therefore, Ted the shaman says, you are not to talk to members of Sheila's family and must carry water in your left hand for a week. Diverse groups comprise larger societies. For this reason the proscriptions and superstitions tend to have a more abstract nature. The penalty for x is y; not just for Ted or Bill, but for all nobles. Societies that are going to incorporate vast numbers need to be structured on general rules.

Cultures that incorporate larger populations being based upon generalities reduces their intricacies and decreases diversity somewhat. General rules for states either treat all as the same or lump citizens into categories. Just the fact that larger states reduce the number of cultures in an area reduces diversity. This should not, however, blind you to the diversity that exists between states. The Aztecs and the Romans were very different. It also should not fool you into thinking that the demands of efficiency will cause cultural convergence. Some social organizations can galvanize more participants than others. The ability to involve more people does not reflect a conscious attempt for efficiency. Cultures can be violent, stupid, and stable in a wide variety of forms. Advances towards states are not indicative of rational advance that are destined to converge.

Culture takes over

Man is different than other animals. He changes rapidly. Japan was extremely violent for the end of the 19th century and the first half of the 20th. Since that time it has not tried any military conquests.

The study of nature can tell us how exactly how inanimate objects will behave but not living ones. That does not mean that science is, however, useless in our understanding of life. It cannot tell us whether a duck will turn its head or not, but it can tell us whether it will fly North next month or not. Man is even less predictable than a duck. Still, he has tendencies that it is helpful for culturists to be familiar with.

Darwinian principles show us what some of these tendencies are. Left to their own devices, we would expect men to be promiscuous. This explains why all societies put some restrictions on men. Organization avoids disintegration then rules that channel aggression and impulse. Even polygamists are restricted in the amount of women they are allowed to impregnate. Males tend to keep moving on to newer women. Liberation from social control, the lesson is, will lead to social disintegration and more fatherless children. Those who are ignorant of natural science will often create poor policy.

Natural science also teaches us *why* letting men impregnate and run is a bad thing. Evolution's direction has been towards creating flexibility. Instinct has given way to choices. You cannot preprogram reactions without knowledge of the environment individuals are being born into. Nature created childhood so that we can learn the cultural solutions to the environmental situation the newborn finds itself in. Thus the cost of our flexibility has been bought at the inconvenience of a really long dependency of our young. Our economic strength allows children to stay in school and learn for a long time. Father's being around allows helps the children go to college and frees the mother to spend more time with them. We are not chimpanzees or birds; long childhoods of learning are important for us.

We largely absorb culture via imitation and watching those with status. This is not result from a rational thought process by which we independently arrive at self-evident natural law. We come into this world primed to adopt a language and a value system. One can especially see this in babies' amazing growth, children's dependence, and youth's cliques. Many nations are able to garner great allegiance because we are primed to join. People have rabid affiliation with their societies and causes. People strive for status in a pecking order in groups and want to join groups that are powerful. And if status does not come from the larger culture, we see people striving for it in subcultures. Adult males group around teams and those with the most athletic prowess. People will not join these because it makes sense; rather they are primed for absorbing something that gives them a sense of belonging and status.

Natural science teaches us that we are social animals. Absolute individualism is not a realistic option for us. Schools of fish look like they are cooperating. They are not. They do not recognize each other as individuals. They do not specialize. We are amongst the animals that do recognize each other and do specialize. We are more interdependent on each other than the individuals in schools of fish. As do all primates, we recognize individuals and live in more or less distinct groups. Any ideology based on the idea that people are individuals that have nothing to do with each other fails to notice that we are fundamentally unlike fish. We like to belong and hate alienation.

Humans belong to the class of animals that live in groups and defend territory. All humans, at all times, living with other humans and all being territorial is not a coincidence.[234] Human group solidarity is achieved by cultural markers. We dance and speak a certain way, have certain ideals, and Gods, clothes etc., and this helps differentiate those you fight for from those you fight against. Like other animals we have turf and borders. We mark our territory. If we want unity we need to create identification with the markers such as the American flag. This may seem manipulative, but better we announce and use forces consciously than to see default behaviors run wild. To not define and propagate identification with our ideals would disrespect our forefathers and the land they fought for.

Nature's stable patterns are not always functional or for the best. The Argus Pheasant have more progeny if they have more of the feathers the females go ga-ga over. This has created a gene pool where women want big feathers and men have them. This dynamic has resulted in pheasants that cannot run away and are easy bait.[235] They will never decide to stop this silliness. Often these blind systems do not adapt, they just die out. Our commitment to neither guiding identity nor morals might not be rational. Nature naturally evolves species and social systems; these are not conscious attempts at being efficient or rational. To make sure that we are not operating on maladaptive premises we need to constantly scrutinize the wisdom of our assumptions and policies. As natural scientists we should recognize the natural tendencies and pitfalls social groups have. As a culture that takes pride in being rational we must consciously scrutinize and guide our group's cultural defaults.

CHAPTER SEVEN

CULTURISM IN PSYCHOLOGY

Riots and the needs to control society mentally

The police never came during the 1992 Rodney King riots in Los Angeles. Why not? Why didn't the front lines of law and order restore law and order with their presence? Because the police knew that the rioters thought of police officers as the problem. Outrage at the beating of the motorist Rodney King started the riots. Rioting started the night the acquittal of the police officers who had beaten him was announced. When most citizens see a policeman and they are asked to do something they say, "Yes sir!" They are compliant and respectful. During the riots, when a policeman was seen the crowds would exclaim, "Look! It's one of them! Get him!"

Belief is the difference in these two reactions to police presence. Belief explains why the police were actually withdrawn from the 1992 Los Angeles riot zone. The rioters saw the police as an enemy to be attacked, not a friend to be respected. The police had to observe the spread of criminal activity from the sidelines like the rest of us. Cameramen in helicopters helplessly filmed crimes of looting, arson, and the unforgettable assault with bricks on a truck driver named Reginald Denny. The police saw this on television like the rest of us, but they knew they were even more likely to have been attacked if they entered this situation than the average viewing citizen. Their absence reflected their understanding of the importance of cultural sentiments.

Who should you bring in to restore order if the police are unavailable? It turns out that the National Guard is next up on the chain of enforcement. And during this Los Angeles riot the National Guard came in and restored order. Yet, in reality, the National Guard is just another group of young people with guns. In that respect they were identical to the rioters they were trying to stop. The only difference between the groups was their states of mind. Belief, again, has great consequences.

What if the National Guard decided to join the rioter's anarchistic fun? Who would you bring in to restore order? A branch of the military would have to be called in. I hope you have already anticipated my pointing out that the military is, in fact, just another group of young people with guns. The only difference between the rioters, the National Guard, the hiding police, and the military are their beliefs. Armed with this information, the military spends a lot time molding the mental habits of recruits. Recognizing that these are just average young people with guns, they make sure that they aim their weapons at those who they are told to when they are told to without reflection.

What if the military joined the rioter's anarchistic fun? Would you call in the President to restore order? An old man with a limousine in a riot scenario is not liable to do a lot of good. The President's power is predicated on the reactions of a whole lot of people when the red carpet is rolled out and Hail to the Chief is played. "Hey look an old man with a limo! Take it." would be the likely response in a riot situation. His age or rank or some other reason would have to engender a respect for his safety and well being for him to survive the scenario. Ultimately, only respectful attitude towards the old man with the limousine and the institutions he represents can protect the President; that goes for the rest of us too.

Thankfully, only a small part of the city usually has the attitudes, discontent, and anger that fuels riots. The posh communities of Beverly Hills and Santa Monica never had their police withdrawn. If too many communities in a country become lawless even a well regulated Army cannot reel them in. Social order is mostly a matter of getting the vast majority of people to agree to behave without police enforcement. The Police are, after all, only equipped to deal with the few exceptions. But how is social order made? How can such mindsets be instilled? How are the mental attitudes necessary for social order to be maintained? These are the sorts of questions this chapter will seek to address.

Social psychology has found that group creation is natural

In nature, as we saw, the group is often the nexus of sustainability. It is not always easy to tell if the individual exists for the group or if the group exists for the individuals. The distinction shifts when resource allocations and security situations shift. Emphasizing either the individual or group as a focus otherwise results from a matter of interpretation. Psychology shows us that this sort of reality does not only apply to amoebas and primates. Humans also have a reciprocal relationship with the communities and cultures we inhabit. We cannot extract ourselves from our environmental, social, and intertribal contexts. The branch of psychology that was designed to study this relationship between the individual and their context is social psychology.

One of the most widely recognized social psychology experiments was conducted by Philip Zimbardo. In this study randomly assigned student volunteers were given roles to play. They were either to play prison guards or prisoners in a mock prison in Stanford's basement. All the participants knew it was just an experiment, but it had to be called off after six days because the prisoners were having emotional breakdowns and the guards were getting too sadistic.[236] The individuals involved, he showed, were neither inherently passive nor sadistic; they were made so by the role they had within the group. The self cannot be wholly accounted for apart from the situation.

More than the power of roles was attested to by this study. It showed that, like our primate relatives, we have an inborn tendency to identify with our groups. This tendency was dramatically shown in Mazafer Sherif's Robbers Cave experiment of 1954. Sherif brought two groups of kids to summer camps and kept them from knowing about each other's existence. He made the two groups as homogenous as possible. They were all white eleven year old Oklahoman kids that had the same accents, social status, IQ, and lack of familiarity with each other. Sherif created activities in which each of the two groups could bond independently of each other.

When one of Sherif's experimental groups accidentally found out that another group was sharing the same space, their instinct was to "run them off" of it.[237] Before the researchers could initiate the part of the experiment that had to do with competition the groups were clamoring for battle. One group seized the other's flag and fist fights erupted. They then took to raiding each other's cabins at night and collecting ammunition to use against each other.[238] Unbeknownst to the participants their activities exactly paralleled what the anthropological record shows humans have traditionally done to each other and popular dynamics in nature.

Then something remarkable happened. The winning group decided that they had won because they prayed. They noticed that the other group swore. They decided not to swear thereafter. The other group started to identify themselves as the bad kids. The previously homogenous groups began to enforce their differences. Thus two cultures were born! What Sherif observed confirms that cultural differentiation via creation of a group identities and norms happens spontaneously. Once these identities emerged they were reinforced by noticing how different they were from the other group. Whether you like it or not, culturism constitutes a natural tendency in our species.

Just how deeply this tendency runs has been shown using what are called minimal information groups. These are designed to investigate how small a difference can trigger our innate tendency to differentiate. In one often repeated study of this phenomenon groups get created by fictitiously telling folks they had either overestimated or underestimated the number of dots flashed on a screen.[239] Unbeknownst to them neither the "over-estimator" group nor the "under-estimator" group deserves their moniker. In later tests each group tends to denigrate the other group and overestimate their own group's superiority. They will overpay their own sort and underpay the others. This is done without any group bonding activities or other distinguishable features being identifiable. We still run the subconscious "in-group / out-group" heuristics other hominids use.

Universal dividing does not only separate us superficially

Our foray into anthropology showed us that our belief in individual rational actors does not constitute a default in culture.[240] With the increasing prominence of suicide bombers in our lives, many have started to accept this truth. Imagining the mindset that leads one to killing themselves for God challenges us. Recent systematic studies of indigenous groups have shown that "what individuals can think and feel is overwhelmingly a product of socially organized modes of action and talk."[241] The Westerner's deep sense of individuality is not a universal. Ironically, our thorough individualism is a creation of our collective culture. Paradoxically, our reification of the individual was not an individual choice.

New research is showing that cultures have an enormous effect on us before we think. Cultures actually determine the way we look at the world. For example, North Eastern Asian cultures see things in terms of relationships. North Americans see things in terms of categories. When shown a chicken, a cow, and grass then asked which two go together, Westerners say the chicken and the cow do. They are both animals. Asians, on the other hand, prefer the pairing of the cow and the grass. They have a relationship.[242] Even deeper than the way we think, is the way we see. When Asians look at a scene they see and remember the overall setting. Westerners remember objects.[243] Writers who are new to English are often profoundly uncomfortable with identifying the individualistic, context free style of logic that is second nature to Westerners.[244]

These psychological differences are augmented by differences in cultural values. Methodologically rigorous analysis has shown that mindsets and values create comprehensive worldviews that vary from hemisphere to hemisphere. Furthermore it has been shown that some of these value systems result in democracy and wealth and some do not.[245] While this research is valuable proof, it is proof of the obvious. Every high school teacher can tell you that some cultures are more rabid about education than others. There are neighborhoods where men do not raise their children and people shoot each other. There are neighborhoods where there is no graffiti and very few people have guns. It is obvious that the impacts of cultural differences are deep and wide.

Belief in the impact of culture on psychology and the impact of psychology on culture separates culturists and multiculturalists. Multiculturalists base their social ideal on the premise that everyone is basically the same. Multiculturalists believe that when we celebrate diversity we are only celebrating differences in stylistic considerations like costumes and foods. Underneath it all, the assumption runs, we are all the same. Multiculturalists hold that diversity is epiphenomenal. Culturists hold that our differences are more than just a matter of exteriors. Culturists believe that diversity is real. Not believing cultural differences to be important, multiculturalists must attribute all differences in attainment between cultural groups to irrational discrimination. Culturists hold that cultures are diverse and that this diversity has an impact big enough that you can make important distinctions between cultures logically.

Studies showing the diversity of mentalities and their impact on the world highlight the precarious nature of our culture. While cultural mental perspectives deserve respect because they have survived a long time, they are not set in stone. Our individualistic and efficacious way of approaching the world is not written in the heavens for eternity or the universal default. Each culture encapsulates a unique way of looking at things that took hold in a part of the world. If a culture's mindset was lost for one generation, it could be lost irretrievably. If our mode of thought were relegated to a smaller segment of the world its existence would be more precarious. Culturism is not just an attempt to retain a style of dress. Culture is personal, local, historically created, of tremendous geo-political import, and not to be disregarded lightly.

Categorization and our inability to recognize our problems

If you are a Westerner you might have trouble thinking of riots as having anything to do with psychology. As one would expect from the way our culture sees parts instead of wholes, Western psychology is overwhelmingly concerned with the individual in isolation. From an Asian or Islamic point of view the connection between riots and psychology would not seem as odd. Their assumptions are much more culturist than ours. Our individualism and categorizing have caused a hole in our social sciences. Entire neighborhoods are dysfunctional and psychology only offers individual counseling. There is no term for a psychology of the ideological and unconscious assumptions that rule our collective lives. We can call this area of concern culturist psychology.

We learned that culture functions as an adaptation that allows the transfer of information from one generation to another. This allows us to have group solidarity and adapt to environments genetic adaptation could not prepare us for in time. We also learned that we are hardwired to absorb the culture we are born in to. Group survival would not be facilitated by each generation consciously scrutinizing the precepts of the culture and challenging their parents. We learn much individually, but absorb much without reflection. Much of an individual's behavior is the product social attitudes that are acquired from others with little, if any modification. We need to be aware of the contents of the messages we unconsciously accept from our culture.

The riot scenario description was meant to show that humans are not only behavioral, but ideological as well. The reaction to police reflects a mindset, but that mindset, while not consciously scrutinized by most who hold them, has ideological underpinnings. Cultures are mental by way of having shared assumptions. Not only consciously formulated constructs create the patterns by which people live their lives. The poverty that angers gangs is relative. Immigrants to these neighborhoods know that having electricity, cars, appliances, and water makes these residents amongst the richest people in the world. Black immigrants advance faster than locals because they know there is a comparatively huge amount of opportunity in America. Unquestioned assumptions inform lifestyles. They are accepted without much examination of their grounding. These assumptions are extremely pervasive and that results in their adoption.

Asian psychology, again, does not include the ideal of the absolute and abstracted individual. If a high school girl gets pregnant in Korea there is a concentric feeling of shame that radiates out to her family, friends, and school. Her shame and other's reactions will not assume individualism. Her friends will stop talking to her lest others think they are also moral idiots. The teachers will be ashamed of her not having taught the girl well enough. Her family and even the associates of her family would loose vast amounts of prestige. In a way that we would not understand, she would be ashamed of her socialization process. People will no longer be seen with her. She would never consider going back to the school again. Going back would reflect what would be taken to be an incomprehensible level of moral oblivion. Her shame should be hidden, not paraded.

Western schools are exactly the opposite. High school teachers are not allowed to make disparaging remarks to pregnant teenagers. Her pregnancy is considered a private matter and not a proper sphere for a teacher of a particular subject matter to comment upon. The teachers are to create non-punitive make-up assignments so that her private life does not impede her progress. To make a judgment on a personal matter would be inappropriate and possibly damage her self-esteem. Special programs help her adjust and no discrimination can be shown in hiring her for positions in which she interacts with the student body. Not facilitating her success due to her personal life would be a sign of intolerance, discrimination, and prejudice that would likely result in lawsuits. Pregnant teenagers have a right to work in the reception areas of schools just like everyone else.

People ask, "would you rather not have the teen mother educated?" But that question only addresses the individual. Not only are the perceptions of this teen pregnancy not individual, the results are not. Our lack of collective or personal shame has resulted in our having extremely high rates of teen pregnancy. Accepting the actions of the individual mothers creates a culture where teen pregnancy is normalized. The Asian teen pregnancy rate is nearly non-existent. This in turn has economic repercussions. These cultural perceptions shape the form of our families our economies, levels of education, institutional policies, crime rates, and levels of opportunity. Our absolutist individualistic stance refuses to acknowledge that private matters have public underpinnings and ramifications. Balance is needed. Our culture is proud that it allows the individual to challenge absurd and illogical social norms. But our purely individualistic notions of self need to be included in the list of things that are open to question.

These differences have nothing to do with race. Between 1960 and 1992, births to unmarried mothers leapt from 7 to 30 percent in the United States. This did not happen because we genetically mutated as a population. The change can be tied to the rise of consumerism, the idea of civil rights and entitlements, the roaring sixties' obsession with romantic notions of passion or our failure to view ourselves in the context of a public. Likely each of these contributed (as with individuals, historical causes in society are hard to isolate). But those who illogically attribute differences in cultural attainment and social pathology to race exemplify our innate proscription against critical thinking. Race and social pathology have nothing to do with each other. Even if these categories sometimes overlap, their fluctuation within groups clearly shows that social pathology is cultural.

Social pathology has been facilitated by a profound breakdown of our tradition of collectively practicing culturism. Recently attempts at making policy have resulted in lawsuits alleging they are racist. Some minorities drop out of school at a much higher rate than others. Criminal prosecutions result in more black people than others going to prison. These are not the result of racial differences. These other results reflect the fact that cultural diversity is not just epiphenomenal. This depth of diversity should also serve to warn us that if we do not take control of our culture we should not expect middle class values to result. Social pathology happens naturally. Policies that ignore the need to control and teach cultural values and the efforts of individual psychologists are ineffective at stopping social pathologies.

Not only are societies built on mental assumptions, the tools used to analyze them are too. As such we have to be careful of limitations of our conceptualizations. Not having a concept or a word for "awareness of and management of the collective assumptions, ideologies, and mental health of cultures and subcultures" reflects a big blind spot in our vision. This is a Western visual problem. Psychologists look at the gestalt of individuals. Social psychologists use statistical snapshots. Neither focuses on ideology. Philosophers deal in morals, but do not deal in applications. Political scientists do not manage cultures. No one is in charge of our collective mental health. And without such a field we cannot guide ourselves collectively. The ideological and habitual components of a culture are too important to be ignored. Culturist psychology is necessary.

Aristotle's vision for mental health

As with focusing on riots and morals, having a philosopher in a chapter on psychology might seem strange to Western minds. Overspecialization of social sciences has had harmful affects. Like culturist philosophy, culturist psychology must realize that it does not exist as a discipline for its own pleasure. Philosophy and psychology should understand that they are located within a wider culture. Being in a Western context this means being aware of Western history and Western philosophy. The individual is at once biological, political, moral, economic, and historical. To treat a person as an individual abstracted from these contexts is unrealistic. To treat the individual as being separate from their culture harms them and their culture.

It is appropriate to mention the ancient Greek philosopher Aristotle in this context because he, despite himself, is largely responsible for the malady that is being described. Aristotle was a master categorizer. He wrote a book on poetics, another on politics, another on ethics, another on rhetoric, and another on metaphysics. Though his writing fluidly integrates his understandings of these discrete areas of study, his divisions became the model for our belief in the ability to compartmentalize different branches of knowledge. Thus when we treat ethics and politics and art as distinct disciplines we are falling into an Aristotelian trap. His categorizing laid the foundation for the division of branches of knowledge inside and outside of the university. In an attempt to integrate these categories, therefore, it is appropriate to mention Aristotle.

Aristotle's vision of human happiness epitomizes culturist understanding. He notes that there are diverse pleasures.[246] To discriminate amongst them we must know the nature of man. Man is, by nature, a social being.[247] We form friendships. Some friendships are based on mutual pleasure. When the fun ends, these types of friendships end. Some friendships are based on what you can get from the other person. When they no longer provide, you divide. The highest form of friendship is one in which we are concerned with what is good for each other. To do this successfully, you must be a good person. You have to know what is good for people. Bad people unwittingly undermine their friend's achievement by exposing them to bad habits.[248] Helping someone requires knowing the difference between right and wrong and avoiding poverty.

Aristotle, in *The Nicomachean Ethics,* likens government to friendship. The government is like a good friend or a father that inspires you to do your best. We do not naturally have a character suited to the careful cultivation the good life and state require.[249] We must have our characters molded to habitually find happiness in virtue and dislike of that which is bad or we will be spoiled. Government guides people to be better people. Politics is the highest art of man because it aims at making the largest number of people virtuous.[250] Government is friendship writ large. You and the government should not use each other. You will form an enduring bond when each partner wants what enhances the other. This beautiful sentiment was also understood to be a necessity. Greeks were often at war. They needed to be surrounded by good people that cared for each other.

Cultivating culturist mental health requires more than stopping certain behaviors. We must show that our culture can provide a satisfying meaning of life for people. Western civilization can provide a great fount of motivation and meaning; Aristotle's idea of work as public service can make it personal. Contextualizing your search for the good life via an awareness of your family and community gives your philosophy depth and personal meaning. Tying it into Western civilization gives it depth, guidelines, and sublime role models in ethics, arts, politics, and sciences. Not only are social pathologies sins to Western civilization's mission, they are treasonous to your family, your community, and your drive to perfect yourself. Aristotle's culturist vision ties the mental health of the individual to their community and civilization. His vision of mental health connects the individual's passion and psychology to their culturist duty.

Many Westerners would become nervous at this point. The government and morals cannot go together. It defies our current functional bureaucratic vision of government. Our vision of government conforms to Aristotle's second type of friendship, we use it and it provides services. From his vantage point, the community and the government are distinct. This is another effect of our failure to see the whole picture. The people living within our borders are designated "citizens." Being a citizen entails a legal relationship to the government. But it is more than that. Citizenship implies belonging to and caring about the country in which you live. Being an American entails caring about America's future. It requires knowing something about America. If you break our laws entering, send your money back home, fly a foreign flag, and root against America in sporting events, you can hardly be said to be an American in a deep sense. Being a citizen is not just bureaucratic. Citizenship involves caring.

Aristotle's scientific compartmentalization helped to create the West's compartmentalizing mental mindset. Asian culture's psychological propensity to group via relationships comes from Confucius' philosophy being concerned with creating a harmonious whole. These mental emphases are also seen in the fact that Asian essays paint pictures whereas ours assert propositions. Muslims cannot help but see the relationship between religion, the culture, and the people. Other culture's psychology predisposes them to see the big interrelated picture. Aristotle's legacy, unfortunately, tends to leave us seeing unrelated individuals and categorical divisions where none should appear. We are dependent upon each other. Whereas other cultures do not need to be reminded that parts are integrated into wholes, we do.

Individualism and individual mental health

Sigmund Freud conceptualized psychology as search for what was happening deep down inside of our individual psyches. As such he laid the groundwork for conceptualizing the battle for selfhood as finding autonomy from all of the outer claims on your self. Alcoholics Anonymous (emphasis on the latter) perpetuates this vision when they admonish us that mental health is predicated on drawing "boundaries." They assert that our "dis-ease" comes from confusing our needs and other's needs. This model ends up ennobling struggles against "oppressive" social norms. This sort of philosophy views individuality as something achieved via defiance of society. By this logic freedom will not be total until all taboos have been violated. Thus when you are totally solipsistic and anti-social you finally know that you are being true to yourself.[251]

We have achieved what has been called a "Culture of Narcissism."[252] This individualistic orientation can only provide a lonely world interacted with in terms of what pleasures it can provide the self.

The self conceptualized as a bundle of individual wants needing to be satisfied has been taken advantage of by consumer culture. It is hard to conceive of what the meaning of such a selfish life is outside of pursuing the satisfaction of private wants. Ironically, this emphasis on personal happiness has not resulted in personal happiness. This rampant individualism has been held responsible for the huge increase in depression in our society.[253] Nearly all of our evolutionary predecessors lived in groups. This is natural. And as sure as we have a tendency to form groups, being isolated does not feel good to us.

Robert Bellah has noted that our individualistic vision is antagonistic to families. Western youth try to be authentic by breaking away from society and finding their generation's special identity. In our culture it is considered a sign of health when young people break away from their families early.[254] Getting ahead is something you do for yourself and leisure is never burdened with social responsibility. When the ethic of self-fulfillment becomes the basis marriage, each person is only bound to the agreement as long as they are getting what they personally want out of the relationship. Even couples with children break up now because they do not find the arrangement personally fulfilling.[255] Individualism thus undermines the stability of the social bonds.

"Social capital" is a term designating how much the people in a community, neighborhood or society are relating to each other or are involved in each other's lives. Measures of social capital reflect how individually oriented versus how socially oriented people are. Robert Putnam has documented that the amount of social capital is *the* determining factor in child welfare and education, healthy and productive neighborhoods, economic prosperity; evenness of economic distribution, health and happiness, democratic citizenship and government performance.[256] All of these crucial factors rise and fall as a direct result of variations in social capital. The more socially connected we are, the better off we are collectively and individually. This statement does not only refer to ephemeral measures of non-essential characteristics. Purely individualistic psychological and cultural outlooks are pathological.

Furthermore, individualism undermines culturism at the highest levels. The Supreme Court heard Ginsberg v. New York in 1968.

Ginsberg sold a girlie magazine to a 16 year old boy.[257] The Court was trying to decide if such material was *harmful* to the individual youths (instead of discussion of whether or not this material was *healthy* for children). One important witness for the prosecution was Willard Gaylin. He successfully argued that it was not the affect of pornography itself on individual children we should be looking at. Rather it was the effect on the culture of saying that pornography was okay that we should be our focus.[258] In an age of soaring anti-social behavior, looking at the individual's mental health in isolation is a mistake.

Gaylin's suggestion found a remarkable confirmation and extension in the work of Richard Arum. Arum's team showed that court rulings in school discipline cases that were only based on the rights of the individual undermined the collective good. Arum found a correlation between trends in the over 1,200 court cases he studied and school discipline policy. Interestingly, it was not the specific cases, but the "court climate" that influenced practice.[259] Thus Gaylin was correct that the implications as well as specifics of a ruling are important. More importantly yet, Arum found that the students' impression concerning the fairness of discipline in schools was eroded by legal challenges. And the efficacy of discipline is more related to the students' perception of it as fair than by its actual strictness. Collective understandings exist and have importance. In the end Arum asks that the legislature reset the perception of those in school communities. Arum's analysis recommended this tact over "simply accepting the dysfunctional character of public schools as an unavoidable price paid for the general expansion of individual rights."[260]

By definition, individualism undermines our sense of community. When all behavior becomes a private choice, no community standards can be accepted as legitimate. When the local level of self-governance loses clout, the Federal level becomes the only level at which we are united. Individualism combined with absolute rights means no one, from the teacher to the neighbor, can tell anyone else what to do. This undermines any potential attempts to foster a sense of common identity, standards or feelings. We cannot be united except on the basis of our common isolation. Pure individualism does not resulted in individuals being financially, physically or mentally healthier.

Individuals are better served by having culturist awareness.

Divesting

Robert Reich, President Clinton's Secretary of Labor, wrote of the dangers posed by the business elite no longer feeling a sense of solidarity with our population. When the rich no longer feel a sense of connection with the rest of the nation they send their children to private schools, hire private security systems, and no longer feel a need to fund the infrastructure of the country at large. This exasperates financial divisions that, in turn, increase the mental distance. Schools and local infrastructure and, ultimately, the strength of the nation are imperiled. When our sense of cultural connectedness diminishes the lower classes get unfunded and our nation is threatened with fractures.

The business elite's decision to withdrawal from our country is usually based on the idea that wealth is the creation of lone individuals struggling individually to take care of themselves. Adam Smith's assertion that the basis of wealth is individual greed launched this thought pattern into our collective consciousness. It is, however, not true. John Kay has shown that wealth is a community effort. In this day of international trade, Hollywood still dominates films because you can conveniently find everything you need to make a film there. Hollywood is a film community. The Silicon Valley dominates computers and New York finance for the same reason. These enclaves of economic sector dominance grew up organically, if you will, as people filled niches. Individuals got wealthy filling the sector's needs. And their wealth would not have happened without the community context.

Cultural diversity aggravates this problem of individuals and industries not feeling allegiance to the countries that fostered their wealth. Someone who wears a turban and beard because a 10th prophet who emerged in wars between Muslim and Hindus is going to reappear (a Sikh) is hard for most Americans to find common cause with. When the poor do not speak the same language as the elite do, their feeling of solidarity with the rest of us is undermined. When the poor eat different foods, have different customs and always refer to other countries as "their" country, funding their infrastructure does not carry as much moral weight. As much as wealth disparity, cultural divisions undermine our feeling of having a common cause and the duties that implies. Cultural divisions also undermine poor people's efforts at lobbying for funding. When lobbying for their class is seen as lobbying for a distinct and separate cultural group it does not garner sympathy from other citizens.

Corporate leaders who think that they can ignore America by doing international trade from remote locations need to reconsider. They should appreciate that America gave them opportunities that they would not have had elsewhere. Communities are necessary. Their universities were communities that helped them learn. The American economy was strong enough that they could go to school. Our infrastructure facilitated their transportation to school. Divestment will undermine opportunities for future Americans. Their dream ends up in isolation and negative feelings about those outside of their security gates. Meetings with cultural strangers in far off lands cannot feel very homey. When all their business dealings are with folks of a different culture, far from home, a feeling of ostracism and estrangement must set in. They should admit that they secretly envy their foreign partner's sense of community and cultural pride. At any rate, unless they are going to retire abroad, divesting in their home country will undermine the comfort and quality of their later years.

Business leaders can be heroes. In Ancient Greece those with money were expected to use excess wealth to sponsor theater and celebrations or give back to their polis in other ways.[261] This earned them esteem and brought a sense of loyalty to the fighting forces that endlessly had to defend the polis from those who would attack them and drag them down into economic and mental slavery. The rich people were given seats of honor at these festivals they sponsored. The mental aspect of this exercise is worth noting. If one did not feel a sense of community with those who you were expected to buy a celebration for, your box-seat would feel like a prison. If you felt a sense of community with those enjoying the celebration, the box-seats would be a source of glory. Being envied is great. But being honored in your country is something that money cannot buy.

Ultimately, our society cannot exist without a sense of community. There are not enough tax collectors to go after everyone. People should pay their taxes because they believe in the government that is using them and that the government is using the money to bolster the well-being of a culture that citizens love. Ultimately, people who do not love their country or feel solidarity with those who their tax dollars underwrite will be able to find a way out of paying taxes if they so desire. In this age of international business nothing can really stop executives from sending factories or headquarters overseas. But this ultimately eats away at the culture that guarantees fair play in business. Ultimately, this is not only bad culturally, it is bad economically. Cultural psychologists need to do what they can to make sure efforts towards creating a sense of cultural connection and meaning reach all economic classes.

Unity

Gangs are, in some ways, healthier institutions to belong to than mainstream society. Much of what they provide fits in well with the psychological propensities we inherited during our long evolutionary history. Gang membership can lead to an early death. So can individualism. Studies show that isolation greatly increases your susceptibility to a host of fatal illnesses. Would you rather die from a bullet or isolation? Gangs are, by definition, a group activity. We would do well to provide people in our society meaningful roles and a sense of belonging. Providing people with volunteering opportunities and community structures to belong to would help us compete against the emotional pull of gangs.

Status is important to males. Getting to the top of the social heap gives males a jolt of testosterone and diminishing status depresses it. You can get your status from passing your calculus exam or your first beheading. Pride in your gang is anti-social from the perspective of the larger culture. But it in the absence of other sources of pride, gang membership becomes a psychological necessity for the individual members. Few things can equal the hurtfulness of the daily knowledge that you are an anonymous loser. As in when we root for teams, we can get our sense of status vicariously. It is very important, for this reason, that males feel a sense of pride in their country. Cultural psychologists should make sure that all are included in celebrations of the accomplishments of America.

Cultural pride can give you a sense of belonging and status. Members of Islamic nations celebrate as a group whenever there is a successful terrorist attack on Western soil. Their people are willing to blow themselves up for their culture. The specter of a dominant China swells the pride of their citizens. The poorest man can find his own importance and dignity in his team's greatness. Emphasis on the greatness of the society of which men are part also humbles men of rank and fortune. It provides a source of unity and lays the foundation for true citizenship. Pride feels wonderful. It gives one a sense of efficacy. It improves your posture. Society should make sure that pride comes from healthy sources.

Gangs provide a worldview for their members. They are also, unfortunately, myopic, and unsustainable. They do not realize that they are, in fact, not tough. When compared to fighting in World War II, drive-by shootings do not take a lot of guts. Gangs do not realize that they are on the wrong side. Were Hitler to have won they would really understand what there is to gripe about in the world. Islamic victory would teach them their interests laid in being proud members of Western societies, not terrorizing them. But human survival has depended on our ability to absorb culture, not an inborn sense of skepticism or critical analysis. Culturist psychologists need to teach young people what worldwide cultural diversity looks like, what poverty looks like, and which society they should root for. The street defense orientation of gangs is normal, but a broad world outlook is more appropriate to our diverse and civilized world.

Gangs are not the only groups who find splitting off from society. Ethnic sources of identity also provide social connections, meaningful roles, status, and ideology. Ethnic enclaves can also be healthy in their contexts. But all Americans need to be reminded of the larger team they are on, where their efforts do the greatest good, what exalts them the most, and where their best interests lie. A problem with multiculturalism is that is often fails to promote that larger group context of which we are all a part. By definition, being predicated on differences, it cannot be a source of unity. Ethnic identification should never be strengthened at the expense of loyalty to Western culture. If the Western world weakens the entire framework of tolerance, freedom, and individualism will be undermined.

The Robbers Cave experimenters tried different methods of reuniting the warring summer camp participants. They listened to sermons on brotherly love and it had no effect outside of the church.[262] They tried leaders summits. These could work, but leaders giving too much would result in their being called traitors. Contact between the groups at pleasant activities increased, rather than decreased, hostilities.[263] What was able to bring them back together was working on goals that neither group could accomplish alone. For example they helped push a broken down us together. Collectively working on superordinate goals reduced hostilities to the point where friendships formed across group lines and different group members voluntarily decided to take the same bus back home. Those who held on to old animosities were marginalized by their groups.[264] By providing a superordinate goal culturism can diminish discord in our society.

Culturist devotion to Western civilization can provide a feeling of belonging that helps, rather than hurts the West. Our alpha male nature means our efforts will be especially effective if our cultural pride is stated with bravado. Pride in the accomplishments of the West can serve as a source of pride and status for every member of our society. Focusing on wonderful nature of foreign traits does not increase pride in America. A belief in ethnic determinism runs counter to the American creed and divides us. Rather than strife, culturism provides us with a superordinate goal that can unite groups. And this is not just for fun. Our values are challenged internationally and anti-social beliefs and behaviors hurt us domestically. The Western belief in the ability of men to guide themselves is a belief that honors each of us. We are strengthened by common purpose individually and collectively. We need to be united as Western culturists.

Culturism provides values

The use of the word culturism can be useful on many levels. First and foremost culturism fosters discussions about something higher than the individual. Even if the person uses the word to denounce culturism, they are entertaining the idea that there might be a value that could be a legitimate criterion upon which to base policy other than the individual. For those who agree that culture is a value that we should consider, it necessitates a discussion concerning the definition of the values that comprise our culture. Diversity provides no moral guidance. Neither does individualism. Ways in which we are diverse and individuals cannot guide you. At best they advocate tolerance, but advocating tolerance weakens our ability to act as much as it provides guidance. Culturism provides a source of values that can sustain our very particular and valuable culture. The use of the word culturism implies a morality that can help bind and guide our culture.

Plato, Aristotle, Jesus, and our Protestant based traditions all agree that our thoughtful and spiritual natures are higher than our animal drives. None would tell us that our highest good lies in rubbing ourselves against strangers, undermining our brains through substance abuse or ignoring education. Western culture tells you that freedom results from overcoming the temptation to have our biological nature override our spiritual nature. Whereas it might be difficult to provide an absolute basis upon which to say that spiritual and thoughtful goals are better than sexual ones, you do not have to look far into the Western tradition to find effort to substantiate the claim. Our current failure to find anything shameful is only conceivable in a culture that has completely forgotten the Western tradition.

Culturist awareness implies understanding that your actions affect your community. Dressing like a bum indicates that you fail to understand responsibility, the nature of the geo-political world or the sacrifices that have been made in creating the West and your freedoms. Dressing like a whore shows that you are not aware that sex involves making children and conscientious beings do not enter into such relations lightly. Being a proud whore either represents a failure to grasp, or spiteful rejection of, the understanding of the spiritual enlightenment upon which our freedoms are based. Using foul language shows a total disregard for other people's sensibilities. Healthy cultures have a sense of shame and pride. Culturism implies being conscious of the effects of your actions. Your actions do not happen in isolation. All of your actions send a message to the public. We are all role models.

Basic morality can also be garnered from economic considerations. Without a first-world economy, our choices and opportunities are undermined. There are few schools to attend in poor countries. Poor countries are not full of opportunities. A first-world economy being necessary for much of what we mean when we discuss liberty, responsibly means only having children you can support. Excessive borrowing leads to economic bondage and bankruptcy. Not taking advantage of the educational opportunities afforded you not only shows ingratitude and ignorance; it shows you do not understand what a first-world economy is based upon and that it cannot be taken for granted. Gambling is money poorly invested and shows you are either immoral or addicted. Divesting from Western countries is wrong. To the extent that you are undermining our economy, you are undermining our collective strength and freedoms.

Culturist pride comes from doing what is right by your culture. Being a citizen has been conceptualized as a legal status. Beyond this however, there is being a good citizen. Being a citizen means rooting for the country in which you reside. For Americans, this entails understanding our mission and being dedicated to fostering it. This does not require you to join the military. It does, however, require that you take some pride in our country. When you are dishonest in your business dealings, you lower the value of the American word. When you are lazy, it ruins the image of the hard working American. Knowing that you are a helpful part of a country that leads the world in freedoms and democracy is an awesome feeling. We should feel at least the same amount of pride in our collective existence as the racist Chinese and fanatical Muslims do. Our flag represents a vision we should be proud to carry forth. All healthy activities can be doubly celebrated in this light.

Culturism being used makes those adhering to Old World divisions accountable. Using culturism means that different levels of attainment in education, crime, and levels of health will not be automatically attributed to racism. These differences being seen as the result of diversity will cause groups to take responsibility for the results of their norms. Talk of racism disempowers everybody. When a policy affects every sub-cultural group differently, as it inevitably will, this does not mean the law is racist; it means that diversity is a real and important entity. Culture being malleable communities can do something about their situation. Invoking racism or non-cultural factors means that measured differences become a source of anger. Such talk creates hostility towards the society at large and disempowers the groups involved. Culturism creates a way for groups to monitor both the progress of subcultures and the culture at large.

Individualism does not create a healthy sense of community and, ultimately, it undermines our morality. Graffiti shows a disdain for the culture. Sloppy dress, again, says you do not care what others think. It also shows a lack of pride. This can be seen to be the result of not having anything noble to aspire to. Only discouraging not going to school or doing drugs on the basis that it will harm your career makes it a personal choice. If you do not care there is no moral leverage to be found. There is no sense of team. Under a purely competitive model, another person's victory implies your defeat. Accomplishment just becomes another selfish act. Shame and pride have no context in which to exist. Ultimately, being told that every choice is purely individual leads to a feeling of despair and abandonment. Society says you are on your own and what you do is your own business in an individualistic model.

Culturism ultimately posits a positive value source. People that feel an attachment to their society's status are happier. Rooting for your side is something all sports fans can appreciate. Those who conceive of their fellow citizens as being compatriots forge stronger community ties. This increases the levels of interpersonal trust that are ultimately necessary for a functioning society. Mental health and wealth result from pulling together. Leaders challenging average folk to make our noble superpower stronger should especially appeal to males (many of whom have gotten very wimpy). But the point of culturist psychology cannot only be to make the individual happy. Were that the goal it would just present another form of hedonism. Our important values' success will ultimately require a real culturist mindset.

Perspective and vision

Often what immediately benefits you and what benefits society are the same. Sometimes what immediately benefits you does not benefit the culture. Our Founding Fathers were acutely aware of this when they met to create the Constitution. To attain a disinterested perspective they deliberated in secrecy. Had they not done so their status as local politicians would have forced them to take the limited perspective of their states or some faction within them. They could not have advocated limiting their local government's power in public. Secrecy allowed them to consider what was best for the fledgling country overall. When buying products made in America it might cost more, but it shows a cultivated awareness in that you are taking a social perspective into account. You are thinking of others. People do not naturally put their society first. The Founding Father's choosing to meet in secret should serve as a reminder for us that actively cultivating a wide perspective is a virtue.

Our failure to battle illegal immigration provides one example of our failure to consider the broad picture. The academic community has not been a leader on this issue. Overtly culturist historians, linguists, political scientists, lawyers, philosophers, psychologists, and sociologists would bolster the common sense view that unrestricted and unselective immigration hurts the West. They are discouraged from straying from their areas of expertise. Professionalism dictates that academics just stick to the facts. Worse, within their specialty, these same standards require that they aim for the impossible and impractical goal of impartiality. Thus, unlike their counterparts in other cultures, our scholastic repositories of leadership are emasculated and removed from the culture they could lead. They are not recognizing that they exist within the context of a cultural mission.

Business leaders have also been abstracted. Once upon a time businessmen were seen as community members with the traditional duties of other good citizens. Now their bottom-line only refers to money. Immigration only means cheap labor to them. Whether this undermines the sovereignty of the nation and efforts to reduce crime and drugs; whether it strains the local schools, infrastructure or the idea of loyalty to those whose ancestors built the country they live in is "immaterial." Business leaders are wrong about their ability to abstract themselves. If the Chinese dominate and downsize or America fails they will not be able to comfortably take up residence in the third-world country, racist Asia or the Islamic Middle East. But we cannot realistically expect business leaders to advocate for anything that is not tied to their company's profits.

We cannot expect those arguing on behalf of illegal immigrants to ask "What is good for America?" That is not their job. It would be silly to expect them to do so. China's refusal to repatriate the 40,000 Chinese illegal immigrants we now hold at a cost of over 667 million dollars does not surprise those versed in cultural politics.[265] The Chinese government advocates for those policies which benefit China and people of Chinese descent. That is their mission. The Mexican government's job is not universal justice. From the stand point of self-interest, it is sane, consistent, and rational for them to argue for their citizens having their universal rights recognized in America while denying them to foreigners in Mexico. Individual immigrants, especially as they are foreign, are not naturally oriented to put America's interest first. Their own fates are their primary concern. One would not expect foreign nations or nationals to take a Western culturist perspective.

Unfortunately, it is largely inane to ask politicians in a democracy to ask "What is good for America?" In the current state of democracy politicians are largely limited to being either concerned with themselves or their political party. These activities require that they pay attention to big donors and do not make anyone angry. They are not political leaders, they are politicians. Logically, they will point out, they cannot legislate in the general interest of America and Western civilization if they are not re-elected. They must take the safe route on all issues and give a special listen to their biggest donors (businesses who have little allegiance to America). We should expect them to pander to people, not ask them to sacrifice for America. Unfortunately we can only expect them to ask, "What is good for America?" in a manipulative way.

Expecting citizens to constantly be vigilant observers of the legislative process is not realistic, but it does imply two workable corrections to our present system. First, the legitimization of culturism in the academic community and general citizenry would make asking, "What is good for America?" normal again. Funding academic research projects could be chosen on the basis of their implications for Western Civilization. Much of the general public still has an instinct that makes it reflexively ask, "What is good for America?" The term culturism provides them a handy catchphrase to throw at politicians and others who justify their impotence in putting America first on the basis of abstracted and universal freedom, individualism, rights, and an inappropriateness of government delving in morals. Widespread use of the word culturism would pressure them to do the right thing and give them a reason to do it.

Secondly, getting Western Civilization's priorities put first could also be facilitated by the formation of a Federal Department of Culture. Nearly every other nation on earth having such a Department shows that this is not a bizarre or unrealistic goal. So many countries having a Department of Culture (usually named the Ministry of Culture) also shows that most countries have recognized the promotion and management of their national cultures, culturism, as an important function of government. Those in this Department would be better situated to watch our legislators in the interest of our culture than most individual citizens. This source of employment and funding would encourage academics to take a culturist perspective into their work. Creating a Department of Culture would teach the American people that our country and its culture are important enough to deserve legal consideration. Those in the Department of Culture could be the West's ultimate culturist psychologists.

Department of Culture

Part of recognizing that our culture is not universal is realizing that other cultures might have practices to learn from. Where ever you go around the world, the governments are seen as advocates for the ascendancy of their country and culture. Every major city in Mexico, for example, has an enormous Mexican flag flown in prominence. This only engenders a shallow level of attachment to one's country, not a deep understanding of the values of the culture. It has, however, facilitated great nationalism in a populace who does not receive much more than abuse from its government. What it fosters is more akin to patriotism than culturism. But if your goal is engendering pride and unity, it works. Culturist psychology must ultimately, though, convey more ideologically rich content.

Culturist psychology must address ideology at a deeper level than at that of superficial patriotism. Our culturist efforts have to be intelligent and respect our heritage of individual thought. Statues celebrating the greatest citizens are widespread in most countries. Oppressive, tyrannical countries are compulsive about such public displays of affection. Appropriately, as soon as freedom is allowed, the statues of these tyrants are torn down. These are statues of bad men. Their being torn down immediately belies the fact they were just propaganda. Erecting such statues just becomes another source of resentment to the citizens in an otherwise repressive and exploitative country.

Yet it would neither violate the purposes of government nor just be cheap propaganda for our country to make statues of our greatest citizens. We have fabulous persons to revere in our history. Our political leaders have been near paragons of virtue. Though some of their actions failed to reach perfection it was not for lack of trying. Their failure to achieve pure morality can be used to teach the lesson that achieving perfection requires constant struggle. And their ideals of perfection can serve as inspirations to good behavior and respect. The proposed statues should be accompanied by plaques that explain who the person did and what they contributed to our freedom. Their deserved recognition could serve as models for responsible concern with our country and its standards of behavior. They would personify ways of meriting glory for generations to come.

Much of what makes a healthy culture is a shared narrative. Having a large amount of first generation immigrants makes public works explaining our culture especially important. Many know nothing of our Founding Fathers or the Puritans, let alone Socrates. As with talking to an individual, cultural psychologists must use words in their communications to their patients. Those in our riot zones were acting on premises. Those ideas and presuppositions must be addressed verbally. Solitary pictures of our heroes on our money do not provide enough context for these narratives to be understood. Public murals are an internationally used tool for fostering such understanding. They are large colorful and can have linguistic explanations that accompany them. Musicals, plays, and public celebrations concerning our history would also effectively convey our narrative, bond people together, and help to propagate knowledge about our collective reason for existence and glory.

Earlier we defined social capital as an indicator of community networking. We have a generation gap in America. In the world of niche marketing, our older generation has lost its ability to convey its values to the younger generations. The generation that has the highest rates of social capital is that was raised in the Depression and fought World War II. The power of perspective can be seen in this generation having sacrificed so much for this country, having lived in deprivation through the thirties and yet being more patriotic than any other. Their perspective has to get into the public square. Locally sponsored outdoor World War II and Korean War film festivals would help youngsters understand this generation's attitudes in a public space, surrounded by community, in a format they would enjoy. Festivals for this generation of veterans would create a mechanism by which elders, in an age of broken homes, could transmit traditional values.

Whereas noble ideals and persons should make up these public activities, America also has lighthearted and fun themes to celebrate. Movie stars, the invention of the television, cars, and air conditioning would also make fabulous themes for public art and parades. If you include all that our technology and popular culture have created, the potential variety of American themed celebrations becomes nearly inexhaustible. Imagine a festival, parade, play, museum and statue dedicated to the American inventor of television, Philo Farnsworth! Popular statues being publicly unveiled could foster local civic pride. This being locally funded would create a sense of culturism amongst those who erect them. It could also create a revenue base through expanded tourism.

The Department of Culture could instigate and provide seed money for such events. But, each local person involved in the projects garners more social capital and pride. Citizen, not professional, involvement and control should be the goal. These events would make citizens more aware of the impact of public space. Citizens coming together would create unity in the ideological realm, but it would also be more personal. It would be an opportunity for local people to get to know one another by working on projects together. People would possibly see their neighbors at such events and trust would thereby be increased. These efforts might also get a generation of artists to think in more culturistically edifying ways. There would be other echo effect of such projects. All of these effects are very much needed and would have minimal side effects. These efforts certainly need not wait for the establishment or blessings of a Department of Culture.

Americans, to their credit, are always afraid of indoctrination. But far from promoting tyranny, celebration of our cultural heroes provides an inoculation against it. Every play depicting George Washington presents a threat to tyrants everywhere. No government intent on violating rights would sleep well knowing it was surrounded by thousands of Thomas Jefferson statues. Benjamin Franklin is not one of those overbearing heroes of other countries that would engender civic withdrawal. Our Founding Fathers being celebrated publicly would not encourage power for power's sake. They would not cause people to be mindless followers of government schemes. They provide symbols of intellectual freedoms and political rights we hold so dear and rebellion against tyranny. Public art celebrating our past would constitute a defense against indoctrination.

The importance of public art in the mental landscape of a nation can be seen in the impact our "Statue of Liberty" has had. But even it, it turns out, needs a cultural context. The granddaddy of all culturist projects suggested by this need for context would be "The Statue of Responsibility." This would teach the ultimate civics lesson: *without responsibility you cannot have liberty*. Whereas the Statue of Liberty faces away from our nation, on the East Coast, The Statue of Responsibility should be on the West coast facing towards the middle of our country. This posture would suggest that those who have arrived inside of the country have domestic responsibilities. This statue could potentially change the overall ideological understanding of our nation. Its text could mention the difference between liberty and license just to make the message extremely clear. Any locality that sponsored the creation of this statue would generate enormous tourist revenue. But, the message being national and the costs prohibitive, the Department of Culture should oversee this project.

Qualifications

Culturist statues, parades, museums, murals, and events should be instigated to create a sense of unity and pride in Western Civilization. Incan Gods and ceremonies would be excluded. They have nothing to do with Western Civilization. Beethoven is great, but his not being

American would make him more problematic to us than an American composer. Just as the government in Peru is concerned with Peru's success and the government in Thailand should be and is dedicated to Thailand's success, our government should be biased in favor of our country's success. It is not un-American or unreasonable that we should promote awareness of our cultural icons to the exclusion of those from other countries. It is time that we brought this international example of common sense to our shores.

Caesar Chavez monuments would be questionable. His success as a labor leader cannot be compared with that of Samuel Gompers or Eugene Debs. We undoubtedly should celebrate labor's part in creating our nation. Chavez's celebration, however, often focuses on him as an icon of diversity and Latino race pride. Both of these themes foster division. Celebrating him outside of the area in which he was born or worked would foster division. A diversity of ideas is welcomed. But celebrations tied to race are un-American and can only foster division. Celebrating Gompers or Debs because they were white would be equally wrong. Promoting divisions, racial or otherwise, is not the job of our government.

Deciding what is appropriate will not always be easy. The Constitutional prohibition against government establishing a religion would not preclude much of our public art. Fortunately a miniscule amount of our cultural heroes were overtly religious. Public art could be, however, controversial for other reasons. Malcolm X and Eugene Debs are obviously controversial figures. Debs could be excluded on the basis of his not being very famous. But if you have not heard of Malcolm X you have a large hole in your basic knowledge of United States history. So here we have a case where a very controversial person should be known. Excluding figures based on partisan considerations would lead to disunity. Pollyannaism weakens culturism. A true reflection of the mistakes and struggles we have endured makes us appreciate the gains we have and the work that cultures take. To the extent that Malcolm X can be seen as a symbol of a person working towards inter-racial harmony and bettering America, his celebration would be beneficial.

Standards of civic discourse should also inform the level of vulgarity associated with these public events. Remember we are promulgating public standards. The public sphere and the private sphere are different. Recall the example where censorship was thought of, not only in terms of whether it would harm a child, but in what it said the public was willing to esteem. If the public underwrites acts of youth sexuality, it cannot then expect youth to have any doubts about the acceptability of pre-marital sex. The same can be said of vulgarity. If nothing else constantly resorting to the same four letter words shows a poor vocabulary; it also shows a lack of concern with other's sensibilities. Western culture has traditionally held things of the soul to be higher than things of the body. Public art should ennoble and not degrade us or our historical sense of decency. The public being discriminating as to what it will underwrite does not mean that private citizens are prohibited, in any way, from freedom of speech.

Culturist realpolitik thus provides a value by which we can determine the content of our common public space. Form is an artistic choice. Civic parades, concerts, and festivals are appropriate. It is an artistically unfortunate fact that much of our culture is cerebral and is tied up with ideals. Colorful tribal dances and costumes have never been America's forte. Puritans hated show. Still and all, parades and concerts in honor of our historical battles, ideals, and great artistic achievements should strive to avoid being overly dry. This does not mean public support of foul angry passionate bands that have a very limited intergenerational appeal. Social capital and good times are best generated by having participation. Our artistic strength lies in our not being tradition bound, we should explore new participatory art forms.

Culturist efforts will work be more affective if they have a local origin. National parades would not be as effective as locally produced ones as they would be seen as propagandistic. If bureaucrats in Washington D.C. put up signs in an Atlanta Inner-city neighborhood that read, "Men in this neighborhood do not lie," they would be laughed at. If local mothers did so it would be taken more seriously. Culturist efforts created by people you know can instill the element of peer pressure that national efforts cannot. No one can, however, force psychological attributes. Individuals have the right to completely ignore such activities as much as they have the right to change the channel. Any culturist efforts that implied or used compulsion would be un-American. In the end, however, peer pressure constitutes an important cultural force. And though you would not require people to show up at an event, asking those at the event to sing the national anthem is not in bad taste. People must be given a reason to join together as communities

Can Western civilization think?

"Can Asians Think?" is the title of a widely-read book and essay by Kishore Mahbubani. One of the reasons he gives for asking such an audacious question is that during the long period in which the West had cultural and economic ascendancy, Asia put its head in the sand. While we expanded, Asia became more conservative. Asian inability to follow our ways seemed to us to represent an inability to think. We considered thinking to be synonymous with adopting new ways. Now, as Western civilization starts to lose pre-eminence, we still hold many destructive ideas to be truisms that we seem unable to question. We refuse to advocate any sets of norms and give due process to the point where our laws are meaningless. The current situation requires that we ask if Western Civilization can think.

We are incapacitated by a host of bad concepts. We have failed to realize that rights only exist if they are backed up by a culture that can sustain them. Unchallengeable individual rights mean that we are unable to protect our culture. Multiculturalism and individualism have caused us to retreat from making any value judgments whatsoever. Your right to be a vulgar, drug using whore and mother of five by three different men at the age of 19 cannot interfere with your right to government services and approval without judgment. We do not discriminate on based on culture, religion, creed, level of depravity, nationality, education level, sense of responsibility or any other criteria. Culturism's use legitimizes the right of the public sphere to protect itself and provides a basis by which to say some behaviors are wrong. If you cannot make distinctions, one would be hard pressed to find a basis upon which you could be said to consciously think.

The disdain for Victorians and Puritans is based on the idea that they were shallow. They were not shallow. They knew that sex existed. They were also aware that civilization requires curbing our instincts. Manners did not show that you were ignorant of the animalistic nature of man. It meant that you preferred civilization and realized it requires us to have a consciousness of what is socially acceptable. Victorians shunned people who had transgressed because they were unable to rise above the level of animal instinct. Victorians' reasoned disdain for irresponsible behavior brought the rate of children being born out of wedlock down to three percent and saw a nearly fifty percent decline in indictable offenses in four decades.[266] Our half-baked Freudian equation of bestiality with authenticity has led to the explosion of irresponsibility that any Victorian could have predicted. People do not analyze, but absorb culture. It is time we realized that our sneering at Victorians is not based on our depth and their shallowness. If we cannot shake our uncritical somnambulism on this topic, we cannot claim to be wise.

Imagine waking up this morning and not knowing how you got here! On the one hand, it would be wonderful. You could make a fresh start. On the other hand, it would be terrifying. You could be held responsible for crimes you did not remember committing and have no basis upon which to dispute the accusations. Imagine you woke up in the Aztec empire and were told blood kept the sun in the sky. People not knowing where they are or how they got here is not a solid foundation upon which to make decisions. Much of our voting public is in this predicament. Countries have not always succeeded. Rights are not eternal. North America is not just a place. Our ignorance makes us liable to believe anything and disconnects us from our cultural trajectory. People are not born with anything but a temperament and an ability to absorb culture. Culturism suggests reconnecting with our past in order that we may not suffer from symptoms of amnesia.

Our lack of historical and global perspective is the source of many of our problems. Many Americans think we are the most racist country ever. We invented race sensitivity and can hardly be said to be racist in comparison to Asian countries. Many think that we are consistent violators of rights. We invented democracy and Islamic countries still kill citizens that blasphemy. We are thought to be militaristic. All civilizations reduce war. They can be defined as an area over which peace is enforced. Tribes are largely built and sustained by the constant killing of outsiders. Many think that a terminally abused and disrespected America cannot fall. All nations are fragile entities. Because we do not have a religious or racial basis we are more fragile than most. If we fall, man's potential for depravity will be less controlled. Our experiment testing the hypothesis that people can govern themselves and maintain liberty will have proven that we cannot. This will justify repression. It would be much better if we did not learn this the hard way. One Dark Ages was enough.

Our very physiology reveals a need for culturist assertion. We are different than animals in that we can think with words. A benefit of being able to think with words is greater behavioral flexibility. Culture is the way that the accumulated wisdom of the past is passed down to the new generation. Rather than being born ready to be independent, our youth are born ready to absorb culture. We are reticent to inculcate because of our unrealistic adherence to abstract individualism; we want the child to find out who they are on their own. But the child must exist in a culture. In the name of individualism we have renounced our human mandate to pass on our culture. The opposite of socialization is not (as Puritans or Victorians could have told you) freedom. People are not preprogrammed. They will absorb whatever culture surrounds them. If Western values of rights and the dignity of man are not evil, socializing people to believe in such values is not evil. If we do not socialize in our image we should not be surprised if those who consider rape and killing to be sources of pride emerge. If we do not like brutality we need to say so.

Our abdication of thoughtfully guiding our culture is based on ignorance. We must realize that our species requires upbringing. We must recognize, as Aristotle did, that we are social beings. We must remember that rights and democracy are new concepts that were earned at the cost of much struggle. We must see our blindness. Islamic countries are creating fanatical adherents. Chinese citizens never lose sight of the fact that they exist in a cultural, geopolitical, and historical context. Whereas heavy-handed culturist countries have managed to create direction and devotion, the West's refusal to advocate for itself has given it the aimless apathy symptomatic of a beaten vagrant in a riot zone. Our cultural ideals must be overtly and verbally communicated to the culture at large. We must dialogue with rioters as a group and particularly via those in the community

with status. Western Civilization alone needs to remember that it is
not composed of lone individuals that somehow woke up in the same
space. We need to recall that we share unique values. We haven't
always been here. We created our cultures' economy and respect
for the individual by conscious struggle. We need to regain culturist
consciousness. We need to think!

CHAPTER EIGHT

CULTURISM IN PHILOSOPHY

Idiots

What is an idiot? "Idiot" is a Greek word that denotes someone that does not participate in their political community. It shares the same root with idiosyncrasy and idiom. These words all refer to a lack of context. Thus a populace that has no connection to the community or country in which it resides can literally be said to be idiotic. According to this definition, more and more of us are becoming idiots. This trend can be seen both in fashions that show no concern for the impression made on others and corporate theft.

Idiocy is not very American. One thing that Alexis De Tocqueville noted during his 1830 tour of America was how civic minded we were. Rights often make people anti-social. They can be asserted in opposition to community pressure. Last year people that did not get their individual needs met sued school districts across America for hundreds of millions of dollars. These people punished the community for its not catering to their needs. When people exert their prerogatives at the expense of the community in which they live they can truly be said to be idiots. Worse, they are idiots with lawyers. To all who care about our social fabric, this is scary stuff.

We have already seen that early Americans distinguished between license and liberty. Whereas license leads to bad situations, true liberty requires self-control. Early Americans also realized that the self-control that liberty requires was attained easier in a community that did not place too many temptations in front of you. The original American settlements being threatened with extinction made the settlers realize the costs of degeneracy could be high. We also noted that when Revolutionary War era Americans "spoke of their rights, their 'liberties, immunities, and privileges,'" they almost always conceived of them as communal.[267] The United States could not have beaten England without uniting. Our very nation being the first modern experiment in democracy resulted from a team project.

This vision of collective liberty goes further back in Western history, however, than America. Like the derogatory word "idiot" it goes back to the Greeks. The Greeks had a painfully present concern with the viability of their community. The frequency of their wars meant that they did not have the luxury of having an idiotic orientation. As such, the idea of an ethic outside of the social world they inhabited could not make sense to them.[268] All Greek societies shared a traditional and common understanding that conscious collective political action gave form to the people and if the people were not strong they would be history.[269] Philosophy was a public concern. It was not idiotic.

Idiot also has, of course, its modern meaning. An idiot is someone who is really stupid. Such a person would not know to put on a jacket when they are freezing. Our survey of cultures in nature showed us that cultures are not naturally reflective. Cultures are entities that hold information more than entities that question information. In that sense, cultures are idiotic. Our culture's claim to fame is that we are self-governing. That means that we consciously choose our social forms. To consciously choose – to avoid being an idiot collectively - we must all be philosophers and be wary of any systems that would strip us of our ability to make choices.

Greek philosophy

Plato and Aristotle are the most influential Western philosophers ever. They set the philosophical agenda for Western Civilization. Therefore, as Western culturists, it is vital that we are familiar with their works and thoughts. The most salient feature of their political writings is the constant concern about the reciprocal affect the political association and the populace have on each other.[270] They were very concerned that the people would corrupt the government and that the government would corrupt the people. But above all, both Plato and Aristotle were concerned with the nature and survival of the Greek polis.

We have already looked at Aristotle. We saw that he analogized the relationship between government and citizen to that of friends. The best friendship is one in which both people want what is best for the other. They support and guide each other. Plato's main work, *The Republic,* concerns the nature of justice, ,which he finds in the ordered state. He analogizes the individual to the state. In the individual, as mentioned before, reason should direct the appetite via will. In the state that means that the philosopher kings (reason) should direct businessmen (appetite) via will (army). Sound judgment and justice in the individual require that he be in control of himself; the same holds for the state (discussions of the relationship between reason and passion are old hat in our culture). Better to have philosophers, with rigorous training and no access to money rule us than those driven by the love of money or power. Either of the latter options will cause chaos in individuals and states. With all doing the job that fits their ability, and all knowing their place, the state will be just, wise, and prosperous.

Aristotle is sometimes derided as a defender of slavery. The opening of Aristotle's book *the Politics* is largely concerned with justifying this institution. The extent to which this is held against Aristotle, though, reveals the biggest pitfall of philosophy of the last few hundred years. The criticism fails to take cultural contexts into account. Slavery has meant different things at different times. Many of Athens' bankers were ex-slaves. Aristotle himself was a not a citizen of Athens. This meant that he could not vote, but that he also did not have to fight in battles. Greek categories were not ours. Taken as a whole, both Aristotle and Plato's greatest strength is that they are quite sensitive to the realistic contingencies that constrain political decisions. Neither were so naïve as to insist on absolute definitions, rights, and freedoms without regard to their historical contexts or social ramifications.

Neither of these founding philosophers would be pleased by blind adoption of their programs to our age. Both catalogued what the different sources of corruption are for different types of government. Aristotle noted that oligarchy and demagoguery are dangerous to a democracy.[271] He thus suggested manipulating voting requirements so that not too many or too few voted.[272] Who voted would depend on the situation. Plato's observation that uncensored media creating a "theatrocracy" will lead to pandering and moral corruption remains accurate.[273] Freedom of speech, he said, must be placed in a context of moral stewardship. Our contention that there are absolute guarantees regardless of their political and moral contexts would offend both Plato's and Aristotle's sense of practicality.

Specialization has undermined Plato and Aristotle's common sense approach. For them, political policy could not be considered separately from an understanding of the psychological nature of mankind. Laws could not be considered apart from their moral consequences. Economics of the polis were assumed to be a result of the virtues of the body politic. Art was not a separate entity without a connection to the rest of society or the nature of man. Education had to be concerned with the needs of the state. The way you treat the aged will affect the way the youth see their relationship to society. Everything is integrated. Psychological, political, artistic, religious, social, military, economic, moral, legal, and "personal" considerations cannot be realistically isolated.

Plato and Aristotle's political science masterpieces are not solely works of political science. They did not just think of themselves as philosophers. They were concerned with all things human. They did not view man as an entity that could be abstracted from his inner and outer context. Though both thought a lot about ideals, practicality was never far from their minds. Culturist philosophy advocates restoring these tendencies both on the merits of such thinking and as homage to tradition. Decontextualized abstractions tend to be unrealistic and destructive. No philosophy that views man outside of his cultural contexts will create realistic ideals. No philosophy that postulates ideals outside of cultural contexts will create viable policies.

The rise of universal principles

Via a slow historical process political thinking has taken a turn towards abstract universal concepts that neither Plato nor Aristotle would have approved of. Universal absolutes are those concepts that are taken to be true in all places and all times regardless of the historical or contextual situation in which they are applied. Neither Aristotle nor Plato would have entertained ideas of rights completely divorced from the ability of a state to survive or provide them, as desirable or workable. Yet our hallowed and unrealistic belief in the supremacy of the individual postulates just these sorts of rights at the expense of the community.

Aristotle has a very ingenious thought experiment in which he makes clear that cities cannot be an abstraction. He notes that if two countries created reciprocal treaties that guarded property and enforced judicial claims between citizens, they would not thereby become one larger country.[274] Mexico and America are different countries despite NAFTA. Germany and France remain different despite the European Economic Union. A state is not just a legal concept. It has a cultural heritage and traditions that produces affection in the inhabitants for one another.[275] People of completely foreign customs do not even become one if they are united against a common foe. Aristotle wrote that the mere association of people forged by legalistic means would not cause inhabitants to look out for each other's interests.

To be sure, Plato did have idealist tendencies. But he did not do so unreflectively. Even in his most idealistic depiction of a state, *the Republic*, he pauses to note that it is just an ideal.[276] Furthermore, his characterization of being too ideal overlooks the fact that both of his major works, *the Republic* and *the Laws*, concern the running of states. These are not just ideal for ideal's sake. He thought ideals important as they give us something to measure ourselves against. And he held that we would never reach them. But, his overriding concern was the order of the good state. Those who see him as an idealist also forget that he actually tried to put his ideal of a state run by a "philosopher-king" into action. He tried creating a rational philosopher-king out of a man who, ironically, had the name of the God of ecstatic drunken and sexual excess, King Dionysus the Second. Plato ended up being arrested and nearly sold into slavery. Plato failed, but his trying shows that he was *very* serious about the practical applicability of his work.

The true origin of totally universalistic abstract philosophical concepts is to be found in Christianity. Christianity is both universal and local. It is universal in that it claims to have the truth for the whole world. It applies to everyone. All men are valuable and can be saved. Indeed it enforced a unitary set of beliefs on Europe for nearly a thousand years. Christianity's local character manifests itself in the certainty that it alone constitutes truth. Jesus said, "I am *the* way and *the* truth." If you do not agree, you do not have a different point of view; you are wrong. During its hegemony Catholicism gave universal dignity to its own people, but branded all others as heathens and heretics. Those outside of the community were seen as alien and, therefore, bad.

As the hegemony of the Catholic Church declined new sources of ethics and social organizing principles had to be found. Meeting this challenge resulted in the philosophical movement, discussed before, known as "The Enlightenment." This movement cemented our current attachment to abstract universalism. The Enlightenment was a scientifically based philosophical movement. Great advances came from this movement. Scientifically, it was noted, the King is just another man. As we are all just men, it is not fitting that one should rule another. Democracy and equal treatment under the law were born of this demystification of the monarchal system.

The scientifically based Enlightenment ideal that one should only believe in what one can measure did much to undermine superstition and the persecution of "witches." Its promotion of science helped make the silliness of religious wars obvious. The Enlightenment insisted that we make laws based on rational principles. This conscious application of mind to the problems of society led to laws to help the poor and the end of torture being used to garner confessions and conversions. It can be argued that our governmental system of checks and balances is the greatest triumph of the Enlightenment. It was a fantastically successful application of rational principles to the problem of governance.

Though many of the results were good, the underlying theory was not. The longer a theory is around, the more of its subtle implications have time to manifest. Immanuel Kant lived from 1724 until 1802. His was the most systematic exploration of the underpinnings of Enlightenment ethics ever. He justified Enlightenment ethics on the presupposition that all humans are rational and should live up to exacting rational principles. As you rationally would want to live in a world with everyone having rights, we should all have rights. Rationally, you could not will it to be otherwise. Unfortunately the world is not full of rational beings doing what logic would dictate. Furthermore, what rational individuals would will and what can actually happen in this world are not necessarily the same.

Rights, as substantiated by Kant's methodology, are inalienable. You can demand the right to have education provided to you in the language of your choice regardless of whether or not the school system has the resources to provide it. We do not discriminate based on creed or religion. Punitive morality, by Kant's reckoning constituted a logical oxymoron as all real morality comes out of rational deliberation. So rationally, morality has to come from letting people be free to learn about the irrationality of their mistakes. Many still believe that suicide bombers and headhunters will be turned into German logicians by adoption of rational precepts. Kant and the other Enlightenment figures had a nearly Christian level of faith in the redemptive power of rationality.

Cultural particularism (elevation of local truth) was one of the banes of the Enlightenment.[277] Christianity turned out to be just one of many religions. As a local phenomenon it was demoted from the status of a universal truth. Enlightenment figures wanted to postulate mental states and rules for governance that were, like science, truly universal. And as the Western cultures that the Enlightenment values thrived in were just particular cultures, they were devalued. Finding the New World and its many exotic cultures had exaggerated this sentiment. So a predisposition to prefer one culture's holiday above another, was seen as just seen as a silly local eccentricity. The Enlightenment philosophers did not hold cultural particularities in high regard. Valuable knowledge rested upon on Universal principles. Again, it was *the* Enlightenment, not *an* enlightenment.

The "social contract" theory of society came out of the Enlightenment. Social contract theories concern the origin of society. They all postulate that societies exist as a result of contracts between the original members. According to one version, men are so violent that they contracted with a king to keep the peace. Thus the legitimacy of the King resulted from his enforcing order. Another version sees us as joining together to mutually protect our property rights. Thus the government's legitimacy stems from its ability to enforce contract and property rights. Both versions bolster the claim that the government's ultimate claim to authority should rest on the will or benefit of the people it serves. These yarns have obvious beneficial applications.

As anthropology, nature, world history, Aristotle's thought experiment of tying two countries together, and Plato's misadventure show, countries are not just legalistic arrangements between random individuals; they are cultural constructs. The Enlightenment was based on a scientific worldview. Science deals in universals, not particulars. The laws of science are considered laws if they apply everywhere equally. The rights and freedoms rationality dictates, therefore, were not considered laws if they are subject to qualifications. But this universalism is predicated on a universal culture that does not exist. All preconditions in science are the same. Diversity means cultural preconditions for creating social policy are not the same. Though it resulted in benefits that the Western world should never regret or retreat from, the Enlightenment also laid the philosophical foundations that have undermined our healthy sense of culturism.

The metaphysics of rights

Universal rights are the result of the Enlightenment's search for a post-religious, scientific basis of morality. Rights, thus derived, find their grounding in universal Kantian reason. This assumes, again falsely, a world in which all people are playing by rational rules. Yet one could postulate both my right to take advantage of you and yours to not be exploited. In this hypothetical test one right would interfere with another. A diversity of desires exists. Conceptually universal rights can only exist in a world where ideas do not conflict. Kant would ask about the logical desirability of a world in which people took advantage of each other. In doing so he would be acknowledging that even within the within the metaphysical world of logic, rights have to be contextualized.

Rights are shown not to come from universal principles everyday. Rights only actually exist in the context of a state and culture that are willing and able to recognize and provide them. The right to an education cannot be realized in poverty stricken countries. Economic rights are not universal. They are something that your culture purchases. Your right to free speech only exists if there is a legal system to protect it. You can logically prove that there should be gender equality, but the cultural milieu in which the pronouncement takes place might cause the decree to ring hallow. Universal rights are violated in every war zone. Rights are shown not to be universal every time a person starves to death.

People often liken the granting of a new right to the finding of a new scientific fact. The Nineteenth Amendment to the United States' Constitution gave women the right to vote. What is the meaning of the verb "gave" as used in this sentence? It literally means that it was conferred by the federal legal system. The phraseology whereby rights are "recognized" seems to imply that they had an actual existence prior to the state's granting them. Rights, however, disappear. Under the Taliban in Afghanistan women lost the right to go outside. The temporal nature of rights means that they are not real entities that are waiting to be recognized; they are constructs. They can be conferred but, as they did not exist before, they could not have been found. Scientific laws are *not* temporal, context-dependent entities. Scientific laws sit waiting to be discovered and then hold true, at no expense, for all time. Rights could not be more different.

When we talk of the proliferation of rights, we have to recognize that rights cost money. The right of the handicapped to have access to my restaurant will not be cheap. The phraseology that sees rights effortlessly being recognized and proliferating conflates them with metaphysical entities. Realistic phraseology would convey the sense that rights are gifts that your culture has decided it will try to purchase for you. Think of rights as something purchased would mean that rather than insisting on rights, those who sue for them would be asking if they could be purchased. This monetary understanding could be extended to consider cultural costs. We could ask what the cultural costs of allowing dual citizenship are. Rather than asking about recognizing rights, we would ask if we wanted to implement the right. The cost analogy would allow us to say there are rights that enforcing would be too expensive to implement. Being realists we could then elect not to enforce them.

When we fail to recognize the cultural context of the rights that are being purchased for members of society they often become destructive. Something that operates without respect to context can run counter to the context. Then, instead of being seen as coming from Western culture, they can be used against Western culture. Being a pornographer next to a church or an elementary school can be seen as your right. Non-citizens can sue us for not processing their applications for citizenship fast enough. People demand free emergency health care from hospitals that cannot afford to provide it. Decontextualized rights are free to be asserted against the very communities and institutions that create them.

Even when a culture can afford to enforce rights, they do not always exist. Saudi Arabia has a lot of money, but women still do not have the right to drive there. More than money, collective assent is required for rights to be enforced. French people, it would seem, have the right not to have their cars set on fire. India has tried to end the killing of women whose entire dowry is not paid on time. But such behaviors persist. Rights are only possible in a culture that has mores and economies that can support them. Even that is not always enough. Immigrants to countries that forbid female genital mutilation still persist in the practice. Rights only exist if cultural precepts that believe in them exist.

Rights are so integral to Western culture that we have trouble imagining a world without them. Because we see them everywhere, we are predisposed to believe that they are universal. Western civilization's meaning is based upon more than legal decisions. Rights are not a result of universal metaphysics. We appreciate and understand our rights more when we recognize that they are only figments of the Western cultural imagination. Furthermore, we must realize that they can only be manifest if our culture is solvent. If we do not take care of our culture we may be thrown back into a world without rights.

Recognizing that rights are not metaphysical necessitates creating policies that sustain them in the real world. In this light we must ask many questions. Can we afford to buy the right of each student an individualized education program that meets their special needs? In a world where higher GNP results from expertise, might we be better off prioritizing the rights of the gifted? Because we may not be able to afford both, we need to choose. Can a community battered by drugs and violence afford not to be able to search suspicious cars? During an era of terrorism, can we afford to give foreigners the right to political asylum in our country regardless of country of origin or cultural affiliations? In an era of closing hospitals we can ask if we can afford to give you free emergency medical care. In a time of state debts we can ask if we can afford to give prisoners cable television. With high numbers of irresponsible pregnancies can we morally afford to give single mothers under the age of twenty-five welfare? When we recognize that rights cost money and can only exist in the context of a solvent community we are given a new set of questions to answer and we can answer them more flexibly.

The evidence against Universalism as an outlook

Globalism bases its hopes on Enlightenment presuppositions. The Enlightenment was a time when science was first being widely employed as a tool of understanding. One by one the mysteries of the world were being understood. Social sciences were being employed to understand the universal institutions that underlay societies. The hope was that all societies could one day all be conscious creations based on logical principles. Many are still of the faith that all cultures of the world will see the parochial nature of their positions and drop them in favor of a rational choice of global cooperation, laws, and consumerism.

The hope of universal unity based on universal laws results from social contract theory writ large. However, social contract theory is derived from a faulty premise. Individuals did not meet in the forest by accident and decide to band together for mutual benefit. Neither do ants or chimpanzees. Enlightenment figures asserting that all human governmental organizations grew out of a political decision reveals their rationalist bias. Even in the relatively rational West, the Puritans were a collective before the Mayflower compact. And our country existed before the Constitution. Countries, cultures, and tribes do not owe their existence to rationally designed constructs.

Culture predates politics. Culture predates man. As previously mentioned, rats are alternately kind and brutal depending on scents that identify friends and foes. Western Culturism does not, of course, celebrate this brutality. Hutus killed Tutsi's without a trace of the compassion that Western man would hope is universal. They acted in defiance of rationalism. And unfortunately, they are far from the only one to commit such irrational atrocities. Pol Pot killed a third of his population. Race has nothing to do with this. The cultural and biological composition of man has everything to do with it. Rational considerations are only a part of what drives people.

America's involvement in Iraq provides a pertinent example. America's attempt to turn Iraq into a representative democracy is failing due to clearly an irrational tribalism. Rationally, the Shi'ite and Sunni populations have more in common with each other than with the infidels patrolling them. They share a history and a country. Furthermore, when a peaceful brotherhood based on common interests is attainable, their constant warfare in defiance of this outcome seems insane. Hopefully the people of that region will act based on their enlightened self-interest. But at the time of the printing of this book the destructive terrorism in that region showed no signs of subsiding.

Moreover, even if universal rationalism were adopted worldwide, we cannot say what it would look like. Asian societies are more culturist than we are. The Confucian ideal that rationality means the individual should subjugate themselves to the demands of their role is not irrational. Radical authoritarian militarism within the context of a competitive world can be supported rationally. If survival is a rational goal, you could argue that creating a theocracy that has a work ethic internally and violent hatred externally comprises your best bet. It is not clear that the ideal state would not be based on a submission to God or recognizing China's right to rule. Our faith that globalism means everyone drops their parochial traditions and agrees that our version of individual rights and democracy represents the ultimate good combines arrogance and ignorance. Our view that rationalism leads to a liberal democracy based on radical individualism is very parochial. It confused our local preference for a universal truth.

British imperialists strove to export their world view. They saw their value system as conducive to making business deals that made sense to all parties. This system was based on commerce being the ultimate value. Rational arrangements best provided for the free flow of goods and efficient creation of new ones. British imperialism could be considered a social science experiment to test the validity or the rational nature of the social contract. The results do not support the hypothesis. The seemingly obviously compelling British-style constitutional, rational, and economic bases of social organization were not adopted. Rational choices are not the glue that cements societies.

Only the Protestant colonies succeeded in becoming liberal capitalist democratic successes. This was not due to race. White skinned communities succeeded because they "had the outlook and institutions favorable to progress which Asiatics and Africans seemed to lack. They offered [the right items to] customers with European tastes and money to spend."[278] Our tastes are not universal. Our institutions did not catch on. African tribes kept raiding each other. Shopping for goods was not everyone's priority. Africans even reverted to their indigenous tradition enslaving each other after many British efforts to wipe the practice out. Despite this historic proof, many hold to the old British idea that cultures will all be reshaped based upon rational market principles. Some will, many won't, and those that do will not thereby shake their attachment to their local cultural realities.

Diversity exists. Our survey of anthropology should be enough to convince anyone of that. But even current cultures have different visions of the good life. A kiss is not a kiss. For some it is nearly an engagement. For some it unites two families. For some it is mere erotica. Some cultures are order and achievement crazy. Some value large families. Some build banks, others places of worship. Those advocating universal concepts have to postulate that all cultures that are not liberal individualistically based free market democracies are developing in that direction. For differing from our culture they are called backwards and developing. Culturism acknowledges that the other modes of life exist and may be just as satisfying as our own.

Even if there really is a universal standard of truth, using it as a basis of policy is dangerous. For example, the West's allowing massive immigration from Islamic nations is based on the idea that we are all going to get along assumes there are no differences between cultures. Meanwhile, the other team has not embraced and, in fact, remains openly hostile to the idea of universal cooperation. If an American football team decided to not protect its quarterback based on the fact that we are all equal it would be disastrous. Even if it is true, until both teams have acknowledged that there are no sides and competition does not exist, guarding ones quarterback seems prudent.

An American response to universals

Traditional Western philosophers (every philosopher's favorite whipping boy) might scoff at the types of proofs being offered in support of a culturist philosophical outlook. Immanuel Kant, for one, would say that philosophical rigor requires formal propositions and proofs for or against a claim. Such objections reveal the continuing Enlightenment influence and our bias towards what is perceived of as scientific thinking.

The very act of philosophers wanting sound and rigorous arguments for the reality of culturism would, in fact, provide them. If philosophy were universal it would look the same in all places. Not all cultures look for Germanic rule-based logic chopping in their philosophies. Neither Buddha nor Jesus nor Muhammad included major and minor premises in their proofs. Thus the insistence on rigorous proofs in philosophy is the result of a historical development in a particular culture. The request for rigor proves the culturist basis of philosophy.

Kant remains a very influential Western philosopher. He was Prussian. However, culturism dictates (using Kantian logic) that my final philosophic school of choice should be American. To put it in a way that would hopefully satisfy standards of rigorous logical proof: Culturism requires you favor your own culture (major premise), pragmatism is a philosophy from my own culture (minor premise), therefore American culturism should be based on pragmatism (conclusion). With this logic in mind let us now leave Prussia and turn to America.

Pragmatism is the United States' largest contribution to the world of philosophy. Though pragmatism still has prominent proponents, it hails from the late nineteenth and early twentieth century. Pragmatism's earliest formulation was created by Charles Saunders Pierce. John Dewey and Josiah Royce were advocates of pragmatism. However, William James, who lived from 1842 until 1920, was pragmatism's most renowned exponent.

John Dewey wrote in *The Quest for Certainty* that the hurly burly of life had driven man to seek physical and mental shelter.[279] Philosophy and religion have historically created safe havens in which we escaped from this world of constant change. Scientific experimentation helped steer us away from religion's revealed and eternal truths and towards a more realistic approach to the world; science validated lived experience and discovery as ways of knowing. Kant went half way towards the naturalization of philosophy when he said the truths we seek are not in the spiritual realm but based on our reason.[280] But Kant, like his religious and philosophical predecessors, Dewey noted, was still dealing in universals.

Overall, pragmatism agreed with the overview of philosophy given so far on two counts. First of all, pragmatism overtly rejected universal truths. James believed that there was no way around the fact of "moral dualism."[281] Secondly, pragmatism agrees with the critique of overly metaphysical philosophies. James said, if there were no people there would be no morality. If there were only one person on a planet, there still would not be a right and wrong, only consequences would exist. Ethics comes when there are two people who must deal with each other. These two inhabitant's morals will have to be negotiated in real situations. No truths exist, metaphysically, outside of specific people and their changing situations.

For our purposes, Pragmatism's methods are even more important than their rejection of metaphysical universal truths. Pragmatists get truth from practical applications. Rather than trying to ascertain whether free will exists, we should ask, "What would be the consequences of believing in free will?" The ultimate metaphysical truth about whether or not we have free will cannot be known; but accepting free will means that we can hold criminals responsible for their actions. So whether free will is real or an illusion, we *should* believe in it for practical purposes. Some might say that this pragmatic approach takes us off of the path of finding real truths; genteel and erudite philosophers were repulsed by James' search for "cash value" in propositions. But, these situational methods are particularly well suited for policy formulation.

The practical character of pragmatist analysis can be seen in the case of racial profiling. First of all, this phenomenon is misnamed; it is cultural profiling. When you wear gangster clothes, drive a gangster car, and blast gangster music, suspecting that you buy into the whole criminal lifestyle is not unreasonable. Race is not the deciding factor. Assimilation into cultural behaviors does not depend on race. Herein we have another example of where separating culture and race can help us think more clearly. People of all races do and do not dress as gangsters. But while pragmatism does not eschew common sense, it does not simply advocate acting on hunches. Pragmatism is scientific and finds truth through verification.

Pragmatists hold that policy should be based on scientific verification of practical goals. If no difference in arrests result from stopping those who fit the gangster profile, your assumptions were wrong. If more weapons and drugs are seized than random searches would yield, your hunch is verified. Pragmatic definitions of truth come from verification, not just speculation. People who believe in absolute definitions of morals might still be bothered by this. Pragmatism, fortunately, can even deal with perceptions flexibly. If crime was really low, you would create more peace by ignoring those posing as gangsters. But when a lot of crime exists, you would create more peace by profiling and enduring the bad feelings of those who believe in justice in the abstract. Goals and verification permeate this methodology and give it a realistic and flexible bearing.

James' version of pragmatism stressed the power of words to create reality. If you go with the abstract paradigm that *all* cultural profiling constitutes an injustice, crime may not be effectively addressed. Your goals and beliefs affect outcomes. Even the methodology you choose will have an outcome. Abstract formulations of right and wrong are impervious to evidence. If you believe that all profiling is wrong, evidence cannot be considered. You will not be able to profile even if statistics and common sense recommend it. Pragmatic methodology is flexible. If the gangster fashions mutate, you follow. If people stop living the gangster lifestyle, you drop the whole concept. Pragmatism creates paradigms and monitors them in relation to the world as it actually exists. Pragmatic policy changes as the world changes.

Pragmatism has not been greeted uncritically. Josiah Royce noted the main critique of pragmatism and tried to address it. Royce was worried that pragmatism led to moral relativism.[282] If I believed that killing children leads to happiness, I could verify that hypothesis using the pragmatist technique. I want to be happy, I try killing children, it makes me happy, and therefore, killing children is good. Royce circumvented this pitfall with the concept of loyalty. He showed that loyalty to a cause gives you meaning, direction, and community. Royce's caveat for stopping moral relativism is that the cause you are loyal to should never diminish someone else's loyalty. Killing children destroys an object of loyalty for parents and so it is wrong. Royce's philosophy of loyalty is wonderful. Unfortunately, as loyalties often conflict, it is hard to put into practice.

Dewey provided another mooring for pragmatist morals when he suggested asking if they lead to progress defined as personal and social growth.[283] Like Royce's concept of loyalty, this grounding also dovetails nicely with culturism. The question, though, then becomes what does progress mean? If progress means more efficient killing of children is it right? Though extreme, the reference to killing children provides a real moral conundrum in a post-holocaust world. Post-Kantian metaphysics fans said the danger of moral relativism shows that we must always, in the end, rely on abstract metaphysics to get our ultimate sense of right and wrong. Otherwise we can verify whatever horrible practice we like via pragmatism and call it truth.

Another attempt at pragmatic grounding can be found within the work of William James. In an attempt to reign in the negative potentials of ungrounded pragmatism he said that some propositions, like the killing of children, were not "live" options. By this he meant that they were not valid options for someone of a particular cultural background. He was not overt and consistent, however, in naming and using this criterion. In one place he said an option was made live by a measure of inclusiveness, in another he said being live resulted from social consensus. He was on to something and intuited that diverse belief systems were culturally grounded. If we want to successfully ground our pragmatic morality, we need to be more overt and clear about this than James was.

To put ethical parameters on pragmatism we should use the term "cultural pragmatism." It overtly indicates that ideas are "live" because they fall within the scope of our cultural traditions. Thus the idea of progress towards the killing of children can be ridiculed as falling outside of our cultural tradition. The cultural moniker also allows us to advocate, as Dewey wished, certain progressive behaviors. But progress here gets defined culturally as reflecting our democratic, individualistic, liberal history and the concomitant Protestant ethics. Since this philosophy is both cultural and pragmatic it can consistently say that both criminal lifestyles and heavy-handed violations of rights are wrong. But because cultural pragmatism comes from experience with the real world, these moral definitions do not prohibit action.

Cultural pragmatism may seem overly commonsensical. It does not propose an esoteric metaphysical truth of the sort we have come to associate with philosophy. That is the point. Within the world of philosophy, pragmatism's commonsense approach was and still is radical. Pragmatism does address metaphysical subtleties. James was very sensitive to the idea that truths are made, not found. He wrote extensively on religious experience and the nature of the universe from a pragmatic perspective. But, for our purposes, pragmatism's value does not lay in its ability to be esoteric. Pragmatism is necessary because it resituates philosophers in the real world, fighting pertinent battles in a common sense way.

Modern Philosophy's attack on culturism

Decontextualized rights are actually out of step with modern philosophy. Modern philosophy has moved away from fixed truths. Poor Kant has been besieged on all sides. Whereas we in America created the pragmatic method as a guide in a world in flux, Europe took another path. It has taken what has been termed a "linguistic turn." This means that, rather than make statements about meanings, it examines the nature of sentences themselves. Deconstruction has helped us get more out of sentences by making us approach them differently. But, their all out attack on meaning goes too far. Whereas American philosophy adapted to the loss of universals by embracing a provisional definition of truth, European philosophers jettisoned truth.

Deconstruction dominates modern philosophy. It not only feeds on the beaten corpus of Kant's work, it deconstructs all positive attempts to construct truths. Take the sentence, "John got a hair cut." Deconstructionists would contend that as much meaning remains excluded from this sentence as included. Why am I mentioning a male? Why a male with a typical American name? Am I privileging

American / male dominance? In modern jargon, the reality that Latino females reading the sentence experience has been "marginalized." The subtle message of the sentence is that her life story happens outside of mainstream America. In the sentence, her reality has been silenced. Even if we took the Latino females' perspective, who can really tell us what that ultimately means? There are always excluded meanings.

The same objections to our sentence concerning a haircut have been leveled at national stories. If all assertions encode power relations (by way of what they exclude and what they include) our national stories (which are frequently termed "narratives") constitute the worst examples of marginalization. Our portrayal of our history as a good thing silences and marginalizes the truth claims and lives of those for whom it was not so beneficial. Our narratives do not tell of the disruption of the traditional aborigine way of life. The lack of attention to women and harm to the environment also get marginalized. Ultimately, every positive statement about our national narrative can be said to be complicit in atrocities.

Deconstructionists make the following mistake: they assume that if a truth is not universal, it cannot be regarded as a truth. The discovery that a truth is only applicable to one culture's particular sensibilities, for them, disproves its value. They have unwittingly absorbed the Enlightenment demand that truths be universal or false. But just because we describe wood as lumber does not mean that elements and combustion rates do not exist. Rather than either being true or false, truths appear on a spectrum from certainty to debatable to false. Filipino reality does not get obscured in discussions of the Founding Fathers; there were no Filipino fighters in the Revolutionary War. When we discuss the Revolutionary War we simply are not discussing the South Pacific. The Philippines' place in the Spanish empire might have indirectly impacted the American Revolution. That is debatable, but the topic is not being marginalized when we do not discuss it. It was already marginal to the topic when we started.

Deconstructionists' assumption of Western methods actually confirms that all thoughts happen within a cultural context. The logic splitting Kantian methodology they use can be traced back to Socrates' obsession with definitions. Socrates split hairs to defend truth from people who, like deconstructionists, thought truth was just a matter of language claims. These people were called sophists. They were like today's lawyers; they would argue any side for a price. Deconstructionists' discussions have deep roots in Western heritage. Their very linguistic methodology supplies subtle proof of culturist parameters of truths in philosophy. They would get less subtle proof if they went to Muslim countries and started deconstructing the Koran. Jail or execution would result. Debunking the government of the People's Republic of China in China or on Chinese media would garner similar results.

Deconstructionists have turned to Marxist and, ultimately, more nihilistic attitudes towards truth.[284] When they say that our discourse is "oppressive" of other realities, they minimize the harsh and physical nature of real repression. Rather than absolute projections of Western ideals, they should use real history and anthropology as standards for judgment. As with the Filipino example, assertions interact with realities. Deconstructionists lingering attachment to universal truths makes their comparisons destructive. Chaffing at all sentences for not being all-inclusive and using this to debunk narratives has consequences. Deconstruction erodes our ability to make positive culturist statements. Just because we cannot include all truths in our statements does not mean that they are not provisionally true to us. We need to advocate our provisional truths from our vantage point.

Deep reasons

David Scott's very insightful book about rituals in Sri Lanka investigates the relative status of knowledge. Buddhists of Sri Lanka believe Yakku were cannibalistic demons that used to inhabit their land. Buddha banished Yakku, but allowed them to glance backwards from an invisible position. These glances, along with human glances, emanate energies that can cause varieties of misfortunes.[285] Priests can get the Yakku to stop the energies that lead to the misfortunes by speaking to the demon when it inhabits the body of the accursed.[286] A sort of exorcism in which the afflicted person goes into trance and the demon speaks through them allows us to beg the demon to forgive and forget. This moment provides the only way to mitigate the harm of the Yakkus' cursing energies.

After his account of the Sri Lankan ideology, Scott goes on to criticize prior anthropological accounts of Sri Lankan culture that use terms like "ritual" and "demons." These words, he notes, assumes the British colonialist discourse concerning the rational and objective worldview of the Western anthropologist and thus perpetuates a view of the abnormality of the natives in question.[287] Sri Lankan reality gets marginalized by the form of the linguistic discourse. He wishes that we would give that tradition's discourse as much respect as our own by looking at their strategy from the point of view of the practitioners. This strategy is advocated to circumvent our imposing our paradigms on our explanations of native cultures.[288]

Scott's strategy likely does cut away some of our obvious Western conceptual impositions. But it ultimately cannot overcome cultural biases. No Westerner will ever really take this cosmology seriously. Invisible beings invading your energy and using exorcisms to get rid of them is not scientific. The concept of strategy which he uses to undercut his bias itself constitutes (as Scott might agree) a Western imposition. Even after their goals are appreciated, no Westerner will actually experience authentic fear of these Yakku "glances" (let alone appreciate what it means to have a supernatural being speak through you). We cannot authentically enter such a world. The objective viewpoint Scott and other anthropologists wish to attain remains an impossible ideal.

Beyond its impossibility, the search for a non-judgmental appreciation of other's equally valid cosmology is undesirable. Our obsession with Western scientific objectivity is very Western. The very attempt to be objective contains bias. We will never be able to see these Sri Lankans as they see themselves. We are much better off, politically and philosophically, admitting and accepting the bias of our viewpoint. Scientific objectivity is something that we Westerners value. We can study demon possession and admit that our considering their cult bizarre is only our bias. But we cannot help finding it wanting from our scientific perspective. And our scientific perspective has helped us go to Sri Lanka and study locals. It facilitates the printing of books like Scott's. We should not pretend we can evade our paradigm. The belief that we can view others without bias belittles the depth of the local's cosmology while being disrespectful to our own.

Had Kant known more about cultural diversity he would have told you that universals about diverse cultures presents a logical contradiction. To have a universal truth that applies to diverse cultural milieus denies that they are diverse. Consistency requires that either diversity has to go or universals have to go. Diversity exists. James would tell you that universalism in the cultural arena is dangerous. If we stop advocating for and believing in our particular culture because it defies universal, scientific truths or if we stop advocating for ourselves because disillusion with the quest for certainty has turned us to absolute relativists (while others continue to fight for their cultural vision) we can end up in a lot of trouble. The truth that there are varieties of cultural groundings for perspectives, Dewey and James would point out, does not mean that there are not coherent desired outcomes.[289] Just because our truths are particular, interested, and local rather than universal does not mean they are not truths. My preference for Western values is real. And, as James claimed, real and different consequences result from diverse outlooks.

Why is the maintenance of Western civilization a valid goal for us? It is our goal because we cannot choose to do otherwise. We value this civilization that values individuality because we cannot help but value individuality. Even knowing that, in fact, individuality is largely an illusion borne of our cultural programming, we cannot choose but to be for it. Throwing out individualism and rights are not live options for us. That is one reason why members of Western civilization do not have to worry about tyrannical impositions in the name of Western culturism. Tyranny of the individual is not a live option for us. "Give me liberty or give me death" is more than a national motto. We deeply believe that a life that we do not get a say in is not worth living. We are Western.

Meeting the Genocidal attack

We judge ourselves harshly due to the crimes of the Second World War. It has been noted that the scientific method will tell you how to eliminate Jews, but not if it is right.[290] Science has been tainted in philosophical circles because it was used to implement the Nazi war crimes. The crimes were industrial. It is interesting to note that this condemnation of the West on the grounds of universal standards does not get directed so mercilessly at the Japanese. Perhaps this omission stems from guilt that theirs is a marginalized or silenced discourse. Perhaps this omission reveals an assumed culturist realization that we cannot judge them by our standards. Perhaps it just reveals a permanent bias against the West by many of our social critics. We are not the only culture to have committed atrocities in the last century by a long shot.

Those who reject ethical universals are haunted by the specter of cultural relativism. If nothing can be universally condemned, the basic formulation asks, can we then say that the Nazi atrocities were wrong? The standard pragmatic answer says Nazis were wrong because they lost. Their vision for society was not sustainable. Democracy was shown to inspire people and mobilize resources more efficiently and so is right. This response to the charge of cultural relativism founders on the fact that many oppressive regimes have thrived for a long time. During their tenure, according to the pragmatic answer to cultural relativism, would we say that Soviet gulags were right? Having to say that they were ethically kosher during the time in which they ruled makes pragmatism's response to the problem of cultural relativism unsatisfactory.

Culturist philosophy provides a satisfactory response. We condemn Nazi atrocities on our own Western cultural grounds. We do so because the overarching theme of Western history concerns an increasing respect for individual conscience and the concomitant fight against tyranny. From Achilles, to Socrates, to Jesus, to Martin Luther, to George Washington, to Martin Luther King we have striven in this direction. The Nazi's violated principles that we hold sacred and their values ran counter to our long held traditions. Respect for individual lives has been a logical corollary to respect for individual conscience. If killing individuals in peacetime can be condemned by recourse to our traditions, killing groups of people without noticing their distinctions as individuals constitutes a double offense. During their reign there were ample legitimate historical grounds, repeated by Winston Churchill, Franklin Delano Roosevelt and others, which provided a solid culturist basis upon which to condemn the Nazis.

We haven't always upheld the value of the individual to the extent that we now do. But, all and all, we have respected the prerogatives of citizens. The Greeks and the Romans did so to an extent still unparalleled by much of the world. During the era of Catholic dominance we did not value individual conscience or even life as much as now. Recall, however, that at that point our historical memory was lost. We call this time period the Dark Ages precisely because of our amnesia concerning our past and the resulting transgressions against our long held traditions. The renaissance was a rebirth of memory concerning our traditions. It was followed by the Enlightenment and democracy. In our long history the Dark Ages comprises the exception that proves the rule. And the atrocities during that era remind us that our ethics are best grounded when we remember our history and its meaning. Whenever we forget the lessons of the past, blindness and unimaginable atrocities are likely to follow.

There is, however, no universal abstract basis upon which to denounce Nazi style atrocities. If another culture values genocide for power's sake, we should affirm that they are to be condemned from our point of view. We may have to utilize argument and warfare to try to stop their vision from taking over the world. Our victory will not be guaranteed, however, by destiny or the inherent moral structure of the universe. A belief in rights and opposition to racism and genocide are Western values. Within our cultural context they are wrong. Values can only be realized within the context of a working, living community. Our community could not will itself to be Hindu. Islamic fundamentalism is not a "live" option for us. Nazi actions and values are wrong to us, in a very real sense, because our culture dictates that we cannot choose to think otherwise. They epitomize evil in our eyes. The best way for us to stop genocide, racism, and rights abuses from reappearing in the world is through implementing sound culturist policies that amplify and protect our particular cultural vision.

In the context of discussing our particular historical grounding for denouncing Nazi philosophy, mentioning that the Germans have repeatedly and thoroughly apologized on such a basis seems noteworthy. The fact that the Japanese have not apologized and refuse to teach their young about Japanese atrocities also teaches us a valuable lesson. Honor and morality argue against the admitting of defeat or anything that would mar personal or national pride in the Japanese tradition. Japan has a racial democracy. Saying things that injure Japanese nationalist pride does not win elections in their culture. We should not expect that democracy equals toleration or universalism. It is not my point to judge Japanese morality. Theirs culture may turn out to be more satisfactory and sustainable than ours. But we should note that morals are not universal and that German apologies confirm our ethical heritage.

Cultural contextualizing

In addition to being a source of disunity and destruction for Western civilization, decontextualized universals cause unemployment for philosophers. For this reason they can be said to be *the* ultimate Western philosophical problem. Decontextualized individualism means society can never tell anyone what to do and decontextualized rights mean that there are no countervailing considerations to be weighed. The decontextualized love of diversity, like tolerance, validates the ultimate absence of values. No one can say that my ways or art are any better or worse than anyone else's. Thoughtful commentators need not apply! Decontextualized universals are decided once and for all. Fortunately, culturism allows for temporal, cultural, philosophic, and historic considerations.

Were culturism a decontextualized system it would not provide employment for philosophers either. Western culturism should never come close to saying that all questions can be answered by asking what best for the state. We would become stagnant and petrified like Sparta. The West is a progressive culture that values individualism. Those hoping to turn culturism into a tyrannical system would be countered by deeper culturists reminding us of the questions of Socrates, Jesus' rebellious streak, and Jefferson's mistrust of government. Tyranny is not a live option for us. Culturism should never be treated as an absolute. Absolutes shut down discussions; culturism seeks to foster discussions. Maintaining real individualism and a culture dedicated to liberty means that compromises must be adjudicated.

Instead of the silence that comes from absolutes, we need a vibrant debate that is worthy of a democracy. Can we require community service on the part of citizens? What level of antisocial behaviors is tolerable? Does giving vasectomies to those who have kids and need welfare unnecessarily compromise realistic individualism, liberty or license? Given our traditions, how much anti-social behavior should we permit in what forums? What are the moral messages, goals for individuals, and cultural implications in laws being considered? Too often such questions are met by the shrill assertions of those defending absolute prerogatives of either individuals or rights rather than the nuanced discourse of those who recognize the balance that contextualized ethics require.

Answering the questions above requires that we have a current understanding of the state of the culture and our cultural heritage. Measures designed to foster the unity that leads to crime reduction would not have been appropriate during the Great Depression. Measures to stop infidelity would have been superfluous the 1950s. In the 1950s school programs teaching us about the diversity of cultures might have been a laudable goal. Currently programs teaching about the particular virtues of the West would be more appropriate. Pragmatic culturism means that we always apply our reasoning to moving targets in specific contexts. In a dynamic world, the cultural pragmatist's job is never done.

One of the most important job of a culturist philosopher will be announcing and defining our standards. Different times require different standards of greatness. Wartime requires a Themistocles. Times of poor art need a John William Waterhouse. Philosophers must then know about history and all Western areas of greatness. Our greatness can be best assessed and inspired in relation to people like Michelangelo and books like *The Republic*. The ability to ward off of malevolent demons and cruelty of tyrants are not the basis of Western virtues. The problem that advocates of tolerance and diversity face is that they advocate nothing in particular. If everything is great, nothing is particularly worthwhile. Exorcism and binding women's feet become as good as anything else. We have culturally specific beliefs. We do not traditionally value sloth, headhunting or racism. We value excellence, creativity, and self-control. Nothing can be said to be a worthwhile action outside of a living cultural tradition.

A reliance on tradition does not mean that we stop inventing the future. Asian art has traditionally striven to embody traditional forms. Western art has tried to create bold new forms. Western art history involves constant change and rebellion. But, modern art gets derided as a farce because of its reliance on being new and daring without relevance our to cultural tradition. At one point Kandinsky's abstractions were shocking to a tradition. Now his followers are just putting meaningless splotches of paint on the canvas that are not historically or culturally relevant. Our current search for originality in fine arts is done against a very shallow historical background. Conscious progress (a Western value) in any discipline requires awareness of long traditions. Without such awareness, any change comes to be synonymous with progress. Progress implies direction and therefore requires knowledge of the past. Only with historical awareness can we say to have progressed since neo-classical art or the ethics of 1895.

Our general conceptions of cultural and individual virtues should take place within our traditional Platonic, Aristotelian, Protestant ethic based, Progressive definitions of self-governance. Pornography makes a lot of money. But all of our sources of tradition privilege the uniquely human spirituality over the bodily functions. They are concerned with the ability to rationally direct our collective lives. Random sex leads to complications that undermine the sustainability of the community. Lastly, pornography is not Shakespeare. In comparison with our fantastic cultural heritage pornography can be seen to be shallow, degrading, and destructive of our traditional sense of mission and self. Without recourse to our traditions, pornography cannot be said to be any more or less worthy than any other example of diversity.

The Western tradition provides coherent, sustainable and ennobling standards for value judgments. Ultimately political realities require that we ask ourselves if our actions increase faith in man's ability to be self-governing. Our actions are bad to the extent that they provide evidence of a vicious world where heavy-handed culturism can be justified. Our actions are good to the extent that they persuade people that unmonitored men can be trustworthy stewards of their own destiny. We thus get a graded and situationally sensitive sense of right and wrong. This approach to values respects our ability to make decisions; to differentiate right from wrong. Universal rules that hold that it is not and never will be appropriate to do X rob us of this capacity. Contextualized ethics are the only way you can devise truly thoughtful policy.

A plea for culturist philosophy

Culturism necessitates that our focus is on Western philosophy. It is natural that those brought up in the Western tradition should do so. Western civilization provided Western philosophers schooling and electricity. It supports Western philosophers economically. Western philosophers should easily identify with Western cultural figures. And note that their connection with Western civilization is not just due to unreasonable bias or pigheadedness. Working in philosophic traditions outside of the Western framework is not a viable, live, option. Even if they wanted to advocate Zulu or Asian philosophy, the language barrier would prohibit them. Their research would have to rely on translated second hand sources. Furthermore, they would be unfamiliar with the basic lay of the mental landscape. The values the foreign heroes epitomized would not be transparently clear to them.

Philosophers often do not pay enough attention to the cultural context they work in. Jacques Derrida's speech at John Hopkins University brought deconstructionist philosophy to the American shores in 1965. This event has spawned a generation of attacks on the validity of Western culture and the Western narrative. Ironically it also showed that philosophy only happens within a cultural context. Had he made the same speech in Saudi Arabia it would not have had much of an effect. All things being cultural, it immediately garnered a large following and spawned a movement in the United States. We love rebellion, upsetting the status quo, and advances.

Deconstructionist philosophers deride and denounce the validity of the society that surrounds them. It would behoove them to become culturist philosophers and try to deepen our connection with our traditional philosophic heritage instead. Our tradition is rich in sources of standards for them to uphold and propagate. This would raise their esteem and help eradicate the shallowness that social critics rightfully decry. As critics of cultural standards that we could all understand they would become arbiters of good taste. They could enlighten us by comparing our art to its historical predecessors. This would imply good taste exists, give us standards to emulate, and elevate all of us.

Philosophy has to be less academic and more culturist. Our diversion into the universal has disengaged us from appreciating the virtues of our particular traditions and history. Universal philosophy struggles to deny being culturally relative and thereby fails to be culturally relevant. The current trend of undermining attachment to a particular culture is destructive. It makes philosophy worse than irrelevant. Societies need relevant philosophies to help guide them. Philosophers have traditionally been concerned with the state of cultures within which they work. It is natural that they do so. They should resume this practice.

Western philosophers acknowledging that they are Western philosophers would allow them to reclaim their heritage. Greek philosophers were very much concerned with the fate of Greece. This did not mean that they were only propaganda mechanisms for the state. They researched politics, art, ethics, culture, science, and even linguistics. Socrates thought he served his culture best by being a "gadfly" that kept Athens from philosophical slumber. He ultimately drank hemlock rather than going against his conscience and so strengthened Athens. Being a Western philosopher does not mean that you check your conscience at the door. But we should be careful to avoid the Western fallacy that your integrity exists to the extent to which you defy your culture. You do not need to be dishonest to find value in Western heritage.

Kant's project required incredible rigor. And he was not trying to undermine his culture. His undermining it only came as he decided that his standards were universal and for all times regardless of context. But this was done in the service of mankind, not abstraction for abstraction's sake. Only in retrospect have we come to recognize that Kant's contributions were extremely Western. They assumed that so-called scientific objectivity was *the* most honest method. His efforts show us that Western efforts at creating Western beliefs can be rigorous and need not be cheap propaganda. But he also showed us that it is nearly impossible to think outside of one's own culture. Lastly, Kant shows us that even the most rigorously derived pretenses to be universal fail.

Philosophy should be in the midst of the history of ideas doing battle. The love of wisdom being less esoteric will disabuse us of the concept of the expert philosopher whose field of inquiry is divorced from anything you would naturally bother yourself with. *Philosophy should treat cultures as embodied philosophies. Living cultures are where the battles for the minds of men happen.* We have to define and redefine what is best in our day according to modern conditions and determine what ought to be encouraged and discouraged. When philosophers realize that defending a thought system means defending the culture that holds that thought system to be self-evident, they can help guide us. We need to establish a hierarchy of taste and ethics or accept that nothing can be considered better than trash. Were the Department of Culture to become a reality Western philosophers could lead it. As such they would be the ultimate culturist psychologists. Outside of a cultural milieu philosophical statements have no meaning.

Traditional cultures do not need as much help as we do when we try to maintain our identity and civilization. They do not have the natural instability that comes from a progressive tradition and the correlated disdain for history. Our philosophers have a more difficult battle to engage in. Just as Plato updated Achilles' philosophy for the Athenian Golden Age and Saint Augustine updated Platonic ethics for the Christian era, Western philosophers must constantly update our traditions in different fields. In our changing and progressive culture, issues from polygamy to rap, from racial discord to business ethics, from immigration to anti-depressants keep popping up. We will always need guidance. Western philosophers must be constantly ready to hazard a guess as to what Jesus, Plato, and Aristotle would say about new and unforeseen situations.

Western philosophers must avoid the complacency that comes from assuming that someday all will agree to our universal ideals. They must engage in this battle of ideas in a diverse and competitive world. They must explain the advantages and nobility of the chaos inherent in the Western tradition. They must help us to understand the neighboring civilizations we live with. They must also make our positions clear to other cultures. They must also keep us from dogmatic, impractical, inflexible, universalistic assertions that those who are unaware of our progressive history advocate. And at the same time they must keep us from those who say that no basis to esteem any thought or activity over any other exists. Culturist pragmatists must know their target; living cultures are where philosophy manifests most strongly. Western philosophers must be the guardians and guides for the culture they are embedded in. They must do so in the context of the emerging international future in which the West hopes to be a player.

CHAPTER NINE

CULTURISM AND
MULTICULTURALISM

Culturism's relationship to multiculturalism

Culturism is opposed to multiculturalism only to the extent that multiculturalism discourages belief in the Western World's having a positive and unique cultural heritage. All cultures have subcultures within them. Culturism is just a corrective. Western culture is not hostile to individualism or cultural diversity, and Western culturism does not seek to get rid of individualism nor does it require that we suppress all non-mainstream cultural elements. To do so would in fact be anti-Western. Culturism involves, rather, making sure that sub-cultural affiliations are recognized as being subcultures within a larger cultural context. Appreciation of individuals, rights, and liberty are not cultural defaults; many cultures are hostile to these concepts. These values are only at the heart of the Western tradition. If the larger cultural tradition of honoring these values is weakened, the ability to sustain the individualism, tolerance, and liberty that allow for multiculturalism will be gone. In a very real sense, then, Western culturism is the protector of multiculturalism.

The question addressed in this chapter is not whether or not we have subcultures in our dominant culture. No one would deny that. Nor is the question investigated in this chapter whether or not America and the larger Western world have distinctive cultures. Any anthropologist would tell you that we do have a distinctive culture. The question addressed in this chapter is whether we are better

off emphasizing our diversity or our similarities. Culturism implies
questioning those strains of multiculturalism currently afloat that
would deny the centrality of any special characteristics to our country's
culture. The choice is not really between absolutes or extremes. The
question is whether or not we should emphasize our differences or
our similarities. The question being addressed herein is, "Would we
be better off being more multiculturalist or more culturist?"

Methodological introduction

Celebrating diversity as an absolute good is a default of our
modern public discussions. Notions of diversity being the American
way and contrary views being labeled as racist have made dissent from
multiculturalism risky. Alhambra, a typical small American town near
my home, lined its streets with banners celebrating diversity. It is
interesting that Alhambra is named after the place where Catholic
Spain finally threw the Muslims out of Europe. Perhaps the hidden
historical message conveyed by this coincidence is a positive one. It
might be taken to suggest that, instead of war aimed at expulsion,
allowing the Muslims to stay in Spain and cultivate their separate
culture would have been preferable. This chapter will investigate the
merits of this suggestion for our time.

The push for diversity is not just idle sloganeering. In its name,
we are now embarked on an unprecedented transformation of our
demographics and public policy. When implementing huge changes
in social policy, simply being comforted by a banner on Main Street
America is not enough. In undertaking such an experiment we should
look at what the costs and benefits might be. If unintended negative
consequences were to become manifest we would need to be ready
to suspend the experiment; if the gains truly are great, we might want
to accelerate the process. But we should make a systematic evaluation
before we embark on large policy adventures.

Undoubtedly, deep reasons underlie the push for diversity. We
cannot evaluate those here; we are concerned with results. The gravity
of this radical experiment necessitates rigorous monitoring. When
undertaking an experiment you should use the scientific method for
evaluation. This involves setting up formal criteria. And as is proper
for a rigorous appraisal, we will first formally define the terms involved

and the hypothesis being investigated.

Mul·ti·cul·tur·al·ism (mŭl-tē-kŭl-chər-əl-ĭź-əm) *n.* **1.** Of, relating to, or including several cultures. **2.** Of or relating to a social or educational theory that encourages interest in many cultures within a society rather than in only a mainstream culture.[291]

Hypothesis: Nations would be better off overall if they adopted the policies and cultural attitudes implicit in a multicultural outlook. Falsification of this hypothesis would be achieved if it were shown that potential costs outweigh potential benefits.

Culturism has already been defined. Whereas multicultural and culturist policies can and will exist side by side, we need to treat them as absolutely distinct for the purposes of this comparison. After setting forth the two possibilities, we will consider what the potential outcomes of adopting each outlook would be across several variables. After considering the potential outcome for each variable individually, we will compute the overall costs and benefits. Results indicating that a multicultural outlook will likely cause more costs than benefits would falsify the claim above. Since the opposite of multiculturalism is culturism, falsification would suggest that Western nations would be better off overall if they adopted the policies and cultural attitudes implicit in a culturist outlook.

In any good experiment one must choose variables to measure. Research in the soft sciences involves more variables than that in the hard sciences. We can know with certainty what the result of mixing two chemicals will be. It is harder to predict what the mixing of two cultures will lead to because so many complicating variables are involved in social interaction. The historical record often provides approximations to situations we face, and social science experiments can indeed help us. However, holding all the variables you are not testing constant is impossible in social sciences. We cannot expect a definitive answer to our question. Social science investigations cannot tell you what *will* happen. We can know for certain, however, what the outcomes of multiculturalism or culturism *might* be. These potentials can be listed. Without specifying these variables our overall

pronouncements are often too global, too vague, to be meaningful.
Multiculturalism and culturism, promoting contrasting values, can be
expected to hold contrasting potentials, and to lead to contrasting
outcomes. These potentials can be listed.

The assignment of culturism and multiculturalism to one side
of our comparison chart or the other may seem inappropriate in
some cases; in other cases the assignment will seem intuitively
correct. Again, for experimental purposes we must treat culturism
and multiculturalism as mutually exclusive though they are often, in
fact, only distinguished by emphasis. In cases where it seems either
outcome is as likely from either culturism or multiculturalism, neither
course can be recommended via this method. In cases where the
likely outcomes from either culturism or multiculturalism seem more
obviously divergent, we can more confidently recommend one option
over the other.

The following list shows the possible effects of each, which will be
discussed in detail below:

Multiculturalism	Culturism
Tolerance	Intolerance
Instability	Stability
Diversity	Uniformity
Inefficiency	Efficiency
Group	Individual
Past orientation	Future orientation
Belonging	Alienation
Excitement	Boredom
International Peace	International War

The reader is invited to tally scores using the above chart while it is
discussed below. This would be done if you wanted a numerical tally as
to which policy is preferable. Towards this end you could put a check
mark next to the item on the side of the pairs that seems preferable.
You might then want to add weights to the check marks. Avoiding civil
unrest would be at least ten times as important as avoiding boredom.
So whereas the "stability" (if preferable) might deserve ten checks,
"excitement" (if preferable) might only merit one. Finally, you can

tally the total on the bottom of the chart. This methodology should give you an idea of the potential cost, benefit, and merit of either policy.

The variables being used here are meant to apply only to the consideration of Western values. Western culturism seeks to promote individualism. Muslim or Asian culturism do not aim to cultivate a Western sense of individualism. The judgments we make ultimately reflect the biases of our cultural heritage. This does not invalidate the conclusions; it only limits their applicability. Culturism is predicated on the assertion that each culture has its own truths. As this comparison is being considered for its applicability to Western civilization, it is appropriate that we use Western values in reaching our conclusions.

In each case, the variable in the left side of the column and title headings represents the result of adopting the policies and cultural attitudes implicit in a multicultural outlook, while the variable in the right side of the column and title headings represents the result of adopting the policies and cultural attitudes implicit in a culturist outlook.

Tolerance versus intolerance

Intolerance, at its best, informs positive public standards. We might start disapproving of weeknight drinking and dropping out of high school. Whereas we now err on the side of acceptance, limited intolerance would discourage vulgarity and unethical behavior. Intolerance at its best is seen in low-crime, high-achievement countries like Singapore and Korea. This sort of intolerance can strengthen and elevate the standing of the country in which it is practiced.

However, intolerance at its worst stifles freedom of speech and certain people would experience the shame and restrictions of the judgments directed against them. Homosexuals, controversial artists, and single mothers could end up feeling very uncomfortable when discussing their lifestyles. We could end up with a stifling uniformity that would deny many their chosen modes of pursuing happiness.

Tolerance at its best allows for a diversity of lifestyle choices and results in public approbation for each of them. With tolerance we can take pride in our differences, our uniqueness can be more fully explored, and people can avoid being standardized. People will possibly be better adjusted and harder workers because they are energized by the fact that they are living their own dreams and that their lives have resulted from their own free choice.

Tolerance, at its worst, degenerates into anarchy. Crudeness and socially irresponsible choices flourish. Teen pregnancy, drug use, and ignorance would not be met by disapproval. In an entirely tolerant society, reprehensible practices such as female genital mutilation (pardon my culturism) would have to be applauded. Furthermore, the public would have to subsidize these activities to show it was not discriminating.

The permutations on this variable help clarify the limits of the binary methodology being used here. Quite often societies do not have to make "either/or" decisions. We can be simultaneously intolerant of some things and tolerant of others. Thus the opposition taken up here (along with the other oppositions) is an artificial construct. The two sides of the binary opposition represent what might be tendencies or goals in policy; they do not represent mutually exclusive absolutes.

Culturism has an advantage over multiculturalism in this regard, because it is more flexible. It has been estimated that 74,000 women in Britain have undergone female genital mutilation and that 7,000 girls under the age of 16 are at risk.[292] To be consistent multiculturalism would require that we are accepting of such practices. To be consistent a multiculturalist would also have to accept alternative lifestyles that include heavy drug use and the cloistering of women. If a multiculturalist judges such behaviors, he can be called hypocritical for being intolerant of diversity. Such multiculturalism would run the risk of "degenerating" into culturism. Culturism, on the other hand, can be nuanced without being inconsistent. Western culturism advocates diversity within traditional and pragmatic bounds.

Instability versus Stability

Advocates of multiculturalism sometimes market it as a way to minimize the potential for ethnic conflict. The claim is that celebrating diversity leads to appreciation of differences instead of conflict over them. As a result, the historic tensions between different groups in our society (e.g., between blacks and whites) will not recur. The view is that assertions of cultural superiority or primacy lead to conflict, that intolerance breeds resentment, and that resentment breeds, for example, riots. A positive appreciation of differences is thought to make for a more respectful and peaceful populace. This logic argues that stability belongs under the multiculturalism column.

This argument for multiculturalism, though, tacitly acknowledges that diversity brings the potential for instability, and thus stability might belong in the culturism column. Indeed there has been a startling increase of race riots between Latinos and blacks across our country's high schools. [293] The riots this diversity allows can feed on itself and go beyond the bounds of the high school. If a community is long settled in a place and another comes in very quickly, the original community might resent being squeezed into a smaller space. When many in your hometown do not speak the language of the historic majority anymore it can create discomfort. The original community might try to pass discriminatory measures that would spark resentment and conflict. Emphasizing differences always invokes the potential conflict over differences. The fact that conflict usually reflects divisions and diversity, indicates that stability might belong under the culturism column.

Multiculturalism's focus on diversity also challenges liberal democracy. These challenges take two forms, according to two different types of situations. One type of situation comes about when the original group and the new group start voting solely in the interests of their community. Immigration control, affirmative action, and resource allocation are just a few of the issues the groups could potentially be divided over. Ultimately, the result of this tendency would be for our country to no longer fit the definition of a community of citizens. Instead there would be two competing cultural groups occupying the same space. Since democracies are timid and do not like to upset their constituents, the government would become less able to act decisively.

The second threat to liberal democracy posed by diversity is the potential for civil unrest. Civil unrest is not conducive to liberal democracy, because when it arises, governments reduce civil liberties. Freedom of association and speech get limited. In many ways, this has already happened with the war on terror. Were there no large

Muslim communities in America the Patriot Act would not have been justifiable or considered; diversity has already cost us some liberty. Even *the potential* for civil strife undermines liberties. The inchoate potential for violence underlies my decision for putting "instability" under the column of multiculturalism. When you emphasize and increase diversity you inevitably create and reinforce fault lines that can lead to conflict.

Ultimately these differences can lead to widespread violence and war. The definition of war is loose. Our war on terror is not a conventional war. Basque terrorists' bombing the rest of Spain in order to gain independence does not qualify as a full-blown war. Israel and Palestine engage in so much carnage that the "occupation" and "terror" can seem like real wars. No clear standard exists to separates increasing internal violence between groups from civil war, but Yugoslavia's dissolution shows us how quickly communities can separate, polarize, and become extremely violent antagonists. Rwanda shows us just how horrible the results of emphasizing ethnic differences can be. The potential for civil war within the emphasizing of differences cannot be taken too seriously.

Whatever you call it, civil unrest is always met with responses that compromise individual rights and autonomy. Cars and people get routinely profiled and searched. If secession movements are successful, the resulting states will likely be less liberal than the original state. These new states will necessarily be ethnically-based and exclusionary; they will not represent the ideals of liberal democracies. Furthermore, since hostility and discord will linger, it makes sense that the two resulting states will be much more martial than the original state was. Civil strife in a democracy can only lessen the area in which the Western ethic of individualism and rights holds sway.

A survey of international wars and civil wars would show that wars are far more likely between two different groups than between similar groups. People tend to not fight their own kind. One exception that quickly comes to mind is the American Civil War. But while the diversity of populations (and the existence of slavery) did not necessarily cause the Civil War (it need not have happened), diversity made it possible (if our nation had only been comprised of Europeans it would not have happened). In pockets of Europe there has been talk of creating autonomous regions ruled by Islamic law, and there are groups in the United States dedicated to reclaiming our Southwest region for Mexico. These movements' struggles for official recognition of their distinctive culture and sovereignty will not necessarily lead to discord or war, but they do not help stability. Thus, again, it seems counterintuitive to put stability under multiculturalism.

Multiculturalism's strategy of appreciating diversity seems doomed to create more instability than culturism's strategy of stressing commonalities. Increasing and celebrating diversity may be a formula for minimizing conflict. Israel's celebrating Palestinians probably wouldn't stop the conflict. Perhaps Spain celebrating Basque contributions would. We know, however, that breakaway republics and divided voting blocks are not likely in homogeneous societies. So we can at the very least say that instability is a possible result of diversity. And, in the worst case, we may conclude that liberal democracies and celebrations of diversity are antagonistic. Lessening the risk of civil war or anything approaching it provides the strongest reason to diminish diversity and awareness of diversity. Of all of the negative events imaginable, war is the worst. Western nations therefore need to constantly monitor whether their experiments in diversity are increasing or decreasing harmony.

Diversity versus Uniformity

Culturism is predicated upon an acknowledgement of diversity, because it assumes that specific cultures have specific values, metaphysics, lifestyles, psychologies, etc. Furthermore, the differences in values and lifestyles lead to different results. Some cultures encourage having lots of babies early in life. Early and continued reproduction leads to the blessing of large families. On the other hand, large families are not conducive to high levels of education and first-world economies. Furthermore, culturists realize that the diversity of mankind is so great that it encompasses headhunting, condoning drug use, and celebrating violent gang initiations. Culturism is based on the assumption that diversity is real, wide, and significant.

Ironically, multiculturalism has a very shallow vision of diversity. Multiculturalists acknowledge that people have different clothing, foods, and customs. But deep down multiculturalists hold that we are all fundamentally the same. This shallow view of diversity can be seen in the advocacy of policy that asserts that we can unproblematically co-exist, communicate, and agree on values. Our fundamental sameness is also implied in the assertion that we can form a coherent society based on appreciating our differences; diversity can never be so extreme that fundamental disagreements can arise. Furthermore, multiculturalists do not believe that any significant negative outcomes result from diversity. Always taking the position that an ethnic group's different levels of material, health, and educational achievement are due to bias assumes that these differences cannot be due to cultural diversity. Also, short of the real extremes of human behavior, multiculturalists assume that there is no reason for preferring one culture or another.

Culturists qualify their appreciation of diversity more than multiculturalists. Multiculturalists complain that narratives have been marginalized and they are correct. Western culturists, as the designation would have it, acknowledge that Western countries were designed on Western principles. For example, industry is based on science, which came out of Western Europe. Madison, when he framed our constitution, looked to Western history for models. Furthermore, Puritan values were instrumental in our creating a first-world economy. America's rise to greatness had very little, if anything, to do with Asian or Islamic precedents or philosophies. We can investigate and acknowledge that these cultures have something to offer. But Western culturists would hold that, with regard to the United States, they are not nearly as central to our achievements, history, or present as our Protestant, Enlightenment, and scientific orientations.

Culturism can provide values. Recognizing the specific cultural heritage which created this country, culturism in the context of the United States also involves appreciating and preferring sobriety, thrift, ambition, diligence, concern about the public morals, and other values associated with the Protestant work ethic. Culturists take culture seriously. It has consequences. Multiculturalism, on the other hand, does not recognize a core tradition to advocate. At some level, they feel that all cultures are equal, interchangeable, and have added equal amounts to this country's creation. Multiculturalists advocate policies that stress no particular culture or cultural attributes. Multiculturalism tends to paint all attempts to make value statements that "privilege" a particular cultural tradition as oppressive and irrational. Thus multiculturalism discourages positive value statements. Culturism, by contrast, advocates a positive value system.

Culturism does not advocate the removal of all hints of the existence of other cultures from the public sphere. Western culture is the most open of any on the planet. While the Chinese do not welcome non-Chinese populations into their country, and Muslim countries do not celebrate tolerance, emphasizing our Western heritage is compatible with acknowledging that people in our country have and will continue to have cultural affiliations with their countries of origin. In a country such as ours a stifling uniformity cannot be taken seriously as a goal or fear. Our natural fear of such a state will preclude its consideration. The debate involved herein is based on whether or not we acknowledge a unifying cultural strand that has been central to the building of Western nations. If there is a core culture, then assimilation and emphasizing moral standards become possible, and thus culturism becomes possible. It would not be true to our cultural heritage to force people to do anything. Western culture acknowledges people's right to disagree and live their lives the way they want to. The real question concerns whether or not we have core values.

Wealth versus Poverty

There are reasons to believe that having a diversity of cultures within a country can help it economically. Internal diversity can increase the ability to understand international norms of negotiation. Having a population in which multiple languages are spoken enables a country to efficiently engage in international trade. Having a pool of cheap labor is also thought to be beneficial for the economy. Much of China's economic rise has been due to its ability to create cheap products, and this ability results from its having a large pool of inexpensive laborers. The United States and some other Western countries also get cheap labor by admitting and using immigrants. Furthermore, it is argued that the aging populations in Western countries require immigrants to supplement the declining number of young workers. These are some ways in which diversity and immigration can help the economy.

Others have noted that diversity can create inefficiencies. Linguistic skills are necessary for international business, and international businessmen generally learn English for this reason. Domestic linguistic diversity means, however, that you are unable to speak with many others within your country. Occupational mobility is stymied by sectors of the economy being linguistically segregated. Minority language citizens are unable to fully realize their potential because they are linguistically excluded from the higher echelons of the economy. Multiple studies have shown that linguistic heterogeneity is nearly always correlated with economic underdevelopment and that linguistic uniformity is virtually a necessary precursor to economic success.[294]

Economic issues are very much predicated on cultural ones. Culturists would point out that in some cultures people live for education, have low rates of teen pregnancies, and believe that diligence can lead to a better tomorrow. Countries that fit this cultural profile are rich. Countries that do not follow this path have large tight-knit families and good times, but they do not have first-world economies. Diversity also affects a country's knowledge base. Students who do not speak the classroom language well or know about George Washington slow down classrooms and school districts. Multiculturalists do not think that diversity need have any negative economic outcomes. They hold that cultural proclivities, in and of themselves, can have no significant impact on the economy.

However, culturism is about prioritizing cultural considerations. Ultimately economic issues need to take a back seat to those of culture. Cultural integrity and longevity are important in their own right. A wholesale replacement our population with a Korean one in order to increase our economic performance would make no sense. Were we to replace our population with a Korean one, George Washington's memory, respect for the autonomous individual, our stand against racism, and our strong heritage of rights (among other things) would suffer. Culturists realize that getting low-skilled jobs done by the current population, rather than by immigrants, might necessitate raising wages and that inflation might result. But culturism is about cultural longevity, not economics. Assuming that diversity is an economic boon, culturism would still argue that we should not sell out our culture for monetary gain.

Group versus Individual

Individuality has long been considered a solvent in the melting pot. In the play that coined the phrase "the melting pot" the protagonist escapes his cultural ghetto and marries outside of his the bounds of his forefather's tradition. He thinks of himself as an individual not a member of an Old World community and thus becomes American. Much of this is based upon the idea that America is the Promised Land of opportunity. As a Jew, the protagonist's family came here to escape oppression. But the kernel of that freedom implied his freedom to even escape his community's constrictions. Thus his transformation into being a full American means striking out as an individual. And thus the hard divisions of the Old World melt. This traditional understanding of liberty is celebrated by American culturists.

Multiculturalism is in favor of abandoning this traditional understanding. Multiculturalists advocate citizens maintaining their Old World based group allegiances and traditions. To ask a person to leave his old traditions, they claim, is to rob him of much of his identity. America has always contained many ethnic enclaves. As a result, one can suppose that there is no American culture to blend into. Being American and true to one's Old World traditions presents no incongruity for multiculturalists.

The multicultural argument that we should celebrate the traditions that prevailed in the countries that Americans came from is based on two notions. One is the idea that America itself is not a special country. Our nation will stay united because, at heart, no cultures are really different from each other. The abandoned old country was just as good. We just need to acknowledge that each culture is roughly equivalent and we will have harmony. A second similar reason multiculturalists want to celebrate their ancestor's country stems from the belief that America not only does not have a special culture, it has no culture at all. Therefore, there is nothing to assimilate into. Remembering your ethnic heritage fills the void being an American entails; it provides you with a culture.

Culturism asserts that we have traditions. These traditions are unique and we cannot help but see them as preferable to those of the country people chose to leave. The details of our unique cultural heritage were detailed earlier. Individual responsibility and initiative comprise much of this tradition. Americans have long defined themselves in contrast to the stagnant hierarchies and backwards-looking tribalism that have been a violent check on personal freedom from time immemorial. Our heritage propels us towards self-governance and progressive change. Our cultural icons are rebels in the name of progress. This shared heroic characteristic forms the backbone of a unique cultural heritage. And we do have traditional artistic forms and heroes. Racial, backwards looking, Old World, ethnic sources of identity are confining and keep us from recognizing our commonality as Americans *and* our potential as individuals.

Multiculturalism holds superficial diversity to be nearly racially inborn. People of past traditions necessarily have connections to them that will not melt away. Culturists are heartened when they see groups of young Americans of different ancestry together. Nearly always, they are so assimilated in language and character that they are indistinguishable. Assimilation into the common culture has worked. Multiculturalists would hold this ability to change as an illusion. They insist that these young Americans are essentially culturally different and have not assimilated. Multiculturalism believes that we must forever define people by precedents in the past. Western culturism believes in change, fluidity and self-invention.

The implied policy distinctions in this section revolve around assimilation but ultimately concern the identity of America itself. Multiculturalists hold that one's identity should always be pegged to the Old World; they see no alternative. Culturists recognize that Old World identities may help a new immigrant adjust. But ultimately Old World distinctions retard assimilation and the adoption of America's unique cultural vision of individualism and progressivism. They retard the process that ultimately melts us together. Again, if multiculturalists are right about the shallow nature and impact of diversity, this is not a significant issue. But if culturists are right about diversity, it is a very important issue.

Past versus Future

What may be called progressive history involves the story of man going from primitive conditions to modernity. Progressive history did not always exist. For most of man's existence there has only been what is called cyclical or mythic history. Cyclical history is a story of beginnings that usually stops shortly after creation; it never includes events within memory of the living. Traditional cultures revere the past. The very notion of tradition implies an engagement with and respect for the past. Tradition is pure to the extent that it never changes; it is meant to be static. It does not inspire one to seek changes or the new and improved. It looks back to a golden age from which we have permanently fallen. It harkens to events behind us. It projects no impending change or bright future.

Herodotus wrote the first Western non-mythic history. It was written so that we might learn of the valorous deeds and mistakes of the past. Though it looked backwards, we were to learn from history and improve ourselves. Learning implies getting better. This history includes history lessons. Herodotus' goal in writing history was to aid the creation of a better future. Thus non-mythical history is progressive history, and the world's progressive societies owe a great deal to this notion of history. Progressive societies see the past as a nightmare from which we are trying to escape. They do not want to repeat the mistakes of the past. For progressive history, the golden age lays in the future.

Progressive history creates a forward-looking mindset. Battle with the problems of life becomes our natural posture. We employ our Protestant work ethic to create resumes. Our personal stories depicted in these resumes show journeys of growth. Progressive societies are dedicated to improvements that will alleviate the vestiges of Old World faults and the general deprivation of the past. We as individuals are aligned with our cultural vision of life as progress towards goals. Our society reveres youth because the young are our future. They are on the cutting edge of promise that their elders can only look upon with perplexed wonder and envy. Other cultures work to authentically approximate old ways and do things in the ways that brought their grandfathers honor. We have a forward looking orientation.

Western man's propensity to be dissatisfied is grounded in his acceptance of progressive history. America has traditionally been progressive and antagonistic to tradition. Ours is the country people come to in order to start a new life. It has traditionally been called the "New World." Western culture launched a fundamentally new form of government: democracy. We are the modern incarnation of this rarely tried arrangement. We had cowboys roaming the West more than fifty years before Europeans stopped being governed by royalty. Our traditional isolationism comes from our conviction that the rest of the world's preoccupation with the past makes them irrational, dangerous or both.

Multiculturalism looks to the past. It asks you to identify with the country your family came from. Notice that the previous sentence was in the past tense. The vision of multiculturalism, when taken seriously, could mean a return to arranged marriages (Indian cultures) and slavery (Sudan and Mauritania). It might well preclude you from engaging in intercultural relationships. It would preclude you from being an adventurer on the perimeters of the newest lifestyles. In short, Old World cultural traditions are often antagonistic to the freedom of choice implicit in the American promise.

Although we are no longer alone in the race for tomorrow, we should remember that it was our constant search for the new that resulted in the modern world we all enjoy. Cars, electricity, airplanes, the internet, women's rights, universal suffrage, modern medicine, genetic engineering, and computers are just some of the results of America's constant search for the next big thing. To be obsessed the preservation of the past, as the multiculturalists would advocate, is to run against the grain of much of America's cultural traditions, which are our greatest source of identity and best hope for tomorrow.

Belonging versus Alienation

Who is the modern man? He wears a tie. But in the modern world, many wear ties. This does not distinguish modern man as an individual. He has all the modern conveniences, and walks through malls of efficiency. But the chain stores that populate his world are the same ones that populate the lives of others throughout the world. This certainly does not differentiate him. He has no traditions to anchor himself to. He is largely a consumer who lives product-to-product.

We do have a courageous vision of man to which we can aspire and in which we can take pride. The American faith in individual self-reliance and our tendency to judge people by their merit, not their inherited status, has being rewarded with nearly four hundred years of sensational success. Our adherence to these and related values has created dynamic growth and a facility for adaptability. Our institutions are constantly being redesigned and shaken up by technologies. We have successfully met changing demands of economic depressions, the rise and fall of industries, our rise to international prominence, and radical shifts in lifestyles. The contrast between our dynamic society and the stasis of traditional agricultural communities is stark.

Ours is the most mobile population ever. From the pilgrims to the frontiersmen, Americans have always exchanged comfort for promise. As a result, we cannot rest our identity upon the comfort of place. Sixteen percent of the American population moved in the between March 1997 and March 1998.[295] And even if you do stay in one place, the buildings that were there when you were a child have probably all been torn down, many of your old friends will have left, and many of your neighbors will be newcomers. Fewer of the smaller, sleeker families of today stay intact. When American teenagers turn eighteen they are supposed to move out of their parents' home and never return. Traditionally, for Americans, the further one moves from his hometown the more respect he gets. Modern man's identity cannot be based on a sense of place or community.

In the traditional villages multiculturalism lauds, people belonged. Rural folks have bigger families. They are enmeshed in a large circle of intimates from birth. In a traditional, agrarian community your identity would be ready-made as a mother, a brother, a father. Generations would have the same job, farm, and home. Furthermore, the landscape did not change, and so you would always know where you were. People did not move. City folks can easily walk around their environs all day long and not see one person they know. Familiar faces greeted villagers everywhere they went. In a very real sense, not knowing who you are is an unintelligible dilemma in such a setting.

Modernity is alienating and the rate of alienation is speeding up. Disaffection and identity crisis are nearly constant themes in Western art and youth culture. Traditionally you had the same job and lifestyle as your parents. This stability facilitated community and was a core pillar of one's identity. Now each generation is less familiar with the way the previous one lived. Fewer and fewer have lived in a pre-cell phone world. Generation gaps and classifications such as gen-Xers and baby boomers can be a source of identity. But of course this sense of belonging only applies within an age group. Niche marketing undermines any cross-generational or cross-group affiliations.

Culturism advocates considering all the previously enumerated sources of alienation as sources of glory and identity. We are a modern, inventive, individualistic, self-reliant culture. Participating in creating the modern world is a source of common experience. The dynamic nature of our economy can be as much a source of pride as one of alienation. We kick economic butt. Indeed Americans do identify themselves more with their work than people in other cultures do. Every person can connect with other people via sharing in the long individual struggles of our careers, efforts towards advancement, and attempts at self-definition. Our resumes do not bespeak passivity. They speak of a common American fascination with bettering ourselves and our world. This sense of striving and achievement united our exciting and disparate paths.

Furthermore, we should not be overly romantic about the sense of belonging in traditional agricultural communities. Poverty, lack of life options, early pregnancy, low educational attainment, and poor health care are not fun. Furthermore, much of what makes living in these societies a tolerable option is the adoption of American technologies and money sent from abroad. Multiculturalists tend to over-romanticize the old countries they or their ancestors left. It is true, however, that many people do return to their home countries. The frenzied work orientation and isolation of American life often are not considered to be worth the money. Belonging seems more comforting to these individuals than alienation. They cannot stand our frenetic pace.

Alienation is also a result of ideology. Culturists can take pride and satisfaction in Western ideological, political, and material contributions to the world. Multiculturalists do not believe America is special. Therefore, for them, the American story is not a source of pride. America in this view is only defined by geographical parameters; it is not seen as a place that has core traditions or core narratives. It is a world without its own past. Not seeing any cultural or historical coherence in the bustling society around you aggravates the sense of alienation. Multiculturalism is not compatible with a sense of belonging in America. Culturists, on the other hand, can assure you that the story of the West is not incoherent. Culturists belong in the progressive Western world.

Our identity can be derived from our collective choice to abandon the safety and constrictions of the past. As opposed to those who just do what tradition dictates, we have decided to create ourselves in our own image. Ours can be seen as a fight for individual consciousness itself. Consciousness arose from struggle out of the darkness of the animal world. Individual consciousness was born from a protracted struggle with ignorance and tribalism. Our struggle for identity is not only a search for our personal identities; it is part of mankind's ongoing fight for conscious existence. This view is not only fantastic; it is our traditional, mainstream view of ourselves. This framework has traditionally connected us with our ancestors, from Achilles to Jefferson, who engaged in the struggle to escape from the tyranny of their given situations. It unites our individual journeys in a context of a collective mission

Ultimately we cannot say that either multiculturalism or culturism leads to a more satisfying life. Multiculturalism can lead to unwanted group pressures for conformity. Our lack of predetermined roles can become a source of insecurity rather than a blank canvas for dreams. The ethnic traditions multiculturalists celebrate can foster a sense of belonging. But for those whose Old World affiliations are very remote, there is no alternative to our progressive mission to cling to. Multiculturalism can create a safe sense of ready-made identity for new arrivals in our culture. But it only leaves the majority of us who have deep roots in the Western tradition, and no strong tie to any alternative national subgroup or nation, with alienation and an incoherent world. Either way, Westerners are made more valiant by their willingness to be outcasts from tradition for the sake of their individual self-actualization. We can find common cause in our alienation and the individuality and collective glory it has generated.

Excitement versus Boredom

It is often said that having uniformity makes a culture boring.
There is some truth to that. Ethnic neighborhoods draw tourists.
Official "Little Italy" and "Chinatown" designations are sought by
neighborhoods for just this reason. Looking out at a homogeneous
group of people eating similar foods is not a thrilling vision. The
excitement of diversity is one of the main arguments used to promote
multiculturalism.

The value of this argument for multiculturalism depends on the
value you put upon excitement. At a nuanced level, one could say that
this excitement is bought at the expense of a sense of self-creation.
Less subtly, however, it would be hoped that even an entertainment-
oriented culture such as ours would not put the value of excitement
on the same level of importance as the efficiency or viability of one's
country. Liberal democracies are especially threatened by separation
into ethnic voting blocks, the potential for civil unrest, and the
concomitant loss of rights. In a discussion of such potentialities, levels
of excitement seems to be an almost pathological consideration. In
a debate over outcomes of such importance, levels of excitement or
boredom are not worthy of consideration.

International Peace versus International War

Some might say that having representative populations from every
country in the world in the United States lessons our chances of
going to war. We would be reluctant to fight a country that has a fifth
column or voting bloc in our domestic population. The fifth column
could also, of course, by giving the foreign nation more hope in a
war, increase their willingness to wage war against us. The term "fifth
column" was first used to indicate the existence of Hitler's supporters
in Germany's neighbors during World War II. The existence of fifth
columns enabled Hitler's early successes and encouraged him to try
to take over Europe. If Germany did not have large populations of
people identifying with it inside other nations, Hitler might not have
dared to start his wars of conquest.

Foreigners in our country carried out the terrorist acts that drew us
into war in Iraq and Afghanistan. Domestic terrorism is now the official
reason for us being in those countries. That is not to say that war

cannot happen without terrorism. We were previously in Iraq without the precedent of a terrorist event. The first war in Iraq was done to save Kuwait from Iraq's unlawful violation of its sovereign territory. We rescued Kuwait's monarchy in the name of international law. Our current involvement in Iraq is currently dedicated to spreading our values and democracy abroad. Neither trying to make other parts of the world give up their indigenous traditions and follow us nor our laxity in allowing potential terrorists into our country shows a proper understanding of the depth of cultural diversity.

Culturism recognizes worldwide diversity. Cultures are very different. Most non-Western cultures acknowledge this. Asian countries prohibit different ethnicities from becoming citizens of their countries. Thus, Koreans cannot become Japanese citizens and Thai men cannot become Korean citizens due to Asia's widespread codified belief in racial and cultural purity. Islamic countries regard Western ways as an affront to their traditions and thus prohibit them. Diversity is such that assimilation is often impossible. Most Westerners have no stomach for headhunting or affiliation with a caste. Societies that tolerate honor killings would have a hard time adopting feminist ethics. Just as we would hope that they respect our cultural sovereignty, we should respect the cultural sovereignty of other cultures. Insisting that others adopt our cultural values is just as rude and likely to lead to war as their insisting that we adopt theirs.

Multiculturalists do not believe that countries should be able to discriminate. Ironically, those who advocate diversity in America are often those who most strongly advocate imposing a Western notion of rights in other cultures. They do not recognize the tradition of individual rights as being peculiarly Western nor its incompatibility with other cultural traditions. Though they say they respect diversity, they believe that the Western versions of individual rights, democracy, and feminism should be accepted universally. Thus, many who advocate multiculturalism domestically are against it internationally. Internationally, culturist values would hold that cultures approving of or denouncing the ways and values of other cultures is inappropriate. Our failure to recognize and accept that others might want to have divergent cultures is a large source of international resentment against the West.

Culturists are for international diversity. On a global level, part
of maintaining diversity involves maintaining the distinctiveness of
our culture. If America becomes another third-world dictatorship,
international diversity will have taken a hard hit. The best way to
for us to protect diversity internationally is to protect the integrity
of our culture. Changing others is not the best way to do this. Our
reforming other cultures is not desirable or feasible, and even if
it were feasible, it would necessitate our spending a lot of money
abroad. Our country and culture are best secured by investing in our
infrastructure. Furthermore, our meddling in other countries and
cultures creates resentments that can lead to war. War is dangerous and
destabilizing to all parties involved. Multiculturalists would destabilize
us both by having us spread our vision of rights to other nations
and by increasing disintegration domestically. Culturists recognize
and accept international diversity. Accepting our uniqueness and the
right of others to theirs provides a surer way to maintain diversity and
peace.

Conclusion

Domestically, the belief in diversity being a great good is a reaction
to the abusive, racist segregation that used to characterize much of the
United States. The Civil Rights Movement was started to combat this
racist intolerance and hatred. The Christian values of affirming and
respecting others were at the heart of the movement's appeal. The
Civil Rights Movement, however, was not built on an appreciation of
diversity. To the contrary, it took Western values to be a source of unity.
The goal was for all Americans to be thought of and treated as being
the same; to be seen as individuals without prejudice. The Civil Rights
Movement was a battle to erase the concept of an inherent race-based
diversity. The sign reading "I am a man" succinctly encapsulated the
Western ideals of equality, respect, and individualism.

Many who currently battle for civil rights fail to notice that diversity
is real. This failure happens because they are working within a
purely American framework. Black people and white people have
lived together so long that they largely share the same cultural
presuppositions. Black and white people's similarities were encoded
in the understanding that we could be judged interchangeably as

individuals based on the same standards. The multiculturalists would change the aforementioned sign to read, "I am a (fill in the country of descent) man." After asking us to acknowledge differences, today's multiculturalists say we should never judge differences. It would be a painful irony if our dedication to ignoring racial differences should lead to our renouncing our heritage of individualism and acceptance in favor of reified group differences. Furthermore, it would be sad if this perversion of Dr. King's appeal to our nation's heritage blinded us to see it as a special one.

Diversity exists. Logically, to argue that diversity within countries is an unqualified good, one would need to show that its presence always brings benefits and that a lack of diversity necessarily causes problems. Many homogenous countries having very strong economies, a high quality of life, and low incidences of crime and warfare means that cultural diversity is not an essential prerequisite to well-being. Homogeneity is not an unqualified evil; it is compatible with a good life. Diversity's sometimes being a source of war, secession, riots, and inefficiency means that it is not an unqualified good. If diversity is not an unqualified good we have to think hard about its merits and demerits before making increasing it a goal. All totaled our disaggregated consideration of the implications of culturist and multiculturalist emphases shows that more harm can result as a result of the latter.

To conclusively establish the desirability of internal diversity is an overall good we would have to run an impossible social experiment. We would have to take a poorly functioning homogenous country, add diversity and monitor that country's improvement across a wide spectrum of desirable variables. Nearly every well functioning culture in the world would resist being in this experiment. Common sense would tell them that consciously seeking to recruit and import foreign populations into their societies would not be in their self-interest. Their sense of culturism would tell them that their mission is to preserve and protect their cultural heritage and traditions for themselves and their posterity. Even if this were considered an important experiment, it would be difficult to find a country willing to undergo such a dislocation. Social scientists do not have the power to force nations to undergo this experiment.

The closest approximation we have to an experiment on the hypothetical benefits of multiculturalism is being run today in the Western world. If it is a failure, we risk taking a serious hit as a civilization in one or many of the ways the variables considered above suggest. If this experiment results in internal strife Western values will be quickly compromised. Culturists realize that our values are not eternal, the universal default, nor universally applauded. Diversity is real. Were our civilization to disappear much of the bulwark against oppressive culturism would be gone. Large increases in theocracy, oppression, exploitation and brutality would undoubtedly occur. Recognizing the unique value of their cultures, Asian and Islamic countries are very strict in their culturist maintenance of homogeneity. Common sense tells them that their national security depends upon it. We need to monitor the indicators previously delineated and consciously check the results of our multicultural experiment. Otherwise we might be running our unique civilization into the ground just to teach other civilizations what they already assume.

At the very least this investigation has conclusively shown that multiculturalism and domestic diversity are not unequivocally good. We are therefore forced into a cost-benefit analysis. A sophisticated cost-benefit analysis requires that we do not look at either culturism or multiculturalism as a single variable. We must monitor multiple variables. This chapter has sought to outline what some of these variables might be. Crime, literacy levels, teen pregnancy, wealth disparity, and rates of health insurance provide other criteria to measure. Multiculturalists tend to see a single variable, diversity, as an absolute that deserves a nearly religious devotion. We must take a more scientific approach. We must independently measure several indicators when considering whether or not increasing and emphasizing domestic diversity, or the reverse, is strengthening or weakening the viability of our unique culture.

Many answers to social scientific questions cannot be conclusively arrived at. The choice of one policy or another is often argued merely on the basis of personal preference, and sometimes no more evidence than that can be presented. The choice between culturism and multiculturalism is not one of these situations. Ultimately, the preference for taking a culturist stance is based on the advantages it has in making Western civilization more stable. Civil unrest is almost always predicated on cultural diversity. The potential benefits of culturism greatly outweigh the potential harms. Multiculturalism's potential gains do not justify risking the peace and viability a culturist orientation can bring. At the very least, if one deems that the attributions of the outcomes detailed above to one column or another are incorrect, one has a duty to measure and keep track of sources of civic harmony and discord. And if the evidence shows that we are fighting over our differences, we should switch to a culturist approach and emphasize our similarities.

CHAPTER TEN

CULTURIST POLICY IMPLICATIONS

Universal Declaration of Cultural Rights

The United Nations adopted the Universal Declaration of Human Rights (U.D.H.R.) on December 10th, 1948. This document marks the pinnacle of Western power and perfectly exemplifies the tendencies that undermine us. When this document was adopted we had just won World War II. We were powerful. As such we decided that the Western model was the model for the entire world for all times (indeed, as the title suggests, the entire universe). The U.D.H.R. states that, "Everyone is entitled to all the rights and freedoms set forth in this Declaration, without distinction of any kind, such as race, colour, sex, language, religion, political or other opinion, national or social origin, property, birth or other status."[296] It requires nations to disregard all of the spiritual qualities that go into making a culture. Fittingly, this document that claims to be "universal" presents an affront to cultural distinctions and choices.

Lists in which we resolve to be blind are so familiar to Westerners that they do not shock us. Consider it from an Islamic perspective. The idea of not discriminating based on religion is anathema to any monotheistic religion. It is completely corrosive to a tradition based on the unity of church and state. For Asian countries to not discriminate based on race is to attack their very sense of purpose. This is clearly a not an Islamic or Asian document. Being "universal" the U.D.H.R even corrodes Western sovereignty. In a diverse world, not being able to discriminate based on religion, political or other opinions, any status or language, incapacitates the nation's ability to define and defend itself to a dangerous degree. We must realize that not everyone is a Westerner. Only the West believes and supports Western values. Only the West really takes the U.D.H.R. seriously.

As shocking as it was that the delegates were so ignorant as to think that Islamic and Asian nations would just throw out their right to guide their cultures, this ignorance was surpassed by their ignorance of economics. It a state of utopian delusion the delegates conjured lists of worldwide unfunded mandates. "Everyone has the right to a standard of living adequate for the health and well-being of himself and of his family, including food, clothing, housing and medical care and necessary social services, and the right to security in the event of unemployment, sickness, disability, widowhood, old age or other lack of livelihood in circumstances beyond his control." Even the most economically successful societies would have trouble providing this level of entitlements.

Tellingly copying from the very Western American Declaration of Independence it says that these rights are "inalienable."[297] The government is to provide this cradle to grave social safety net without regard to merit. If a culture were successful enough to be able to provide all of these guarantees, a mandate saying no one has to work to enjoy a fine quality of life would undermine it. We must realize that there are no such things as inalienable rights. Even though this is sad, it is true. If your country does not have money, your rights to education, housing, medicine and food are not worth the paper the declaration announcing them is printed upon. Purchasing most of the "rights" enumerated requires a functioning first-world economy.

Recognizing the limitations of this document we need to replace it with a Universal Declaration of Cultural Rights (U.D.C.R.). We need to realize that not all cultures think that universal individual rights are an economically, socially, psychologically and philosophically sustainable premise for society building. Countries have a right and duty to enforce their borders, language, holidays, arts, codes of honor, concepts of an appropriate education, penal codes, military conscription patterns, social programs, and trade agreements as may befit their concept of emotional and physical collective well-being.

No outside agency has a right to intervene in the inner workings of other cultures. Just because we chose not to discriminate due to race does not mean that China must not. We should not. But they are a different country and culture. Our belief that Islamic nations should not discriminate based on religion is not their belief. Their internal sovereignty needs to be recognized. We also have a right to define ourselves and to act on our own behalf. Cultures have rights.

It is only being suggested that the word "universal" be kept in the U.D.C.R. to make it clear which document it is superseding. The West needs this revised document more than other cultures. Other cultures know that they have the right and duty to protect and define themselves. Western countries are the only ones that seriously buy into the notion that inalienable international individual rights supersede the requirements of the culture. Islamic countries have long asserted their right to chop hands off of thieves and kill non-believers. Asian countries do not grant people of other races citizenship. If you asserted your right to wave an American flag in Mexico you would find out that rights are not universally protected. Acknowledging these realities would help us realize that rights and individual sovereignty are particular to us. If we believe in individual rights and democracy we need to promote them in our country. Calling them universal does not secure them, because they are not universal.

The West's not adopting the premises of the U.D.C.R., in principle or reality, endangers us. The idea that our culture has no right to define itself has resulted in our becoming increasingly fragmented and abused. In competition, a team that is consciously fighting for their glory under the direction of a coach can work as a team and be victorious. A team in which all the players demand their right to defy the coach and play regardless of how many practices they miss or their dedication to the team cannot win. And this is no game. The designers of the U.D.H.R. assumed that diversity did not exist. They assumed that every culture's goal was to enforce equality and individual rights. We can no longer afford to be so naïve. The other teams are already playing by the rules of the U.D.C.R. If we do not recognize that there are teams we will likely go down in defeat.

Policy guidelines

Western culturist understandings have been advocated throughout this book. Fundamental to this vision has been the recognition that Western culture is unique and delicate. We have read about the importance of knowing the difference between liberty and license. We have seen that our cultural heritage can supply standards, values, meaning, and role models. Our traditional narrative of struggling towards freedom and esteeming attributes of the soul over those of the body were shown to be essential to our values. Anthropology showed us not all cultures are progressive. We learned that evolutionary group selection pressures explain why we are born ready to absorb cultures. And psychology showed us that groups will define themselves if we fail to provide definitions for them. We learned that the philosophers' weighing the limits of our culturist policies give them a more meaningful role than a reliance on absolute universal rights can. Finally, we saw that culturism provides a balance, not a replacement, for multiculturalism. The use of the term "culturism" has been advocated in all chapters as a mechanism by which we can easily reinforce these cultural understandings.

Specific policies have also been advocated. As cultural improvement movements and creating social organizations have been staples of our culturist past, reinvigorating these traditions was advocated. Immigration laws and guiding public airwaves are not alien to the American way; we should always use these tools. In passing, buying goods from your own country was advocated. Having a Department of Culture to commission and coordinate public art and celebrations of our culture was suggested. Refusing to allow Muslim countries to invest in Western countries for non-fiscal purposes was a more controversial suggestion. Note that this suggestion is controversial if judged in terms of absolute universal rights. But, we need to recognize that other countries restrict Christian proselytizing. Even if it is not in line with universalistic philosophy, governmental advocacy for the health and propagation of our culture is in line with universal practice. Adopting a Universal Declaration of Cultural Rights would highlight and legitimize this function for Western nations. Even so, even minor acts of domestic advocacy and control are problematic for Americans.

Western culture, generally, will have a more difficult time devising appropriate culturist measures than other countries. Other countries can totally override the desires of individuals without compromising their cultural integrity. Muslim's can advocate stern measures against those who transgress against their moral codes without being called hypocrites. Upholding Western cultural traditions requires that individuals have a large sphere of personal liberties. Instituting authoritarianism would constitute treason to our Founding Fathers. China has strict censorship of all media. Insisting on respect and social hierarchy in all of its forms reinforces their culture. Pride in the fact that we allow dissent and protest constitutes on of our most ancient traditions. Stifling political debate in the West would be like condemning Socrates again. Our culturist policies must secure the blessings of liberty for ourselves and our posterity without unduly infringing upon our choices. Here, again, understanding the difference between liberty and license is crucial. But our choices will all involve problematic tradeoffs.

Western culturism also requires dedicated thoughtfulness because we are working in a progressive tradition. We are not trying to go back to a golden age. We are creating a tomorrow that is defined by change. This shows, again, why pragmatism is more appropriate for us than universal abstractions. Peacetime and wartime require different sorts of cultural choices. If we are in an economic slump and competing with a rising fascist power, our culturism will need to be more heavy-handed than it would be during times of peaceful economic thriving. During times in which customs have failed to create an atmosphere of respect and self-control, law must be asserted with more force than usual. We should always have our eye on the ideal of an advancing self-governing republic. Our goals thus have a thematic core, but we cannot simply implement a static model based on a golden age. Devising culturally appropriate culturist policy will forever require astute social scientists who are intimately acquainted with Western traditions and ideals.

The Supreme Court's debates about the Pledge of Allegiance provide an interesting insight into the sort of thinking that needs to happen. In the first Pledge of Allegiance case Justice Felix Frankfurter said the school system had a right to expel Jehovah's Witness children who refused to participate in the Pledge of Allegiance because "[National cohesion is] an interest second to none in the hierarchy of legal values. National unity is the basis of national security." In a beautiful encapsulation of culturist thought Frankfurter said that "[Cohesive sentiment] is fostered by all those agencies of the mind and spirit which may serve to gather up the traditions of a people, transmit them from generation to generation, and thereby create that continuity of a treasured common life which constitutes a civilization." [298] Thus the Court recognized culturist considerations as legitimate concerns.

Just three years later the Supreme Court reversed its Pledge of Allegiance ruling. That this case was revisited so quickly reflects not only the harassment that the Jehovah's were receiving from the patriotic students, but the difficulty of deciding such issues in a tradition such as ours. Justices Hugo Black and William O. Douglas' ruling still rested on creating love of our country. They wrote "Love of country must spring from willing hearts and free minds, inspired by a fair administration of wise laws . . ."[299] And they were culturally astute enough to recognize that the occasion of this ruling necessitated reaffirming that freedom of speech was not absolute. They wrote, "No well-ordered society can leave to the individuals an absolute right to make final decisions, unassailable by the State, as to everything they will or will not do." Frankfurter still held to his decision because the Founding Fathers' were clear in noting that the State legislatures, not the courts, should determine community policy in a democracy. But this was typically Western in that the decision was a judgment call addressing pragmatic concerns based on our traditions, current events and the perpetuation of our culture. Western culturism does not always provide clear answers.

With these guidelines, Western culturism does require that three overriding principles be adhered to. First, culturism must prioritize the viability of Western cultures' viability as an overriding value. Cultural health constitutes a valid interest that deserves consideration in policy decisions. The long history of the Court upholding regulations of speech during wartime confirms this value's validity and legality. But even outside of such extreme situations, cultural and economic viability are necessary for securing the blessings of liberty to our posterity. If Western civilization gets undermined our ideals will not exist without us. Secondly, this goal must be met, to the extent practicable, without violating the Western world's traditional respect for individual conscience. Lastly, when restrictions are made they must be understood to be of a temporary nature that reflects current situations. Western culturism affirms historical change. Any controversial decisions will be implemented with the hope of securing a return to an approximation of greater liberty on a sounder footing. Not advocating absolutes gives culturism flexibility to meet new challenges that absolutist conceptions rights and individualism do not.

Having a culturist perspective provides a better grounding for policy than just observing rights. For example, there are currently stories considering the right of Mormons to have polygamous marriages. They are getting positive press based on the fact that they are relatively well-adjusted people. When only looking at them, the government's position seems irrational. We must, however, take a broad cultural look at such propositions. It may be the case that religiously grounded people can have stable and supportive polygamous families. What will happen when pimps are allowed to marry all of their prostitutes? What will happen to the view of women in general when bad men are allowed to accumulate them? Outside of the particular Mormon families involved, what would such a ruling do to our collective sense of unity? Would legitimizing polygamy not be destabilizing for many non-Mormon communities? Only using individual rights as our basis of decision-making undermines our ability to consider larger cultural dynamics and collective self-definition. Culturist decision-making takes the overall health of the culture into account.

With these disclaimers and guidelines out in the open it must be recalled that culturism is a value system. All assertions of values involve preferring some things to others. By definition preferring some values means not esteeming or permitting others. Some of the options suggested will come closer to violating our traditions than others. None will suggest anything that would be controversial in non-Western cultures. We should take pride in recognizing that our instinctual discomfort with some suggestions stems from a wonderful tradition. We must not respond to suggestions with objections based upon universal assertions. The existence of cultural rights means that we have discretion in how we interpret our tradition and guide our future. We can have self-governance. In the end, if the West falls, the entire discussion about rights will come to an end. Some policy suggestions could only be legitimated in the West by extreme cultural situations. Hopefully, the disagreement will be over the tactics, not the goal. The West must survive and thrive as an island of liberty.

Culturist foreign policy

History has not ended. Western values of rights and free enterprise triumphed over the Soviet Union's version of communism. But economic disparity and Marx's name still haunt the world. Demagogues still lurk. Rival cultural models thrive. Consumer oriented capitalism is not now the undisputed default of the world. History has not provided any examples of any universal guarantees. We can still degenerate into civil chaos. Islam and Asia have not decided to become focused on the universal and decontextualized nature of individual rights. Asia's' economies are ascendant and Islam has commenced its first major attacks on the West since 1492. Diverse players are still advocating, as they should, for their models of life. Unfortunately, they are advocating for their models' expansion. Those who see the world becoming one always expect a future of unity based on Western ideals being accepted by others. This reveals arrogant hubris. History shows that systems are always bucking for ascendancy and that eternal cultural vigilance will continue to be the price of continuing the existence of Western style liberties.

For the most part culturist foreign policy would be, by definition, isolationist. Culturism is concerned with the health of cultures. Violating other's territory undermines their cultures. In realpolitik terms, cultural survival depends on territory. Again, culture exists in heads and heads require food and a place to live. Western civilization is dominant on 24.2 percent of the occupied land mass of the world.[300] Islam reigns as the official and dominant religion in 21.1 percent of the world's land mass. Asia controls around 8 percent of the world's land mass. Land is a measure of vulnerability to disappearance. If the Indians lost India, Hinduism would be over. If Japan were destroyed, Asian values would persist on the Chinese mainland and in Korea.

But Asia's bid for autonomy and hegemony would be set back. The United States constitutes approximately 27 percent of Western territory. These figures noted, culturist control a territory only happens when the locals adhere to your values. "Controlling" an area where no one believes in your values does you no good. Culturism is not metaphysical. Our culture only exists where the institutions and people's that hold to it exist.

Cultures that occupy very small niches are more vulnerable to extinctions than those that occupy vast geographical regions. Europe being surrounded by an expansive Islamic culture presents a cause for concern. But trying to export our culture shows that we sill have not learned the culturist lessons of history. The English were not able to turn Africa into an extension of England. Psychological studies recently documenting cultural differences in thought imply that, " . . . efforts to improve international understanding may be less likely to pay off than one might hope."[301] We may be able to take over other areas militarily, but transplanting our institutions, changing values and creating cultural amity is a long shot. Besides, the U.D.C.R. mandates respecting other cultures' rights. We can encourage others to appreciate and enjoy our cultural products and ways. But, war designed to export our culture fails to respect the rights of others. Violating sovereignty creates a precedent that weakens our own. Recognizing other's sovereignty and strengthening our own culture provides the best policy for ensuring peace and the stability of our institutions.

Our culturist monies and energies should bolster regions that are already Western. The amount of support we give foreign nations should reflect our degree of cultural relatedness to them. If Australia is fighting Indonesia we should, all else being equal, support Australia. They are our cultural siblings on our cultural family tree. Great Britain being the mother country of both of us shows we are related. But this assertion relies on more than historical coincidences. It reflects similarities of long-standing values. We both have stable long-term democracies that separate church and state. We have an uncorrupted independent judiciary, deplore terror, and give our citizens relatively extreme amounts of liberties. Continuity born of our not having had violent transfers of power bolsters the claim of continuity back to our paternity. Our culture can sleep easier knowing that we have a big friend out in the Pacific Ocean. Thinking of Indonesia's largely Muslim population with their tradition of authoritarianism and rights violations thriving does not provide as great a source of calm.

The same culturist principle applies to trade. Western culture is bolstered by a strong Europe. We are not strengthened by a strong Iran. It is in our cultural interest to favor European nations. This is not racist. It is culturist common sense. Giving Muslim nations such as Pakistan and Palestine money does nothing for us. When considering foreign aid we must ask, "What is in such assistance for the West?" Why do we fund Palestinians? Beyond a possible détente with Israel, their stability has nothing to do with the Western tradition. Are Pakistani's our friends? We must be ready to put culturist considerations on par with economic ones. Muslim nations are angry that they had to cede a tiny portion of their dominion to a non-Islamic nation (Israel). We should learn from that. We are aiding those dedicated to lessening the influence of Western civilization. If you reply that we aid Muslim countries out of solidarity with humanity, you do not understand culturism. Of course we should get food to starving people. But the long-term sustainability of the Palestinians is a Muslim affair. Their rightful indignation at our interference in their lands rightfully implies that they are responsible for their own lands and peoples.

The blindness induced by our adopting universalism can harm us. Culture exists. Dubai should not be considered as indistinguishable from rights loving Western nations. When we put out bids to run our ports and borders, economic considerations should be trumped by security considerations. This is not racism. It is recognizing the actual strength of ideology and thought in human beings and culture. It is culturism. Non-Westerners who claim distinctions based on any basis violates universal rights are being hypocritical. Asian countries do not let non-Asians become citizens; we do not need to be impartial when deciding whether or not to do business with them. All cultures and nations make decisions based on their own self-interest; we are entitled to do the same. We cannot be the only culture not taking sides via reasonable cultural distinctions. This should hardly be controversial.

Domestically we have a strong tradition of not discriminating. We should only use culturist discrimination domestically with extreme caution. However, there are times and situations when domestic culturist discrimination is reasonable. Prohibiting recent Muslim immigrants working airline security recognizes the influence of culture on thoughts and action. This is not racism; it is culturism. Discriminating against Muslims who seek to work in banks would violate our domestic traditions for no apparent reason. Discriminating without reason violates our traditions gratuitously and does not bolster them. It would create justified resentment. When considering domestic culturist discrimination it should be controversial. But absolute rights based models that will not allow any distinctions may not be sustainable. Culturist pragmatism increases our flexibility, allows intelligent and rational decisions to be made, and should be employed in domestic security policy. But while discriminating domestically should be controversial, discriminating internationally should not be.

Protecting the integrity of Western territory should be a priority for Western nations. NATO being reconstituted on culturist lines would give it a relevant reason for existing. A recognition of shared our histories and value systems would be the basis for our cooperation. Having a mission statement based upon cultural commonality would boost cultural awareness. Nothing invigorates a culture like a shared sense of identity, a border, and having others defined as outsiders. Nothing more deflates a culture than their lack of these. Confusing our culturally contingent values for universal standards is dangerous. In the former Yugoslavia, NATO defended Muslims against Christians. This was the right thing to do by Western standards and, since it was in the Western zone of influence, might have been the right action. But this action should not have been undertaken in the name of universal rights.

We must recognize that cultures are in tension and compete. When some Europeans argue that it is racist to bar Turkey from the European Economic Union (EEU), they are assuming that cultures are not different. They hold that Western ideals create universal rights that bar discrimination on any basis internationally. Racism is a stupid reason to discriminate. Culturist discrimination is, and has always been, the operating principle of foreign policy. Naiveté about competition between cultures and diversity is astounding and dangerous. Muslim countries would not and should not allow secularists and Christians to flood their territories. We are under no universal obligation to do the reverse. We must not allow Turkey into the EEU.

If there is a civil war in a non-Western nation it is not necessarily our concern. There is no universal claim on us. This is especially true if it gets us in the middle of another cultural block's conflict. Our interventions will likely create resentment. Our indifference will send a message to the world that we have finally grown up. As Western adults, we are taking care of ourselves and expect others to do the same. That said, when such events happen we are not automatically responsible for the resulting political refugees. These people might not make good American citizens. They are likely traumatized illiterate militants. We do not send political refugees abroad because we take care of ourselves. Just as we have no universal right to citizenship in other nations; foreigners have no universal right to citizenship in ours. Asian and Islamic nations do not give carte blanche rights of immigration to foreign victims of strife because they are, rightfully, concerned with their own stability.

We take all refugees because we think that our standards and responsibilities are universal. Our taking refugees of political oppression without regard to reason for their oppression, loyalties, culture, level of education, etc., when no one else does puts us at an unfair disadvantage. Our recognizing that our values do not extent across the globe does not weaken, compromise or threaten our domestic values. Basing our policy on universal presuppositions does. Ultimately, making sure we survive will strengthen progressive values internationally, but we should not be overly concerned with that. Even if you believe that we have a moral obligation to change people to our way of life, if we do not take care of ourselves first we will not be able to undertake such a mission. Diversity and competition currently exist. If we do not prioritize our strength and survival, no other countries will.

Multiculturalism and Security

A "cleft nation" is one that has two culturally different populations within a single country. History shows us that when a minority reaches a significant percentage of he population and is concentrated in one area, the potential for civic strife grows. World War I was started by the presence of a large Serbian minority in the Austria-Hungarian territory. The leader of Austria-Hungary, Archduke Ferdinand, took a tour of the Serbian majority area to show that his government was still in charge. Serbian nationalists killed him to show that they controlled the area in which they predominated and, incidentally, started World War I. Nearly all wars in history have been between different cultural groups. History provides sounder grounding for culturist policies than declarations about universal brotherhood or other metaphysical wishes. War happens. Familiarity with history can familiarize us with cultural dynamics so that we need not repeat the obvious mistakes of the past.

Cultural ideology, history and geography are real and important factors in maintaining peace. There having been a war between Mexico and the United States increases our potential for animosity and intercultural violence. This, again, is not racism, it is culturism. History does not get swept away by enlightenment principles; animosities linger. Our proximity makes our situation much like that of the Austria-Hungarians and the Serbians. Organizations based on reclaiming the Southwestern United States for Mexico are widespread in the United States.[302] This agenda has only been embraced by a small number of those of Mexican descent. Yet, shootings of a Mexican by an Anglo or vice versa could quickly galvanize sides. Because the population is so evenly divided in the Southwest, battles between the cultural groups would create huge amounts of instability in the Western world. We cannot afford to be ignorant of cultural memories.

One tactic for reducing tensions would be to lower immigration levels so that people have time to assimilate to the linguistic and cultural mores of America. We also need to cultivate a feeling of unity and do everything we can do to minimize distinctions between Americans of Mexican descent. World War I showed us how quickly small acts of violence can turn into general warfare. We need to make sure that hate rhetoric is confronted. It should be repeated often that most Mexican immigrants love the United States. Sherif's experiments at Robbers Cave showed that collective goals unite people. Again, one would hope that declaring love for, and wanting the best for, America would unite everyone on our soil. Division endangers nations. Unity can provide a great feeling of solidarity and protection against unrest.

Historical animosity provides the justification for many wars. Muslims and Christians have been hostile combatants for nearly 1400 years. It should be obvious to anyone who has seen a newspaper in the last year that this animosity has not magically disappeared. History has not ended. Historic cultural animosities do not die easily. For this reason accumulating centers of Muslim population in Western nations undermines our safety as well as our unity. Remember that they do not freely welcome us into their countries. In a poll of English Muslims, 31% agreed with the statement, "Western society is decadent and immoral, and Muslims should seek to bring it to an end, but only by non-violent means."[303] Only a small percentage said Western civilization should be brought down by violent means. But even a small percentage of a large number provides a cause for concern. We have seen in New York, London, Madrid, and Moscow that only a few disgruntled people need take Islamic ideology seriously for terrorism to erupt. An ongoing series of terrorist incidents could, of course, precipitate a destabilizing of civic order. Losses of traditional Western liberties would necessarily follow.

Civil liberties lost in the Western world would not be metaphysically guaranteed in other parts of the globe. The riots over Danish cartoons across the Muslim world and the brutal murder of the Dutch filmmaker Theo Van Gogh in order to stifle free speech have shown that the separation of church and state may not be able to co-exist with a large Islamic population. Muslims rioted for around twenty days in France in 2006. Many newspapers prefer to treat the Muslim identities of rioting youth as incidental. Nevertheless, if inhabitants of the larger Muslim world think their European brethren are being mistreated it could initiate inter-civilization war. When choosing between a foreign individual's desire to move into our nations and Western culture's stability our course should be clear; protecting Western civilization can and must be the priority.

The Western commitment to cultural neutrality will continue to be exploited until we realize that diversity exists. Remember that Muslims do not believe in freedom of speech. Other cultures do not have the concept of Jihad. Those who mention such diversity are derided as racist. Raising the red herring of racism is tantamount to asserting that terrorist tendencies have been encoded in certain people's DNA. No sane person holds such a position. Culturism recognizes that cultures do not advocate the same values and that ideas have consequences. Recognizing diversity and its importance is not racist; it is culturist.

You will often hear the claim that embracing diversity is inevitable in our shrinking, global world. This statement may be true in regards to goods and money, but not in regards to peoples and cultures. Islamic countries have not decided to allow religious diversity. You cannot live in such countries unless you are united in sympathy and custom with the dominant culture. Many Asian countries do not allow people of other racial categories to be citizens of their nations. In fact, the only countries significantly increasing their cultural diversity are the Western nations. Diversity runs contrary to other nations' culturist missions and they know it would likely to diminish civic harmony. The statement that the whole world is diversifying is another example of the Western Nations' conflation of the West and universalism. The West is diversifying because it thinks people have universal rights to move; other cultures are not diversifying. We have seen that diversity is not necessarily a virtue. Our being the only culture diversifying has potential dangers.

Citizenship

American immigration policies should always respond to the question, "What is good for America?" Those who do not recognize or respect diversity are too quick to dismiss this question. Current descriptions of citizenship focus on legalistic concerns that ignore culture. But being a good Western citizen requires that you root for our perpetuation. If we grant a person who hates Western civilization citizenship, they do not automatically become internally transformed. Regardless of their legal status, one who roots against America cannot be properly said to be an American. Love of

America cannot be assumed. Beyond ideological concerns, being a good American requires skills. Those who have never been to school will not automatically be able to figure out IRS forms and grasp the importance of education in our culture. Someone whose first act in entering our country involves breaking our laws will not automatically be concerned with the protection of our laws the next minute. Citizenship, in a meaningful sense, cannot be granted by a bureaucracy. Good citizenship is a matter of the head and heart. This is something that our traditional immigration laws understood.

As with every other nation on earth, when considering admitting people into our country we need to ask, "What are our interests in this transaction?" We must be willing to ask, "What are the potential costs of letting seven hundred more Muslims into our country and what are the potential benefits?" Here again the pragmatic method provides a nice guide for this sort of policy. We can monitor the now nearly steady occurrence of attempted terrorist attacks by Muslims. Our 1924 immigration exclusion experience shows that not replenishing old world communities increases assimilation. As people assimilate and attempted attacks go down, we might consider letting in more Muslims.

People might decry this as "Islamophobia." As with the word racism, Islamophobia is meant to undermine discussion. Here the term culturism can remind us that culture and race are very different. Islamic people come in all races. If the attacks stop, we need no longer exclude Muslims. Were Chinese or European immigrants to commit acts of terrorism, culturist pragmatism would argue that they start being excluded. Moreover, phobias are unwarranted fears. This is not an irrational fear or methodology. Fear of terrorism is not irrational; a particular group's rates of healthcare, educational attainment, crime, literacy, teen pregnancy, terrorism, and homeownership can be measured. It is not based upon irrationality or even speculation. Invoking racism and Islamophobia is meant to undermine rational discourse. Culturist pragmatism provides a measurable, flexible, realistic, rational, and prudent policy formation approach.

We are not under any universal rights-based obligation to admit people. Currently our laws prioritize family reunification as a reason to accept new immigrants and America gets painted as evil when families are torn asunder. When you move to another country there are costs. One of which involves splitting your family. Laws and views which assume a lack of consequences for your actions should alert one to a lack of realism and their having a basis in the destructive concept of universal rights. We need to amend the family reunification statutes in recognition of their effects on us. All laws are experiments, not eternal guarantees. If family reunification needs to happen, it can happen in the person's country of origin. We are under no moral obligation to provide a venue.

It is helpful to analogize your country to your home. You are under no obligation to ask people into your home. People have no right to be there. You are not only allowed to ask questions about who enters your home, you should do so. We should do everything we can to keep criminals out of our homes. Those who have useful skills might be welcome at certain times to do certain jobs. They do not thereby gain a right to stay in my home, move their family in, and have healthcare at my expense. I need not adopt my plumber. This goes doubly if you break into my home and fix my plumbing. Even if you assert that I asked you to come into my home and fix my plumbing, you still do not thereby gain a right to live in my home. Even if you were my maid for 20 years, you do not gain a right to live in my home. And, this is no mere analogy. When someone comes into our country they are living in the same space as our children and loved ones. Accepting someone as a citizen means letting them live in your home.

Physical safety provides the most urgent reason to question what we might gain and lose by letting people into our home or country. We cannot doubt that most Muslim immigrants will not commit acts of terror. Yet having many good Muslims in our country (nearly always unwittingly) provides cover for the dangerous ones. Muslim immigration has certainly made us less safe and united. Appreciating this should make patriotic Muslims willing to accept higher than normal levels of scrutiny. We must earn that trust by not suspecting citizens without cause; injustice creates hostility and all citizens have rights. But rights *always* exist within a context. The Muslim presence in America has already compromised our rights by justifying the Patriot Act. We cannot let metaphysical conceptions of rights be used to incapacitate our ability to protect ourselves in our own home.

We must be clear that people who are not citizens of our country have no rights here. Just as we do not let the entire world vote in our elections, the entire world does not have a right to enter our nation. Asian countries use racial criteria to restrict citizenship. Muslim countries exclude non-believers. They are not wrong in doing so. Cultures have the right to define and defend themselves. Our saying you may not enter our country does not violate your rights as an American unless you are one. Were we to never allow another foreign national to apply for citizenship again, it would not violate anyone's rights. No one who is not a citizen of our country has a right to be in it. We must not feel like we are especially evil for violating universal or individual rights when creating immigration policies that put our stability first. Your neighbor has no right to be in your home, just as you have no right to be in his. We are only responsible for upholding the rights of our citizens.

The Statue of Liberty being associated with Ellis Island shows that restricted immigration is part of the American tradition. Given the historical situation, our 1924 immigration law might have been correct in discriminating against Eastern Europeans. Several Western countries in that period suffered from tremendously destabilizing attempted communist revolutions. Russia had one. Geopolitical realities have changed. Russian immigrants currently agitating for communist revolution cannot be taken seriously as a concern. However, the need to consider cultural affinity for Western values and the ability to assimilate when designing immigration policies has not changed. We must live up to our historic duties.

Though racism is evil, culturism is necessary. We must be allowed to ask if non-English speaking peoples who come from cultures that condone honor killings and keep their wives secluded are as likely to assimilate as well as Australians. Preferring Australians reflects culturism not racism. Culturism gives us a rational cultural basis upon which to discriminate. We should prefer those from countries that value education, are not passionate foreign nationalists, do not abuse their wives, favor the downfall of Western civilization, impregnate children or drink too much. Note that none of my criteria listed above refer to race. Race would be a stupid criterion by which to choose who can become a part of our multiethnic nation. Trying to avoid racism should not incapacitate our ability to make reasonable culturist distinctions. Ignorance and intelligence are not synonymous.

Fortunately, we have a long tradition of assimilation techniques to consider. The previously discussed Americanization movement was a multifaceted program which supported and protected immigrants so that they might be attached to America. Protection from exploitation was provided due to the realization that abuse creates hatred. English and Civics classes were provided because people are generally grateful to countries that provide opportunities and we wanted recent arrivals to pass the naturalization tests. Public ceremonies and parades welcomed legal immigrants and allowed them to show their love of their adopted homeland. At its best Americanization meant mutual admiration between the nation and immigrants; immigrants appreciated America and America appreciated its immigrants. Such culturist efforts at assimilation recognized that citizenry cannot be defined by legal status alone; cultural bonds are psychological.

In a country that lacks a religious, tribal or racial commonality, unity is precarious. Our immigration laws have traditionally been designed to lessen division and help us become, in the name of our national motto, "E Pluribus Unum" (out of many one). Since 1795 those who have become citizens legally pledge " . . . to renounce and abjure absolutely and entirely all allegiance and fidelity to any foreign prince, potentate, state, or sovereignty of whom or which the applicant was before a subject or citizen;"[304] Recognizing that citizenship means more than a legal status, becoming a citizen has always required that you show proficiency in verbal and written English and have a basic grasp of our history. Historical situations do not always demand that we strictly enforce such requirements. But our providing educational opportunities, holding celebrations, and strictly curtailing immigration in 1924 led to affective assimilation by 1940. We may not need to be as sharp as they were in 1924. But, our recent huge tensions over immigration show we need to take citizenship dynamics seriously again.

We need to recognize that we destroy the meaning of the word citizen when we only consider it a bureaucratic matter and ignore skill based and emotional components. Citizenship policy must recognize the psychological needs of holding together a nation as well as the needs of individuals. Dual citizenship, especially between neighboring countries, creates a conflict of loyalty. It is not clear which country you want to benefit when you vote. That is why our laws stress giving up old world affiliation before being considered a citizen. We should ask people who lied under oath when swearing loyalty to choose one nation or another. Limiting the amount of money that could be sent abroad and pegging it to your State's level of debt would be economically sound, encourage investment in our country, and teach people to consider our nation's well being. Proficiency in English is required to legally naturalize. While limited English proficiency might be alright for guest workers, naturalization should not be considered valid without it. Efforts to learn English should be celebrated and supported. People respect countries that respect themselves. If we do not take our citizenship seriously we should not expect immigrants to do so.

Ignoring immigration laws often gets justified on an economic basis. It is virtually argued that we need to get rid of our citizenship laws in order to have cheap labor. And while a business sector might benefit from cheap labor, it should be remembered that some cultural traits are generally incompatible with a first-world economy. Small families and high education levels are the common denominators of first-world economies. Illegal immigrant labor is cheap because no taxes are involved. Poor government income-to-population ratios undermine the infrastructures and educational systems that are also prerequisites for, and define, first-world economies. Importing large amounts of cheap labor undercuts legal citizens' income and inevitably results in an underclass. When this underclass and poor tax revenues combine, social services such as hospitals and schools are undercut and economic disparities increase. In countries with large levels of poverty businesses get nationalized. This happens because poverty fosters demagogues. Our having a large middle-class has been often credited with our unusual stability. In a world where terrorism is a constant threat, having open borders does not make economic sense. Even overseas businesses would take a big hit if America became destabilized. Businesses should realize that their best interest lies in a stable America.

Businesses contribute to America. But they also must show

concern with the fate of the nation that birthed and sustains them. As citizens, they should know that rights cannot be maintained without responsibilities. Actions showing concern for America speak louder than words. Businesses that routinely send jobs and monies outside of the United States need to be reminded that the government has the power to revoke their charters and business licenses. When enforcing naturalization and immigration policies we should never forget that we are impacting emotional and complex peoples who will not be loyal if abused. We do not need to be as sensitive with businesses. Like immigrants, businesses should know that citizenship involves caring and working for our national success. As with individuals and communities, discussions with businesses should seek harmony by asking them to realize that what benefits America also benefits them. They should be made to see that being patriotic does not preclude them from being self-interested. But, not being psychologically sensitive, law-breaking and exploitative businesses can be dealt with strictly and with little equivocation if they abuse the cultural and financial underpinnings of our nation.

Public values

Marjorie Heins, in her extremely well-researched book on censorship, worries about the right of young people to access information being violated by censors.[305] She, again, is not alone in her focus on an individual rights-based interpretation of reality. Asserting the right of youth to get no guidance from society takes the concept of rights out of context. In a context where youth crime, drugs and depression as well as teen pregnancy are at historically high levels advocating for more license is inappropriate. Society must distinguish between liberty and license to survive. Our youth are being outscored in every category of academic achievement. Education is a key factor in successful economies. Cultural influence facilitates scholastic and economic success. Rights result from an ability to buy them. Advocating for abstract rights when our youth are foundering and being outperformed internationally not only overlooks the basis of individual mental health, it overlooks the cultural and economic basis of rights. Reverence for abstracted and absolute rights can cause us to look the other way while our children are being led into some pretty dark corners.

Shame having a physical manifestation (blushing and aversion of the eyes) and existing in all cultures indicates that it serves an important evolutionary function. Shame is a biological mechanism by which cultures guide behavior and values. James Twitchell has documented that television has undermined our traditional understanding of what deserves shame. For television to get viewers it must make you feel good, not bad. Therefore, fun predominates and negative consequences get hidden. We see sex, but no STDs or pregnancy. Being hardwired to love gossip we love dirt. Television has discovered this biological predisposition. When shame has no negative ramifications what used to bring you only shame can now also bring you fame. The more horrible a person's behavior, the more likely it is to get televised. Shunning was a traditional response to transgressors. The person had to apologize to re-enter society. Awarding celebrity to criminals and moral abominations runs counter to cultural mental health. It promotes dangerous and anti-social behavior.

The excesses of our public culture have their deep roots in the separation of church and state. This separation has made us the first culture not officially guided by moral exemplars of some sort. The separation was thought to be radical when it was first proposed. Many had little faith that people without religious guidance would be good. They feared that without church guidance people would not be able to tell liberty from license. Immediate gratification would undermine the morals that lead to economic sustainability. The lust for power would undermine our political leaders' integrity. Man's natural inclination towards depravity would undermine our new and radical experiment in self-governance. These concerns lay behind our long history of public moral crusades. In retrospect, separating religion and government was a great decision. Theocracies rank amongst our strongest competitors. The term, theocracy, deserves its negative connotation. The separation was not, however, intended to justify the separation of morals and government. From the Puritans to the modern FCC, the government has traditionally considered the regulation of public space an important part of its duties.

The Supreme Court has affirmed the right of governments to have "adult movie theaters" zoned away from schools and residential areas.

Advertising for strip clubs used to be regulated and broadcasting pornography has also been regulated. This power validates the moral duty and right of the government to safeguard the right of families to raise their children in wholesome environments. Recall the effect of perception on school discipline Richard Arum found. Courts create cultural climates that echo outside of the particular case being considered. Courts must recognize that there is public space in which morality and psychological health of our culture have bearing. Rolling back the increasing proliferation of strip clubs and erotic advertising would reaffirm that we do not consider a life based on irresponsible sensual desire worthy of admiration. Strict zoning teaches youth that we take our culture seriously; we know and affirm the difference between elevated and base behaviors. Causing people to go into peripheral neighborhoods to get their pornography would help bring an appropriate sense of shame back into our culture.

Culturism takes the connection between thoughts and actions seriously. Rap sends out very strong insistent and negative messages. These messages undermine hope to choose your future. They tell youth that drugs and crime are their best options. They glorify irresponsible sex and offend our understanding of the connection of self-government and morals. Culture goes beyond words, the very posture of rap informs the listeners intimately. Habitual anger and behaviors such as staring people down are trained. Humans adapt culture easily without reflection. This helps us adjust to our environments. But, in turn, these attitudes also shape the environment. Nowhere is this clearer than in neighborhoods where people have negative attitudes towards all institutions.

A young person who had, miraculously, never heard of rap, would not intuit its negative messages. People who group up with wholesome surroundings behave differently. Again, neither gets their default via conscious reflection. Cultures are unconsciously absorbed. We again, need to consciously engage the intersection of words and culture. Here media is very important. Forty year ago, indirect reference to drug in lyrics got you banned from public airwaves. Evidence for the existence of a mainstream in America can be found in the widely shared disdain for gangster behaviors. To the extent that the disdain for gangster values diminishes, we are in trouble. If we currently disapprove, we have to say so. When over 16 percent of black men have been to prison, we can pragmatically justify not publicly promoting violence, sexism, and criminal behavior on public airwaves.[306]

As the psychologist Willard Gaylin argued in front of the Supreme Court, pornography may not harm individuals as much as society's approving of pornography will. The child will hear foul language, but he should here it away from the ears of teachers and decent society. This lets him know that it is held in low esteem. Keeping pornography out of the view of children in markets and stores, or wrapped in paper bags may not reduce the use of pornography, but it sends a message. That message again goes back to the relationship of the body to the soul. It means that we esteem relationships and love more than the vision of using other people as an expedient means to physical spasms. There are stark differences between humans and dogs. Love, as you'll recall, creates the bond that makes parents stay around and care for the child. This allows the next generation to use humans' incredibly lengthy period of dependency on others for learning. Esteeming rubbing your body anonymous people without a sense of social ramifications undercuts love and our love of mind. Teaching that relationships are about transitory pleasure undermines family.

Two unfortunate incidents have discredited cultural guidance in America. One was the attack on the film industry by the House Un-American Activities Committee (HUAC). HUAC's actions did violence to our Constitution. Those accused were not allowed to cross-examine witnesses or know their accusers. Political speech needs a higher level of protection than morally questionable speech. The message to take away from the unfortunate HUAC experience, however, is not that all attempts at guiding our culture are McCarthyism. The use of the term McCarthyism shuts down reasoned dialogue concerning securing the blessings of liberty for ourselves and our posterity. It would be a terrible irony if the result of McCarthyism became that we were not allowed to discuss legitimate political and cultural issues.

The other unfortunate conflation involved the early attacks on rock and roll. This music's introduction to the wide public being simultaneous to the Civil Rights movement and there being a color

barrier on radio broadcasts has caused us to confuse cultural guidance
and racism. The attacks on indecent music were not attacks on black
people. Martin Luther King himself said rock 'n' roll "plunges mens'
minds into degrading and immoral depths."[307] One does not decry
the violence, drug use, and sexism in music because of the race of
some of the performers; one does it because it is offensive to our
traditional culturist understandings. We have an honorable history
of protecting our culture by having guidelines for public airwaves.
Some racism was involved in the initial hatred of rock and roll. But
some legitimate culturist concerns were being raised too. We need
to have the wisdom to separate the two and the collective freedom to
guide our public culture.

Those who bludgeon conversations concerning appropriate media
with references to absolute rights need to be asked if they are in
favor of putting hardcore pornography on primetime television? If
not, they have conceded the legitimacy of some cultural guidance. In
1711 Massachusetts, the home of the Puritans, passed a censorship
law that banned, "any filthy, obscene, or profane song, pamphlet,
libel, or mock sermon."[308] This law's existence provides evidence
that censorship has old roots in America. It is not un-American.
It also shows us that filth and obscenity are old traditions and not
un-American. The traditional culturist question in our society is not
if anti-social behavior will exist, it will. The question is how much will
be tolerated in public.

The Internet gives people access to any type of material they want.
In a world with the Internet the fear that people will not be able to get
information in their homes is unwarranted. Censorship discussions
should not concern what you read in your house or in private
establishments. But we have traditionally regulated public spaces
and airwaves because government has traditionally had a culturist
sensibility. Anthropologists tell us that natural diversity is such that
in the absence of standards to the contrary, fatherless children, drug
use, violence, and childhood sex can become normative. Privately
you can do what you want. But the regulation of public airwaves
and places sets standards that are necessary if we are going to keep
our liberty from being undermined by license. We need to be clear
that regulation of public spaces does not infringe upon your private

freedoms; it bolsters them.

Media regulation can create an island in the information age where children can watch entertainment without imbibing bad morals. Public culturist guidance does not, however, need to be purely restrictive. Culturists need to be positive and creative. Perhaps we could require that television stations include five minutes every hour for local commentary on their programming. The commentary could come from recognized leaders in the community. They may be church leaders who, to avoid legal challenges, could be prohibited from preaching the gospel. The commentators could be parents or politicians. Regardless of content or the identity of the speaker, modeling critical thought concerning programming and discussions of civic considerations would increase our collective I.Q. Even the inevitable mockery of these five minutes of commentary would reinforce that someone, somewhere takes public cultural vitality seriously. Allowing free time for advertising community events and meetings would help build social capital. These are public airwaves. If those holding broadcasting licenses do not like the terms they have the freedom to broadcast privately.

In the 1920s there were successful attempts to create of holidays on patriotic themes such as Constitution Day.[309] The modern equivalent of the public square is the media. The government could create five-minute films explaining principles, battles or persons that helped to create America and Western civilization. Public pressure by moral leaders and political officials could encourage television, radio stations, and movie theaters to present these short messages along side their other programming. Advocating for this media locally will build social capital. Private establishments should, generally, not be forced by government to broadcast information. But public showings as gestures of good will towards citizens and boycotts of businesses that refuse to do so do not involve government force. They involve self-governance, the core of democracy, in action.

A fine line separates, people will argue, education and propaganda. To remove this taint, the topics should be historical and not controversial. All Americans should be proud of the sacrifices of George Washington. Again, if such things are not taught, they will not be known. If such messages are mocked, at least they will be discussed. Our noble and traditional fear of tyranny makes us cynical and leery. A free government requires suspicion about the government. But America should not be the lone nation in which the government must be neutral in regard to itself. Public ceremony has always been a part of the joy of being a citizen. It is not wrong for the government to organize Fourth of July parades or to televise them. Using this approach would create a sense of community without any media restrictions at all. No matter what the content of the films, commentary or announcements, the idea that we have worried about the cultural mental health will serve as a balance to the absolute hegemony of personal desire over public concerns.

The separation of church and state has led us to a point where the government no longer seems to have any moral purpose at all; it only exists to perform bureaucratic functions neutrally. Our government should not be neutral in regards to our country. You will hear it asked, "Whose morals should predominate?" We have traditional morals that put the mind over the body and are based on the need to maintain our fragile republic. If the question is meant to stop discussion based on the idea that we have no common morals, it should be met, again, with the question concerning pornography on primetime. You will find the vast majority of Americans agree that gangster values are anti-social. We have basic morals most of us can agree upon for the public sphere.

Ultimately democracy means we should conceive of our government as a collective endeavor run for and by the people. Individuals have rights; we would not want it any other way. But the rights of a single individual should not override our collective rights. People's rights are especially protected within their private quarters. We have a right to a decent public sphere. In fact, the continuance of our government and individual rights likely requires it.

Schools

Our having established a public school system shows that the populace has a legitimate interest in the fate of individuals. Traditionally schools have been conceived of as culturist tools designed to meet perceived social needs. As discussed in the chapter on culturism in United States history, schools were initially supposed to civilize the child. The Puritan needed to do this because it was obvious that the child was naturally evil and the frontier provided a limited sense of civilization. Horace Mann's instituting public schools was a response to worry concerning social disintegration on ethnic lines. The Progressive's socialization model focused on the adjustment of the individual child during an alienating industrial era. The democratization of education was largely the result of a need to integrate returning World War II veterans. Schools have long had a civic function.

Most schools today consider it part of their mission to foster individualism and ethnic pride. This emphasis on individualism has resulted in a radical child-centered philosophy in which the value of information depends on whether it interests the child or not. This philosophy also gets expressed in the vision of school as existing to further individual's careers. Schools' individualistic career orientation models selfishness. The dependency on children's interest does not foster care about our country. Events on public school grounds are now held to increase pride and give the child a sense of belonging via connecting to racial groups, cultures, and foreign nations. Culturist school policy would ask if there is any evidence that further individualism or reification of ethnic differences are what our society needs now. In one sense the child is the customer in a school. In another, since society is paying the bills, society is the customer and its needs should be considered.

Robert Putnam's investigations have, again, revealed that America is becoming more and more fragmented. He has succeeded in proving that the lack of community amongst Americans has led to widespread social pathologies and in showing the importance of community to a successful democracy. The focus on individualism has its roots in John Dewey's early twentieth century attempts to combat the alienation of industrialization. The emphasis was to be on the individual's concerns rather than the bureaucratic needs of the institution. Unfortunately, in its present form, no considerations higher than personal inclinations serve as sources of motivation for abstaining from drugs or doing homework. Our studies of nature and anthropology showed that groups are important and motivate people. Exile being the usual punishment for transgression, we should expect the focus on our individual fates to lead to more alienation rather than less. Putnam has shown that our culture does not currently require stressing individualism over commonality.

Multiculturalism likely provides a better guiding principle for individuals than raw individualism. Young people, like the rest of us, enjoy group activities.[310] And because natural diversity includes some reprehensible behaviors, having responsible adults designing group affiliations beats a lack of supervision. From the viewpoint of Western civilization, however, multiculturalism has faults. Multiculturalism cannot, by definition, be a source of national unity. Using diversity as source of unity (which it cannot be) necessitates throwing out our traditional source of unity: contrasting ourselves with the Old World. This hurts us in two ways. It undermines our traditional mission of fostering the future. It also conveys the message that our culture has no more merit than any other. Our survey of anthropology showed us that our civilization has reduced war and increased life expectancy. By our standards our civilization has benefited mankind. The recent escalation in school race riots reminds us of the world we are trying to escape. The Puritan emphasis on humility resulting in our nation being the only one that does not take pride in itself is ironic. If it results in our disintegration on ethnic basis it will be tragic.

Western culturism provides a forward-looking basis of community that is consistent with our historical adoration for the individual. Multiculturalism celebrates multiple values. This multiplicity makes the values incoherent and a poor moral guide. Tolerance alone cannot provide positive guidance. It cannot give you a sense of direction. Culturism is a value. Culturism situates us as proponents of the Western tradition. Doing so requires that we appreciate the sacrifices and ideals of those who developed it. This emphasis allows us to praise the potential of individuals while we teach our traditions and the collective knowledge we have garnered. Plato, Jesus, Luther, Michelangelo, Shakespeare, Newton, Washington, and Edison all remind us of the Western ideal of the great active individual achieving and provide standards to emulate. We perpetuate guiding standards when we perpetuate their names. We are also revering the potential within ourselves. Having and enforcing standards provides young people with guidance and our culture's elevation of individual potential gives them a noble cause to identify with.

The individual being the sole source of values strips the culture of the right to make demands upon you. Culturism situates the individual in society at a daily level. Being polite and cooperative shows that you respect others and society. Dressing like a prostitute distracts others and lowers our collective aspirations. Using vulgar language shows that you do not respect the sensibilities of the community. Respecting the teacher shows a proper appreciation of achievement. Our traditions teach that one who has not developed their potential is not really free. Illiterates are headed to a life of servitude. Valuing the soul over the body, the human over the animal, constitutes the key to our success and the backbone of our progressive ethics.

We should explain to students that cultures that do not have an educated populace cannot expect to maintain opportunities. Maintaining our progressive society, having opportunities and rights requires an achievement ethic. As with individuals, our society cannot maintain itself with ignorance. Culturism, unlike individualism, provides a rationale for saying that a person who disrupts and disrespects the learning process loses their educational rights and deserves shame. Culturism gives us practical and spiritual reasons to esteem, require, and protect collective and individual learning.

The bad metaphysics of absolute rights have had a terrible consequence on our schools. The radical individualist posture of schools now has legal backing. The courts have held that different learning styles can be construed as disabilities. Since it is illegal to discriminate against those with disabilities, students who are different need individually designed programs to meet their needs. This has resulted in absurdities such as the inability to punish authority defiance because it results from a protected disability. Even if this were a legitimate diagnosis, culturist reasoning would allow the culture of the school to be taken into account. No school can function when students are allowed to abuse and defy teachers. When laziness becomes a protected disorder that the teachers must work around, the school culture collapses.

Rights are only enjoyed by individuals within the context of a culture that supports them and can afford them. This is a truth that must be taught. The idea that rights are pre-existing and that you are entitled to them by decree represents bad and dangerous metaphysics. Schools need to be able to make this clear. Our schools are overcrowded and our resources are exhaustible. If you do not make an effort to learn, we cannot support your continued attendance. Those who do not do their homework might be asked to reimburse the school for their wasted funds in effort or money before they can retake courses. This policy would increase drop out rates, but it would teach a valuable lesson. This suggestion is extreme. But it is no more extreme than laws that err on the side of decreeing unaffordable and inalienable individual rights regardless of effort. Without a sustainable and protected society all of our rights will be alienated from us. We now encourage students to apply for free and reduced cost lunches so that schools qualify for Federal funds. We should try to create equal opportunity for all students. But at some point the school system must teach that there is no such thing as a free lunch.

Diversity exists and is important. Some cultures do not see dropping out or being kicked out of school as shameful. Others consider failure to get straight A's very embarrassing. Cultural diversity can explain differing levels of achievement between ethnic minorities. But when the achievement gap is mentioned institutional bias gets blamed. Using culturist understandings to explain the achievement gap will fuel competition between groups and make each group self-critical about their collective behaviors. Focusing on race to the exclusion of cultural factors means that all differences in achievement appear unreasonable. Individuals and groups who do not do their work must be understood to have responsibility for the poor results. Engendering a sense of responsibility should be an overt mission for our schools. Explaining the achievement gaps as being the result of racism works against that mission.

Our national cultural viability would hopefully inspire everyone to consider how they can improve our collective achievement. But, failing that, local pride or shame could cause communities to create tutoring and homework centers. If diversity is used to explain different outcomes, communities that did not chose not to employ any culturist mechanisms by which to increase their success might think twice before they blame society for their poor performance. These benefits apply whether we are talking about academic achievement, economic attainment, incarceration, or any other social index of success. Focusing on race at the expense of culture makes people angry and irresponsible. Interpreting individual and group results on a culturist basis will help all of us understand the nature of responsibility.

Western culturism provides a common basis upon which to unite all of our students. Western culturism provides a consistent value system by which to guide individuals, communities, schools, and the nation. Western culturism provides a source of beliefs that does not smother individuality. Western culturism gives individuals meaning; we have a duty to the past, future, and present world. Western culturism helps us realistically face our social challenges. Nature shows us that children are primed to absorb cultures. And anthropology teaches that if we do not provide cultural guidance we should not be surprised if one based on violence and sexual domination of women emerges. Culturist psychologists would tell you that we can do better. Western culture's values provide a great team for us to root for. Go team!!!

Valuing our culture

At heart, culturism asks that we contextualize our individual behaviors. Never was our collective responsibility for ensuring liberty plainer than during World War II. It was clear that if our nation was not strong and unified our rights not only would have been compromised, they would have been beaten, enslaved, tortured, raped, and killed without a trial. On our World War II home front, your right to party all night was not allowed to override our need to have lights out so that our coast line could not be spotted by Japanese bombers. Your desire to eat lots and use all the resources you wanted had to take a back seat to our military requirements. In the military your right to be a slacker was not sustainable. During World War II people understood their individual rights were dependent upon our collective success.

In this light we must recognize that the Zoot Suit rioters were not heroes for individualism and rights in the struggle against silly oppression. They were Americans of Mexican descent who started a fashion of wearing wide clothes and listening to swing music. During peace time this could be considered clean American fun. But during that time material was rationed to help supply the men who were fighting fascism. Partying and wearing excessive materials in such a context should not be celebrated. Sometimes selfish fun needs to be put into context. Having collectively upheld liberty for ourselves and our posterity should comprise a greater source of pride than having defied social norms during war time. Considering public needs is a sign of maturity. Immaturity is a sign of, well, immaturity.

During World War II we also put Americans of Japanese descent and other ethnic groups into relocation camps. Other ethnic groups were interned based on intelligence about them or their immigration status. The Americans of Japanese descent were relocated regardless of their immigration status or their individual loyalty. This has often been described as a purely racist policy. This charge always deserves serious consideration because, again, having a multiethnic country makes us susceptible to division and resentment. But we should not use the word racism to carelessly stop debate. Being able to formulate rational policy affects our national solvency. Had this been a purely racist policy with no possible justification it should constitute a huge source of shame for our country. But our winning the war was not preordained by universal proclamations or the universal nature of rights. As ever, our success required consideration.

Half a dozen incidences of sabotage in our ports or information leaks about our ships departure times might have tipped the balance against us. Using Japanese descent as a barometer for relocation was not arbitrary. As multiculturalists remind us, old world allegiances have a strong pull. The decision to relocate Americans of Japanese descent away from military installations recognized this cultural reality. Indeed millions of dollars were sent from American citizens of Japanese descent to Japan during their fifty-year rampage across Asia. We also knew that Japan was cultivating networks of collaborators. Saving Western civilization required temporarily curtailing the freedoms of individuals and implementing policies that should make any Westerner apprehensive. Ideally we should have given each person relocated a trial. Resources required we prioritize spending on what we could afford rather than make policy based on absolute rights. Realistically, we must always do this. We need to be cautious when not supporting or curtailing rights. But rights never exist outside of a social context. Sometimes our culture *must* prioritize itself.

The decaying relocation camps that survive should be preserved.

But they should not be kept up as a testimony to the racist nature of America. They should be historically accurate. They should tell about the dangers divided loyalty can present to the uniquely diverse Western nations. An exhibit on the anti-American Japanese language newspapers would educate people about the perils of liberty. These exhibits should glorify the sacrifices of these loyal Americans who relocated for their country. They should explain why these noble citizens nearly all peacefully complied without protests about their rights at the time. These Americans of Japanese descent understood that liberty comes with duties towards its preservation. Alongside those who were fighting in Europe and Asia, the relocated Americans of Japanese descent should be counted as heroes in America's ongoing struggle to protect the world from despotism. These relocation camps can serve to remind future generations that rights and individualism must sometimes consider culturism if they are to be sustainable.

Had the Americans of Japanese descent not been relocated during the Second World War, we might not have beaten Germany and Japan. Franklin Delano Roosevelt had to order their relocation even though he knew it would mean hardship. Eisenhower had to order men to fight D-Day despite being nearly certain it would end in their deaths. These decisions were made because we needed to save the world from tyranny. Today people chafe at being asked to move their sex shop. People fight all infringements on their prerogatives with language that suggests we have never had culturist policies and that all hints at control necessarily lead to fascism. Such hysterical and absolutist thinking undermines our ability to thoughtfully create policy. All policies impinge on someone's toes. All cultures try to perpetuate themselves in modes appropriate to their traditions. Our need to do so gets highlighted during war. But our sustainability needs consideration in peacetime too. Culture should merit legitimate consideration in our personal values and public spaces. Our laws must strive to avoid being corrosive of our culture's success.

Inserting the word culturism into our national and individual dialogues is a healthy idea. Culturism puts individual actions in a social context. Using the word culturism can make our society kinder as it implies public decorum and that all of our citizens are on the same team. It can serve as a counterbalance to the corrosive and incapacitating demands of individual license backed up by absolute rights. Culturism is not an absolute. Absolutes limit the areas of human discretion and thereby degrade all of us. Culturism, as a relative value, can serve as a basis by which to make nuanced policies. Much of our cultural identity derives from the value we place on individuals and their liberty. Esteeming and protecting our culture has also been a traditional part of our history. We have long judged behavior by its impact on the sustainability of our freedoms. We need to be able to again enact and enforce culturally healthy laws. Our society would be a better place were we to identify ourselves as culturists.

BIBLIOGRAPHY

All citations preceded by an asterisk are summarized at www.culturism.us

1   Culturist. Dictionary.com. Dictionary.com Unabridged (v 1.1). Random House, Inc. http://dictionary.reference.com/browse/culturist (accessed: July 21, 2007).

2   Culturism Oxford English Dictionary, Second Edition (Clarendon Press: Oxford, 1989), 122.

3   James M. McPherson, *The Abolitionist Legacy: From Reconstruction to the NAACP* (Princeton, Princeton University Press: 1975), 201.

4   *Judith Harris, *The Nurture Assumption: Why Children Turn Out the Way They Do* (New York: Touchstone Books, 1999), 263.

5   Robert Reich, *The Work of Nations* (New York: Vintage Books, 1992), 251.

6   John Kay, *Culture and Prosperity: Why Some Nations are Rich but Most Remain Poor* (New York: Harper Business, 2005), 322.

7   xenophobia. Dictionary.com. The American Heritage® Dictionary of the English Language, Fourth Edition. Houghton Mifflin Company, 2004. http://dictionary.reference.com/browse/xenophobia (accessed: January 01, 2007).

8   ethnocentrism. Dictionary.com. The American Heritage® Dictionary of the English Language, Fourth Edition. Houghton Mifflin Company, 2004. http://dictionary.reference.com/browse/ethnocentrism (accessed: January 01, 2007).

9   jingoism. Dictionary.com. The American Heritage® Dictionary of the English Language, Fourth Edition. Houghton Mifflin Company, 2004. http://dictionary.reference.com/browse/jingoism (accessed: January 01, 2007).

10   patriotism. Dictionary.com. The American Heritage® Dictionary of the English Language, Fourth Edition. Houghton Mifflin Company, 2004. http://dictionary.reference.com/browse/patriotism (accessed: January 01, 2007).

11   nationalism. Dictionary.com. The American Heritage® Dictionary of the English Language, Fourth Edition. Houghton Mifflin Company, 2004. http://dictionary.reference.com/browse/nationalism (accessed: January 01, 2007).

12 nativism. Dictionary.com. The American Heritage® Dictionary of the English Language, Fourth Edition. Houghton Mifflin Company, 2004. http://dictionary.reference.com/browse/nativism (accessed: January 01, 2007).

13 race. Dictionary.com. The American Heritage® Dictionary of the English Language, Fourth Edition. Houghton Mifflin Company, 2004. http://dictionary.reference.com/browse/race (accessed: January 01, 2007).

14 racism. Dictionary.com. The American Heritage® Dictionary of the English Language, Fourth Edition. Houghton Mifflin Company, 2004. http://dictionary.reference.com/browse/racism (accessed: January 01, 2007).

15 Bakari Kitwana, *Why White Kids Love Hip Hop: Wankstas, Wiggers, Wannabes, and the New Reality of Race in America* (Cambridge: Basic Civitas Books, 2005), 82.

16 Peter Richerson and Robert Boyd, *Not By Genes Alone: How Culture Transformed Human Evolution* (Chicago: The University of Chicago Press, 2005), 35.

17 * Edward Hall, *Beyond Culture* (New York: Doubleday, 1989), 7.

18 Rothenberg, J. *Florida Court Okays Class-Action Suits Against Schools.* School Reform News. Nov 1, 1005. http://www.heartland.org/Article.cfm?artId=17919

19 Symonds, W. *America the Uneducated: A New Study Warns of a Slide for the U.S. as the Share of Lower Achievers Grows.* Business Week. November 21, 2005. p. 89.

20 Jia-Rui Chong, "Morphing Outrage Into Ideas," *Los Angeles Times,* October 12, 2005, A24.

21 Samuel Goldberg, *Army Training of Illiterates in World War II.* (New York: Bureau of Publications Teachers College, 1951), 261.

22 * Harold Stevenson and James Stigler, *The Learning Gap: Why Our Schools are Failing and What We Can Learn from Japanese and Chinese Education* (New York: Simon and Schuster, 1992), 54.

23 Michael Harris Bond, *Beyond the Chinese Face: Insights from Psychology* (Oxford: Oxford University Press, 1991), 18.

24 *Brown Center Report on American Education. Part Two: Do Students Have Too Much Homework?* http://www.brookings.edu/gs/brown/20031001.pdf

25 International Association for the Evaluation of Educational Achievement, *Trends in Mathematics and Science Study, 2003.* http://www.iea.nl/timss2003.html

26 *The American Heritage Dictionary of the English Language, Fourth Edition* (Boston and New York: Houghton Mifflin Company, 2000).

27 Willard Gaylin and Bruce Jennings, *The Perversion of Autonomy:*

Coercion and Constraints in a Liberal Society (Washington D.C.: Georgetown University Press, 2003), 8.

28　* Barry Alan Shain, *The Myth of American Individualism: The Protestant Origins of American Political Thought.* (Princeton: Princeton University Press, 1994), 252.

29　* Lawrence Keeley, *War Before Civilization.* (New York: Oxford University Press, 1996), 65.

30　Frans de Waal, *Our Inner Ape: A Leading Primatologist Explains Why We Are Who We Are.* (New York: Riverhead Books, 2005), 172.

31　Richard Nisbett, *The Geography of Thought: How Asians and Westerners Think Differently. . . and Why* (New York: Free Press, 2003), 90.

32　* Alasdair MacIntyre, *After Virtue: A Study in Moral Theory* (Notre Dame: University of Notre Dame Press, 2003), 52.

33　* Dorothy Ross, *The Origins of American Social Science* (Cambridge: The Press Syndicate of the University of Cambridge, 1991), 22.

34　Jonathan Winthrop, *The Penguin Book of Historical Speeches.* ed. Brian MacArthur. (London: Penguin Books, 1995), 66..

35　* Edmund Morgan, *The Puritan Family* (New York: Harper and Row, 1966), 37.

36　Perry Miller and Thomas Johnson. *The Puritans: A Sourcebook of Their Writing. Volume One* (New York: Harper and Row, 1963), 181.

37　Isiah Berlin, *Liberty* (Oxford: Oxford University Press, 1995), 179.

38　Perry Miller and Johnson, Thomas, *The Puritans: A Sourcebook of Their Writing. Vol. 1.* (New York: Harper and Row, 1963), 200.

39　Crane Brinton, *A History of Western Morals* (New York: Harcourt, Brace and Company, 1959), 226.

40　Max Weber, *The Protestant Ethic and the Spirit of Capitalism* (London: Routledge, 1992), 109.

41　* Barry Alan Shain, *The Myth of American Individualism: The Protestant Origins of American Political Thought* (Princeton: Princeton University Press, 1994), 195.

42　Crane Brinton, *A History of Western Morals* (New York: Harcourt, Brace and Company, 1959), 224.

43　Carl Kaestle, *Pillars of the Republic: Common Schools and American Society, 1780 – 1860* (New York: Hill and Wang, 1983), 182.

44　Thomas Jefferson, *Jefferson: His Political Writings.* ed. Edward Dumbauld (Indianapolis: The Bobbs-Merrill Company, Inc., 1955), 3.

45　Alexander Hamilton, *The Federalist Papers* (New York: Penguin Inc., 1961), 110.

46　The author's count.

47　Quentin Skinner, *Three Concepts of Liberty.* Columbia College's Core Curriculum Coursewide Lectures. Oct. 24th, 2003 in Lerner Hall. http://www.college.columbia.edu/core/lectures/fall2003/

48   Patrick Henry, *The Penguin Book of Historical Speeches*. Ed. Brian
      MacArthur (London: Penguin Books, 1996), 91.
49   Willmoore Kendall and George Carey, *The Basic Symbols of the
      American Political Tradition* (Baton Rouge: Louisiana State University
      Press, 1970), 124-125.
50   Alexis de Tocqueville, *Democracy in America and Two Essays on America*
      (London: Penguin Classics, 2003), 86.
51   * Barry Alan Shain, *The Myth of American Individualism: The Protestant
      Origins of American Political Thought* (Princeton: Princeton University
      Press, 1994), 181.
52   Lalo Lopez. "Legacy of a Land Grab," *Hispanic Magazine*, September,
      1997.
53   Encyclopedia Britannica Online, "Treaty of Tordesillas," http://
      www.britannica.com/ebc/article-9380951?query=Treaty%20of%20
      Tordesillas&ct=
54   Andres Resendez, *Changing National Identities at the Border: Texas and
      New Mexico, 1800 – 1850* (New York: Cambridge University Press,
      2005), 22.
55   Ángela Moyano Pahissa, *The Loss of Texas* (México, D.F.: Editorial
      Planeta Mexicana, 1991), 10. Translator, John Kenneth Press.
56   Andres Resendez, *Changing National Identities at the Border: Texas and
      New Mexico, 1800 – 1850* (New York: Cambridge University Press,
      2005), 24.
57   John Kennedy, *A Nation of Immigrants* (New York: Harper and Row,
      1986), 71.
58   Chae Chan Ping v. U.S. May, 13 1889, http://www.tourolaw.edu/
      patch/Chae/
59   Chae Chan Ping v. U.S. May, 13 1889, http://www.tourolaw.edu/
      patch/Chae/
60   Gary Gerstle, *American Crucible: Race and Nation in the Twentieth Century*
      (Princeton: Princeton University Press, 2001), 95.
61   Theodore Roosevelt, "Americanization Day. July, 1915," *Metropolitan
      Magazine*. McConnell Press, Inc. New York.
62   Quoted in John Higham, Strangers *in the Land: Patterns of American
      Nativism 1860-1925* (New York: Atheneum, 1963), 238.
63   John Higham, Strangers *in the Land: Patterns of American Nativism
      1860-1925* (New York: Atheneum, 1963), 44.
64   *Mafia: The History of the Mob in America*. Episode One. A&E, 2001.
65   Julian Jaffe, *Crusade Against Radicalism: New York During the Red Scare,
      1914 – 1924* (Port Washington: Kennikat Press, 1972), 184.
66   Larry Witham, "America's Great Awakenings Date Back to Colonial
      Times," *The Washington Post*, August 25, 1997.
67   Pauline Maier, *Reinventing America: A History of the United States* (New

York: W.W. Norton and Company, 2003), 413.

68 * Clifford Griffin, *Their Brothers' Keepers: Moral Stewardship in the United States, 1800-1865* (New Brunswick: Rutgers University Press, 1960), 51.

69 James Morone, *Hellfire Nation: The Politics of Sin in American History* (New Haven: Yale University Press, 2003), 130.

70 * Clifford Griffin, *Their Brothers' Keepers: Moral Stewardship in the United States, 1800-1865* (New Brunswick: Rutgers University Press, 1960), 200.

71 * (Griffin 1960, 264)

72 Mary Kelley, *Learning to Stand and Speak. Women, Education, and Public Life in America's Republic* (Williamsburg: Omohudro Institute of Early American History and Culture, 2006), 126.

73 Jacqueline Jones, *Northern Teachers and Georgia Blacks, 1865-1873* (Athens: University of Georgia Press, 1992), 110.

74 Richard Hofstadter, *The Age of Reform* (New York: Vintage Books, 1955), 152.

75 (Hofstadter 1955, 133)

76 Jonathan Zimmerman, *Distilling Democrac: Alcohol Education in America's Public Schools, 1880-1925* (Lawrence: University Press of Canada, 1999), 32.

77 * Bernard Bailyn, *Education in the Forming of America* (New York: W.W. Norton & Company Inc., 1960), 22.

78 Michael Schudson, *The Good Citizen: A History of American Civic Life* (New York: The Free Press, 1998), 93.

79 Samuel Bowles and Herbert Gintis, *Schooling in Capitalist America. Educational Reform and the Contradictions of Economic Life* (New York: Basic Books, Inc., 1976), 166.

80 Ruth Elson, *Guardians of Tradition: American Schoolbooks of the Nineteenth Century* (Lincoon: University of Nebraska Press, 1964), 150.

81 (Elson 1964, 145)

82 * Carl Kaestle, *Pillars of the Republic: Common Schools and American Society, 1780 – 1860* (New York: Hill and Wang, 1983), 98.

83 Lawrence Cremin, *The Transformation of the School: Progressivism in American Education, 1876 – 1957* (New York: Vintage Books, 1961), 123.

84 John Dewey and Evelyn Dewey, *Schools of Tomorrow* (New York: E.P. Dutton & Company, 1962), 73.

85 * Charles Taussig, Report of the National Advisory Committee of the National Youth Administration to the President of the United States, March, 19th, 1942. p. 41.

86 * Palmer Johnson. And Oswald Harvey, The National Youth Administration: Staff Study Number Thirteen. Prepared for the

Advisory Committee on Education. U.S. Government Printing Office. Washington D.C. 1938. p. 45.

87   Cyril Houle and Elbert Burr and Thomas Hamilton and John Yale The Armed Services and Adult Education. American Council on Education. Washington D.C. 1947. p. 188.

88   * Eli Ginzburg and Douglas Bray, *The Uneducated* (New York: Columbia University, 1953), 136.

89   Peter Irons, *A People's History of the Supreme Court: The Men and Women Whose Cases and Decisions Have Shaped our Constitution* (New York: Penguin Books, 1999), 267.

90   Mitchel Yockelson, "The War Department: Keeper of Our Nation's Enemy Aliens During World War I" (paper presented to the Society for Military History Annual Meeting, April 1998).

91   Peter Irons, *A People's History of the Supreme Court: The Men and Women Whose Cases and Decisions Have Shaped our Constitution* (New York: Penguin Books, 1999), 270.

92   Michelle Malkin, *In Defense of Internment: The Case for 'Racial Profiling' in World War II and the War on Terror* (Washington, D.C.: Regnery Publishing, Inc., 2004), 111.

93   Korean War. Wikipedia. http://en.wikipedia.org/wiki/Korean_War 2006

94   Gary Nash, *The American People: Creating a Nation and a Society* (New York: Longman, 2003), 821.

95   Ann Coulter, *Treason: Liberal Treachery from the Cold War to the War on Terrorism* (New York: Crown Forum, 2003), 40.

96   Alan Barth, *The Loyalty of Free Men* (New York: The Viking Press, 1951), 63.

97   Vanessa Whitcomb and Mike Benson, *The Complete Idiot's Guide to Modern China* (Indianapolis: Alpha Books, 2003), 33.

98   Des Forges. R. Cultural Centrality and Political Change in Chinese History: Northeast Henan in the Fall of the Ming. Stanford University Press. Stanford. 2003. p. 317.

99   Roger Des Forges, *Cultural Centrality and Political Change in Chinese History: Northeast Henan in the Fall of the Ming* (Stanford: Stanford University Press, 2003), 53.

100   Bernard Bailyn, *Education in the Forming of America* (New York: W.W. Norton & Company Inc., 1960), 27

101   Louis E. V. Nevaer, "U.S. Schools Benefit from Mexican Largesse," New America Media, February 7, 2007. http://news. newamericamedia.org/news/view_article.html?article_id=fca34ed6c5 a2fb5334fa0163a2fc49b1

102   PJ Cain and AG Hopkins, *British Imperialism 1688-2000* (London: Pearson Education, 2002), 54.

103 (Cain and Hopkins 2002, 98)
104 Ronald Robinson and John Gallagher, Africa and the Victorians: The Official Mind of Imperialism (London: The Macmillan Press, Ltd., 1981), 4.
105 (Robinson and Gallagher 1981, 23)
106 Henry Stanley, *Through the Dark Continent or The Sources of the Nile Around the Great Lakes of Equatorial Africa and Down the Livingstone River to the Atlantic Ocean* (New York: Dover Publications, Inc., 1988), 175.
107 Cabeza de Vaca, *Adventures in the Unknown Interior of America* (Albuquerque: University of Mexico Press, 1983), 7.
108 (Cabeza de Vaca 1983, 77)
109 (Cabeza de Vaca 1983, 79)
110 (Cabeza de Vaca 1983, 57)
111 * Raine Eisler, *The Chalice and the Blade: Our History Our Future* (New York: HarperCollins Publishers, Inc., 1987), 44.
112 Camile Paglia, *Sexual Personae: Art and Decadence from Nefertiti to Emily Dickinson* (New York: Random House Inc., 1991), 42.
113 Steven LeBlanc, *Constant Battles: Why We Fight* (New York: St. Martin's Griffin, 2004), 224.
114 Lawrence Keeley, *War Before Civilization: The Myth of the Peaceful Savage* (New York: Oxford University Press, 1996), 90.
115 (Keeley 1996, 33)
116 Steven LeBlanc, *Constant Battles: Why We Fight* (New York: St. Martin's Griffin,. 2004), 154.
117 Diego De Landa, *An Account of the Things of Yucatan* (Mexico, D.F.: Monclem Ediciones, 2003)
118 (De Landa 2003, 79)
119 David Duncan, *Hernando de Soto: A Savage Quest in the Americas* (Norman: University of Oklahoma Press, 1996), 98.
120 Ross Hassig, *Aztec Warfare: Imperial Expansion and Political Control* (Norman: University of Oklahoma Press, 1995), 115.
121 Victor Hanson, *Carnage and Culture: Landmark Battles in the Rise of Western Power* (New York: Anchor Books, 2002), 217.
122 Ross Hassig, *Aztec Warfare: Imperial Expansion and Political Control* (Norman: University of Oklahoma Press, 1995), 121.
123 (Hassig 1995, 121)
124 Peter Farb, *Man's Rise to Civilization as Shown by the Indians of North America* (New York: E. P. Dutton & Co., Inc., 1968), 186.
125 Robert Edgerton, *Sick Societies. Challenging the Myth of Primitive Harmony* (New York: The Free Press, 1992), 207.
126 Ruth Benedict, *Patterns of Culture* (New York: Mentor Books, 1934), 200.
127 Robert LeVine, Culture *Theory: Essays on Minds, Self and Emotion,*

eds. Richard Shweder and Robert LeVine (Cambridge: Cambridge
University Press, 1984), 82.

128 Richard Shweder, *Culture Theory: Essays on Minds, Self and Emotion*,
eds. Richard Shweder and Robert LeVine (Cambridge: Cambridge
University Press, 1984), 46.

129 Elinor Ochs and Bambi Schieffelin, *Culture Theory: Essays on
Minds, Self and Emotion*. eds. Richard Shweder and Robert LeVine
(Cambridge: Cambridge University Press, 1984), 282.

130 Michelle Rosaldo, *Knowledge and Passion: Ilongot Notions of Self and
Social Life* (Cambridge: Cambridge University Press, 1980), 64.

131 (Rosaldo 1980, 39)

132 (Rosaldo 1980, 50)

133 Lawrence Keeley, *War Before Civilization: The Myth of the Peaceful Savage*
(New York: Oxford University Press, 1996), 146.

134 Clifford Geertz, *The Human Experience: Readings in Sociocultural
Anthropology*, ed. David Spain (Homewood: The Dorsey Press, 1975),
23.

135 Ruth Benedict, *Patterns of Culture* (New York: Mentor Books, 1934),
164.

136 Jo-hannes Wilbert, *Survivors of Eldorado: Four Indian Cultures of South
America* (New York: Praeger Publishers, 1972), 49.

137 Paul Henley, *Yanomami: Masters of the Spirit World* (San Francisco:
Chronicle Books, 1995), 35.

138 Jo-hannes Wilbert, *Survivors of Eldorado: Four Indian Cultures of South
America* (New York: Praeger Publishers, 1972), 48.

139 Lawrence Keeley, *War Before Civilization: The Myth of the Peaceful Savage*
(New York: Oxford University Press, 1996), 90.

140 Michael Shermer, *The Science of Good and Evil: Why People Cheat, Gossip,
Care, Share, and Follow the Golden Rule* (New York: Times Books), 90.

141 Michelle Rosaldo, *Knowledge and Passion: Ilongot Notions of Self and
Social Life* (Cambridge: Cambridge University Press, 1980), 56.

142 (Rosaldo 1980, 34)

143 Louise Williams, "Head-hunting revival a gruesome legacy of
Soeharto's failed experiment." Sydney Morning Herald. http://www.
asia-pacific-action.org/southeastasia/indonesia/netnews/2001/
and09_v5.htm#Head-hunting%20revival%20a%20gruesome%20
legacy%20of%20Soeharto's%20failed%20experiment (February 26,
2001).

144 Louise Williams, "I Just Stabbed and Slashed and Cut Off Their
Heads." Straits Times. http://www.asia-pacific-action.org/
southeastasia/indonesia/netnews/2001/and09_v5.htm#%60I%20
just%20stabbed%20and%20slashed%20and%20cut%20off%20
their%20heads (March 3, 2001).

145 UNIFEM, "Violence Against Women – Facts and Figures." http://
www.unifem.org/attachments/gender_issues/violence_against_
women/facts_figures_violence_against_women_20060126.pdf.
(2006).

146 World Health Organization, "Female Genital Mutilation." http://
www.who.int/mediacentre/factsheets/fs241/en/print.html (June
2000).

147 Amnesty International, "What is Female Genital Mutilation?" http://
web.amnesty.org/library/index/ENGACT770061997 (October 1,
1997).

148 Bernal Diaz, *The Conquest of New Spain* (London: Penguin Books,
1963), 137.

149 Ruth Benedict, *Patterns of Culture* (New York: Mentor Books, 1934),
200.

150 (Benedict 1934, 106).

151 Klaus Koch, *Jalé Warfare. In The Human Experience: Readings in
Sociocultural Anthropology*, ed. David Spain (Homewood: The Dorsey
Press, 1975), 288.

152 Robert Edgerton, *Sick Societies: Challenging the Myth of Primitive
Harmony* (New York: The Free Press, 1992), 182.

153 *Justice for my People: The Dr. Hector P. Garcia Story*, Prod. Jeff Felts,
KEDT-TV, 2002.

154 Ignacio García, *Hector P. García: In Relentless Pursuit of Justice*
(Houston: Arte Público Press, 2002), 156.

155 Rene Gazaway, *The Longest Mile: A Vivid Chronicle of Life in the Small
Surprising World of an Appalachian Hollow* (Garden City: Doubleday &
Company, Inc., 1969), 57.

156 (Gazaway 1969, 152).

157 (Gazaway 1969, 138).

158 (Gazaway 1969, 106).

159 Patrick Oster, *The Mexicans: A Personal Portrait of a People* (New York:
HarperCollins Publishers Inc., 2002), 263

160 Christopher Hallpike, *The Principles of Social Evolution* (Oxford:
Oxford University Press, 1988), 239.

161 (Hallpike 1988, 87).

162 * *Civilization: A Personal View. Episode One, The Skin of Our Teeth.*
Kenneth Clark. BBC-2, 1966.

163 * Clive Ponting, *A Green History of the World: The Environment and the
Collapse of Great Civilizations* (New York: St. Martin's Press, 1992), 35.

164 Shepard Kretch TWOI, *The Ecological Indian: Myth and History* (New
York: W. W. Norton and Company, 2000), 42.

165 Jared Diamond, *Collapse: How Societies Choose to Fall or Succeed*
(London: Penguin Books, 2005), 147.

166 (Diamond 2005, 119).
167 (Diamond 2005, 109).
168 Michael Shermer, *The Science of Good and Evil: Why People Cheat, Gossip, Care, Share, and Follow the Golden Rule* (New York: Times Books, 2004), 100-101.
169 Steven LeBlanc, *Constant Battles: Why We Fight* (New York: St. Martin's Griffin, 2004), 139.
170 * Clive Ponting, *A Green History of the World: The Environment and the Collapse of Great Civilizations* (New York: St. Martin's Press, 1992), 82.
171 * (Ponting 1992, 121).
172 Derek Freeman, *Margaret Mead and Samoa: The Making and Unmaking of an Anthropological Myth* (Middlesex: Pelican Books, 1983), xTwo.
173 Steven LeBlanc, *Constant Battles: Why We Fight* (New York: St. Martin's Griffin, 2004), 66.
174 Derek Freeman, *Margaret Mead and Samoa: The Making and Unmaking of an Anthropological Myth* (Middlesex: Pelican Books, 1983), 169.
175 (Freeman 1983, 167).
176 (Freeman 1983, 165).
177 Margaret Mead, *Coming of Age in Samoa: A Psychological Study of Primitive Youth for Western Civilisation* (New York: Morrow Quill Paperbacks, 1961), 84.
178 Derek Freeman, *Margaret Mead and Samoa: The Making and Unmaking of an Anthropological Myth* (Middlesex: Pelican Books,1983), 249.
179 Robert Bellah, "Is There a Common American Culture," *The Journal for the American Academy of Religion*, Vol. 66, No 3, (Fall 1998): 613.
180 Christopher Hallpike, *The Principles of Social Evolution* (Oxford: Oxford University Press, 1988), 319.
181 John Kay, *Culture and Prosperity: Why some nations are rich, but most remain poor* (New York: Harper Business, 2004), 56.
182 Porter Anderson, "Study: U.S. Employees Put In Most Hours," CNN August 31, 2001.
183 Samuel Huntington, *Who Are We?: The Challenges to America's National Identity* (New York: Simon and Schuster, 2004), 73.
184 Bernard Bailyn, *Education in the Forming of America* (New York: W.W. Norton & Company Inc., 1960), 27.
185 Victor Hanson, *Carnage and Culture: Landmark Battles in the Rise of Western Power* (New York: First Anchor Books, 2002), 51.
186 Thomas Jefferson, Thomas Jefferson Memorial: Statue Chamber Inscriptions http://www.nps.gov/thje/memorial/memorial.htm#
187 Sam Roberts, "For Young Earners in Big City, a Gap in Women's Favor," *New York Times*, August 3, 2007, N.Y./Region.
188 Alan Kraut, *The Huddled Masses: The Immigrant in American Society, 1880 – 1921* (Arlington Heights: Harlan Davidson, Inc., 1982), 139.

189 Stace Lindsay, *Culture Matters: How Values Shape Human Progress*, eds
     Laurence Harrison Samuel Huntington (New York: Basic Books,
     2000), 287.

190 Donna Haraway, *Simians, Cyborgs, and Women: The Reinvention of Nature*
     (New York: Routledge, 1991), 58.

191 John Tooby and Irven DeVore, *The Evolution of Human Behavior:*
     Primate Models, ed. Warren Kinzey (Albany: State University of New
     York Press, 1987), 183.

192 (Tooby and DeVore 1987, 200).

193 David Wilson and Elliott Sober, "Re-Introducing Group Selection to
     the Human Behavioral Sciences." *Behavioral and Brain Sciences* Vol. 17,
     No. 4, (1994): 585-654.

194 Raghavendra Gadagkar, *Survival Strategies. Cooperation and Conflict in*
     Animal Societies (Cambridge: Harvard University Press, 1997), 73.

195 Richard Dawkins, *The Selfish Gene* (New York: Oxford University Press,
     1999), 63.

196 Irenaus Eibl-Eibesfeldt, *Ethology: The Biology of Behavior* (New York:
     Hold, Rinehart and Winston, 1970), 344.

197 Frans De Waal, *Our Inner Ape. A Leading Primatologist Explains Why We*
     Are Who We Are (New York: Riverhead Books, 2005), 47.

198 Robert Ardrey, *The Territorial Imperative* (New York: Dell Publishing
     Company, 1966), 44.

199 Edge Foundation Inc., *A Bozo of a Baboon: A Talk with Robert Sapolsky*
     http://www.edge.org/3rd_culture/sapolsky03/sapolsky_p6.html
     (2003).

200 *Why Dogs Smile and ChimpanzeesCry*, Dir. Carol Fleisher, Discovery
     Channel, 1999.

201 Frans De Waal, *Chimpanzee Politics: Power and Sex among Apes*
     (Baltimore: The Johns Hopkins University Press, 1989), 95.

202 (De Waal 1989, 97).

203 Irenaus Eibl-Eibesfeldt, *Ethology: The Biology of Behavior* (New York:
     Holt, Rinehart and Winston, 1970), 360.

204 Konrad Lorenz, *On Aggression* (New York: Bantam Books, 1963), 43.

205 Irenaus Eibl-Eibesfeldt, *Love and Hate: The Natural History of Behavior*
     Patterns (New York: Holt, Rinehart and Winston, 1972), 85.

206 Frans De Waal, *Our Inner Ape. A Leading Primatologist Explains Why We*
     Are Who We Are (New York: Riverhead Books, 2005), 78.

207 Michael Argyle, *Cooperation: The Basis of Sociability* (London:
     Routledge, 1991), 59.

208 Kevin Leland and John Odling-Smee and Marc Feldman, "Niche
     Construction, Biological Evolution and Cultural Change," *Behavioral*
     and Brain Sciences, Vol. 23, Issue 1, (September 28, 2001): 131-146

209 Lionel Tiger, *The Decline of Males* (New York: Golden Books, 1999),

42.

210   (Tiger 1999, 41).

211   Rita Carter, *Mapping the Mind* (London: University of California
      Press, 2000), 131.

212   Antonio Damasio, *Descartes' Error: Emotion, Reason, and the Human
      Brain.*(New York: Avon Books, 1994), 122

213   Robert Wright, *The Moral Animal: Why We Are, the Way We Are: The New
      Science of Evolutionary Psychology* (New York: Pantheon Books, 1994),
      177.

214   Lionel Tiger and Robin Fox, *The Imperial Animal* (New York: Henry
      Holt and Company, Inc., 1971), 150.

215   Erin Swan, *Primates: From Howler Monkeys to Humans* (New York:
      Franklin Watts, 1998), 36.

216   Robert Ardrey, *The Territorial Imperative* (New York: Dell Publishing
      Company, 1966), 44.

217   Konrad Lorenz, *On Aggression* (New York: Bantam Books, 1963), 15.

218   Edward Wilson, *Sociobiology: The Abridged Edition* (Cambridge: The
      Belknap Press of Harvard University Press, 1980), 136.

219   Ralph Holloway, *Primate Aggression, Territoriality, and Xenophobia* (New
      York: Academic Press, Inc., 1974)

220   Konrad Lorenz, *On Aggression* (New York: Bantam Books, 1967), 33.

221   Robert Jurmain, et al. *Introduction to Physical Anthropology: Ninth
      Edition* (Belmont: Wadsworth Publishing, 2003), 173.

222   Edward Wilson, *Sociobiology: The Abridged Edition* (Cambridge: The
      Belknap Press of Harvard University Press, 1980), 132.

223   Frans De Waal, *Our Inner Ape. A Leading Primatologist Explains Why We
      Are Who We Are* (New York: Riverhead Books, 2005), 133.

224   Steven LeBlanc, *Constant Battles: Why We Fight* (New York: St. Martin's
      Griffin, 2004), 82.

225   Frans De Waal, *Our Inner Ape. A Leading Primatologist Explains Why We
      Are Who We Are* (New York: Riverhead Books, 2005), 129.

226   Steven LeBlanc, *Constant Battles: Why We Fight* (New York: St. Martin's
      Griffin, 2004), 81.

227   Frans De Waal, *Our Inner Ape. A Leading Primatologist Explains Why We
      Are Who We Are* (New York: Riverhead Books, 2005), 135.

228   * Peter Richerson and Robert Boyd, *Not by Genes Alone: How Culture
      Transformed Human Evolution.* (Chicago: University of Chicago Press,
      2005), 204.

229   Robin Dunbar, "Coevolution of neocortical size, group size and
      language in humans," *Behavioral and Brain Sciences, Vol.* 16, Issue 4:
      681-735. http://www.bbsonline.org/documents/a/00/00/05/65/
      bbs00000565-00/bbs.dunbar.html (1993).

230   * Peter Richerson and Robert Boyd, *Not by Genes Alone: How Culture*

Transformed Human Evolution. (Chicago: University of Chicago Press, 2005), 125.

231 Robert Boyd and Peter Richerson, "Culture, Adaptation , and Innateness," *UCLA College of Letters and Science,* http://www.sscnet. ucla.edu/anthro/faculty/boyd/Innateness%20ver%204.1.pdf

232 Christopher Hallpike, *The Principles of Social Evolution* (Oxford: Clarendon Press, 1988), 115.

233 (Hallpike 1988, 166).

234 Edward Wilson, *Consilience: The Unity of Knowledge* (New York: Vintage books, 1998), 185.

235 Konrad Lorenz, *On Aggression* (New York: Bantam Books, 1967), 37.

236 Philip Zimbardo, "Why Good Soldiers Turn Bad." *The Record,* May 11, 2004.

237 Judith Harris, *The Nurture Assumption: Why Children Turn Out the Way They Do* (New York: Touchstone Book, 1999), 128.

238 Muzafer Sherif, *In Common Predicament* (Boston: Houghton Mifflin Company, 1966), 82.

239 Michael Mitchell, "In-group identification, social dominance orientation, and differential intergroup social allocation." *The Journal of Social Psychology,* April 1, 1994

240 Richard Shweder and Robert LeVine, *Culture Theory: Essays on Mind, Self and Emotion* (Cambridge: Cambridge University Press, 1984), 193.

241 Michelle Rosaldo, *Culture Theory: Essays on Mind, Self, and Emotion,* eds. Richard Shweder and Robert Levine (Cambridge: Cambridge University Press, 2003), 147.

242 Richard Nisbett, *The Geography of Thought: How Asians and Westerners Think Differently . . . and Why* (New York: Free Press, 2003),141

243 (Nisbett 2003, 91).

244 Fan Shen, *Signs of Life in the USA: Reading on Popular Culture for Writers,* eds. Sonia Maasik and Jack Solomon (Bedford: Bedford/St. Martin's, 2000), 586.

245 Ronald Inglehart, Culture Matters: How Values Shape Human Progress, eds. Lawrence Harrison and Samuel Huntington (New York: Basic books, 2000), 90.

246 * Aristotle, *The Nicomachean Ethics* (London: Penguin Books, 2004), 266.

247 * (Aristotle 2004, 14).

248 * (Aristotle 2004, 253).

249 * (Aristotle 2004, 279).

250 * (Aristotle 2004, 21).

251 Don Eberly and Sam Brownback, *Building a Healthy Culture: Strategies for an American Renaissance* (Cambridge: Wm.B. Eerdmans Publishing Co., 2001), 14.

252 Christopher Lasch, *The Culture of Narcissism: American Life in An Age of Diminishing Expectations* (New York: W. W. Norton & Company, 1991).

253 Robert Putnam, *Bowling Alone: The Collapse and Revival of American Community* (New York: Touchstone, 2001), 262.

254 Robert Bellah, et al., *Habits of the Heart: Individualism and Commitment in American Life* (Berkeley: University of California Press, 1996), 75.

255 (Bellah 1996, 92).

256 Robert Putnam, *Bowling Alone: The Collapse and Revival of American Community* (New York: Touchstone, 2001), 290.

257 Marjorie Heins, *Not In Front of the Children: "Indecency," Censorship, and the Innocence of Youth* (New York: Hill and Wang, 2002), 72.

258 (Heins 2002, 102).

259 Richard Arum, *Judging School Discipline: The Crisis of Moral Authority* (Cambridge: Harvard University Press, 2003), 49

260 (Arum 2003, 214).

261 Paul Rahe, *Republics Ancient and Modern: The Ancien Regime in Classical Greece* (Chapel Hill: The University of North Carolina Press, 1994), 58.

262 Muzafer Sherif, *In Common Predicament* (Boston: Houghton Mifflin Company, 1966), 86.

263 (Sherif 1966, 88).

264 (Sherif 1966, 90).

265 "U.S. Say China Refuses Deportees," BBC News, http://news.bbc.co.uk/2/hi/americas/4811458.stm (March 16, 2006).

266 Gertrude Himmelfarb, *The De-Moralization of Society: From Victorian Virtues to Modern Values* (New York: Vintage Books, 1994), 231.

267 Barry Alan Shain, *The Myth of American Individualism: The Protestant Origins of American Political Thought* (New Jersey: Princeton University Press, 1994), 242.

268 Isaiah Berlin, *Liberty: Incorporating Four Essays on Liberty* (Oxford: Oxford University Press, 2002), 294.

269 Paul Rahe, *Republics Ancient and Modern: The Ancien Régime in Classical Greece* (Chapel Hill: University of North Carolina Press, 1994), 31.

270 Aristotle, *Politics* (London: Penguin Books, 1981), 196.

271 Aristotle, *Politics* (London: Penguin Books, 1981), 310.

272 (Aristotle 1981, 187).

273 * Plato, *Laws* (New York: Prometheus Books, 2000), 77.

274 Aristotle, *Politics* (Oxford: Oxford University Press, 1995), 197.

275 (Aristotle 1995, 198).

276 Plato, *The Republic* (London: Penguin Books, 2003), 190.

277 .(Plato 2003, 100).

278 Ronald Robinson and John Gallagher, *Africa and the Victorians: The Official Mind of Imperialism* (London: The Macmillan Press, Ltd.,

1981), 7.

279 John Dewey, *The Quest for Certainty* (New York: Capricorn Books, 1929), 74.

280 (Dewey 1929, 289).

281 William James, *Pragmatism and Other Essays* (New York: Washington Square Press, 1963), 219.

282 James Conant, The Cambridge Companion to William James, ed. Ruth Anna Putnam (Cambridge: Cambridge University Press, 1997), 188.

283 John Dewey, *Reconstruction in Philosophy* (Boston: The Beacon Press, 1962), 184.

284 Richard Rorty, *Philosophy and Social Hope* (London: Penguin Books, 1999), xvi.

285 David Scott, *Formations of Ritual: Colonial and Anthropological Discourses on the Sinhala Yaktovil* (Minneapolis: University of Minnesota Press, 1994), 43.

286 (Scott 1994, 91).

287 (Scott 1994, 123).

288 (Scott 1994, 209).

289 Richard Rorty, *Consequences of Pragmatism: Essays 1972 – 1980* (Minneapolis: University of Minnesota Press, 1994), 167.

290 Barrington Moore, Jr., *Tolerance and the Scientific Outlook: In A Critique of Pure Tolerance* (Boston: Beacon Press, 1969), 64.

291 *The American Heritage Dictionary of the English Language, Fourth Edition* (Boston and New York: Houghton Mifflin Company, 2000).

292 BBC News "Female circumcision 'on the rise'." http://news.bbc.co.uk/2/hi/uk_news/3564203.stm (March 24, 2004).

293 Susy Buchanan, "The Rift :Evidence of a divide between blacks and Hispanics mounting," The Southern Poverty Law Center, http://www.splcenter.org/intel/intelreport/article.jsp?aid=548 (Summer, 2005).

294 Pool, Jonathan. *National Development and Language Diversity*. Utilika Foundation. Seattle. http://utilika.org/pubs/etc/pool-ndld-asl.pdf

295 Carol Faber, "Moving Rate Among Americans Declines Census Bureau Says." U.S. Census Bureau. http://www.census.gov/Press-Release/www/2000/cb00-10.html (March 13, 2001).

296 United Nations. "The Universal Declaration of Human Rights," http://www.un.org/Overview/rights.html

297 (United Nations 1948, Preamble).

298 Justice Frankfurter. 310 U.S. 586 Minersville School Dist. Et al. v. Gobitis et al. Argued April 25, 1940, Decided June 3, 1940.

299 Justices Black and Douglas. 319 U.S. 624 West Virginia State Board of Education et al. v. Barnette et al. Argued March 11, 1943, Decided

June 14th, 1943.

300 Samuel Huntington, *The Clash of Civilizations and the Remaking of World Order* (New York: Touchstone, 1996), 84.

301 Richard Nisbett, *The Geography of Thought; How Asians and Westerners Think Differently . . . and*
Why (New York: Free Press, 2003), xvTwo-xvTwoi.

302 Mecha "El Plan de Atzlan." The University of Arizona http://clubs.asua.arizona.edu/~mecha/pages/ElPlanDeAtzlan.html

303 Anthony King, "One in Four Muslims Sympathises with Motives of Terrorists." London Telegraph. http://www.telegraph.co.uk/news/main.jhtml?xml=/news/2005/07/23/npoll23.xml&sSheet=/news/2005/07/23/ixnewstop.html (July 23, 2005).

304 (INA section 337 [2], § U.S. Code section 1448 [a])

305 Marjorie Heins, *Not in Front of the Children: "Indecency," Censorship, and the Innocence of Youth* (New York: Hill and Wang, 2002), 257.

306 Myron Magnet, In the Heart of Freedom, In Chains: Elite Hypocrisy Gangsta culture and Failure in Black America, *City Journal*, Vol. 17, No. 3. Summer 2007, 22.

307 Michael Bertrand. *Race, Rock, and Elvis* (Urbana and Chicago: University of Illinois Press, 2005), 101.

308 Marjory Heins, *Not in Front of the Children: "Indecency," Censorship and the Innocence of Youth.* (New York: Hill and Wang, 2001), 24

309 Michael Schudson, *The Good Citizen: A History of American Civic Life* (New York: The Free Press, 1998), 202.

310 Judith Harris, *The Nurture Assumption: Why Children Turn Out the Way They Do* (New York: Touchstone Books, 1999), 263.

Index

Abolitionists, 2, 41-42

Absolutes, 19-20, 37, 40, 66, 201, 222, 230, 234, 260, 288

Alamo, 31, 34-35

Alienation, 20, 162, 232, 244-247, 281-282

Alpha Male, 145-146, 156-157, 182

Americanization, 38-39, 42, 45, 272, 292

Aristotle, 19, 173-175, 183, 196, 199-202, 205, 227, 301-302

Art, 1, 31, 62, 64-65, 67, 131, 173-174, 190-193, 201, 222-226, 245, 257, 295

Arum, Richard, 177, 276, 302

Assimilation, 39, 103, 213, 239, 242, 249, 269, 272

Athens, 200, 226, 293

Aztecs, 91, 111, 160

Beecher, Catherine, 42

Bellah, Robert, 176, 298, 302

Benedict, Ruth, 98, 295-297

Benevolence Societies, 16, 41-42, 45

Bibles, 42

Bill of Rights, 16, 30, 130

Black, Justices Hugo, 259

Boas, Franz, 84

Buchanan, Pat, 6

Buddhism, 62

Cannibalism, 87, 99, 106-107

Catholicism
    Latin American, 68
    Spain, 32-33, 68, 90, 230, 236-237, 296-297

Censorship, 53, 193, 258, 274, 278, 302, 304

Chavez, Caesar, 192

Chimpanzees, 145, 149-150, 152, 155, 157-158, 161, 208

China, 36-37, 54, 61-64, 73, 79, 97, 111, 129, 181, 187, 209, 217, 239, 256, 258, 294, 302

Chinese
    Education, 14-15, 24, 35, 39, 43-47, 53, 64-66, 72, 126-127, 130, 168, 171, 176, 183-184, 194, 201, 204-205, 207, 237, 240, 255, 265, 269, 271, 273-274, 279, 281, 290, 293-294, 298, 303
    Exclusion Act, 36
    History, 5, 2, 5-8, 10, 17-18, 21-23, 25-26, 28-29, 31, 35-37, 39, 43, 45, 49-50, 52, 54-65, 69-71, 75-76, 78, 82, 87-89, 92, 102, 111, 119-120, 124, 126, 129-131, 136, 173, 180, 189, 192, 199, 205, 209, 215-217, 220-221, 223, 226-227, 238, 243, 259, 261-262, 266-267, 272, 275, 278, 281, 288, 291-295, 297-299, 304

Christianity
    Christians, 23, 119, 264-265, 267

Churchill, Winston, 220

Citizenship, 38, 55, 174-176, 181, 206-207, 256, 265, 268-269, 271-274

Civil Rights Movement, 122-123, 250, 278

Civil War, 1-2, 28, 33, 36, 41-43, 45, 49, 53, 69, 120, 236-237, 265

Cold War, 51-52, 71, 122-123, 294

Colonialism, 66

Columbus, 106

Communists, 52

Community, 4-5, 11, 23-26, 29, 31, 36, 39, 44-45, 47, 94, 98, 101-103, 108, 115, 144, 151, 158, 174, 176-180, 183, 185-187, 189-190, 196, 198-199, 202-203, 207-208, 214, 221-222, 224, 235, 241, 245, 259, 279-283, 302

Confucianism
    Confucius, 56, 113, 175

Congress
    Congressional, 134
    Congressmen, 45, 52